Theory for the CONTEMPORARY BASSIST

Approved Curriculum

THE ULTIMATE GUIDE TO MUSIC FOR BLUES, ROCK AND JAZZ BASSISTS

Alfred, the leader in educational music publishing, and the National Guitar Workshop, one of America's finest guitar schools, have joined forces to bring you the best, most progressive educational tools possible. We hope you will enjoy this book and encourage you to look for other fine products from Alfred and the National Guitar Workshop.

This book was acquired, edited, and produced by Workshop Arts, Inc., the publishing arm of the National Guitar Workshop.
Nathaniel Gunod, acquisitions, managing editor
Burgess Speed, acquisitions, senior editor
Timothy Phelps, interior design
Ante Gelo, music typesetter

Cover photos: Karen Miller

Cover models (clockwise, from upper left): Ron Manus, Tish Ciravolo, Greg Hiatt, Rich Lackowski

Guitars courtesy of: Schecter Guitar Research and Fender Musical Instruments, Inc.

TRACY WALTON

Alfred Music Publishing Co., Inc.
16320 Roscoe Blvd., Suite 100
P.O. Box 10003
Van Nuys, CA 91410-0003
alfred.com

ISBN-10: 0-7390-6289-1
ISBN-13: 978-0-7390-6289-0

Table of Contents

About the Author

Tracy Walton is an accomplished string and electric bass player. He studied string bass at the Hartford Conservatory on a Goodwin scholarship as a jazz performance major. He has also studied privately with David Santoro. He has anchored a wide variety of bands in styles ranging from funk and punk to rock and jazz. Tracy currently plays throughout New England fronting the jazz group, The Tracy Walton Trio. His playing has been praised for its attention to time and tradition. He is currently a member of the bass faculty at the National Guitar Workshop. Tracy also teaches bass and guitar at The Kent School and Rumsey Hall, located in Connecticut.

Photo by Timothy Phelps

Introduction

This book is designed to give you a thorough understanding of musical theory as it relates to playing the bass. It starts with basic notation and progresses to using bass lines to reflect and manipulate harmonic ideas in chord progressions. There are 25 worksheets throughout the book that will help you test your understanding of the concepts covered.

It is essential that a bass player be well versed in all aspects of music. This book will give you the knowledge necessary to create and play developed ideas in all styles of music. Immersing yourself in each section will not only give you the understanding of the topics covered, but also the ability to make music with this knowledge.

It is essential that you experiment with the ideas presented in this book. The only way to grow as a musician is to listen and play. Always remember that your goals are to make the song sound great and make it groove. The greatest theoretical ideas don't work if they don't serve the song.

If you don't already read standard music notation, I recommend you get a method book and learn—you will never regret it. Check out *The Complete Electric Bass Method* by David Overthrow, also published by the National Guitar Workshop and Alfred.

It is my hope that this book will open many musical doors for you and lead to further investigation of the ideas covered. My book *Musicianship for the Contemporary Bassist* includes ear training and sightreading, and I hope you'll include that book and CD in your studies, as well.

I would like to thank David Santoro for all of the knowledge he has shared with me. –TW

For Sheila

The Basics

The goal of this chapter is to provide a solid foundation for the rest of this book. Make sure you thoroughly understand all of the concepts covered before continuing.

The Natural Notes

The musical alphabet is as follows: A–B–C–D–E–F–G. These notes are known as *natural notes*. The distance between these notes is measured in *half steps* and *whole steps*.

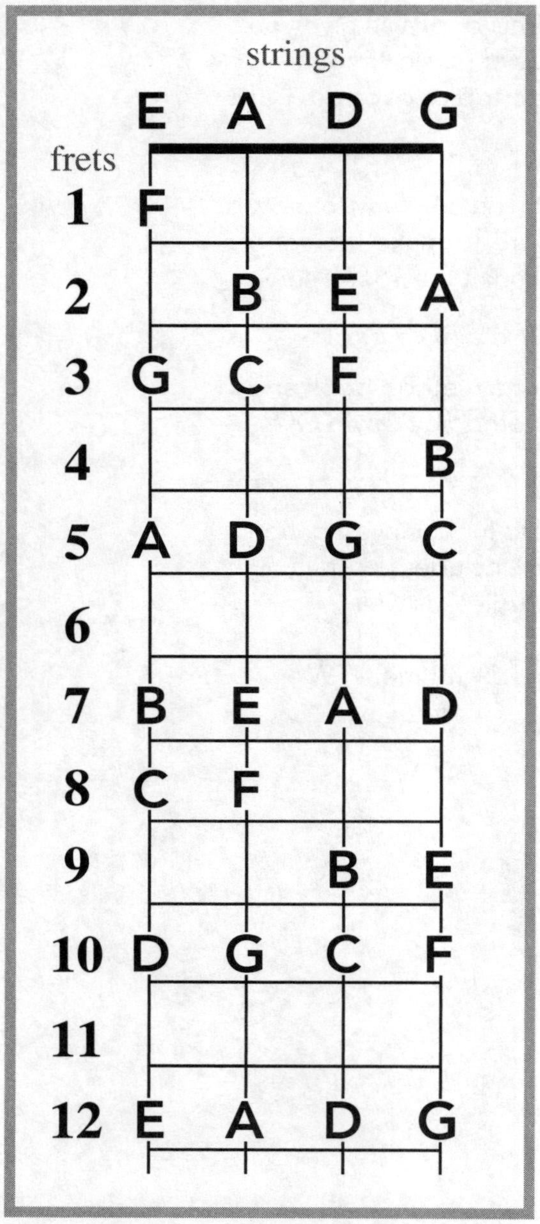

A half step is the distance between adjacent frets. For example, on the D string, the 2nd-fret E and the 3rd-fret F are a half step apart. Notice that on the E string, the open-string E and the 1st-fret F are also a half step apart.

A whole step is equal to two half steps, or two frets. For example, on the E string, the 1st-fret F and the 3rd-fret G are a whole step apart.

Notice on the fingerboard chart that E to F and B to C are always a half step apart. All of the other natural notes are a whole step apart.

Here is a list of the half steps and whole steps as they occur between the natural notes in the musical alphabet.

Whole steps	**Half Steps**
A–B	B–C
C–D	E–F
D–E	
F–G	
G–A	

Memorize the open strings first. From lowest to highest, they are E–A–D–G. Next, begin to memorize the natural notes on the first five frets. Any note can be found an *octave** (a distance of 12 half steps) higher by moving one whole step higher and two strings higher. For example G can be found on the 3rd fret of the E string and the 5th fret of the D string.

* An octave is the closest distance between two different notes with the same name.

Pitch Notation

THE STAFF

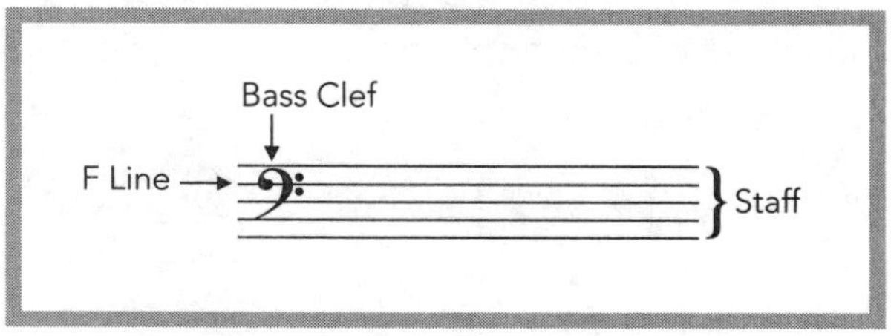

Music is written on a *staff*, which consists of five lines and four spaces. Each line and space has a name from the musical alphabet. A *clef* is placed at the beginning of the staff to tell us which line and space has which name. Music for the bass is written in *bass clef* 𝄢. The two dots surround the F line on the staff, which is why this clef is sometimes called *F clef.* Always make sure your chart is in bass clef and not treble clef 𝄞.

Notes are placed on the staff to indicate specific pitches. These notes are always read from left to right. The higher or lower a note is placed on the staff, the higher or lower it sounds.

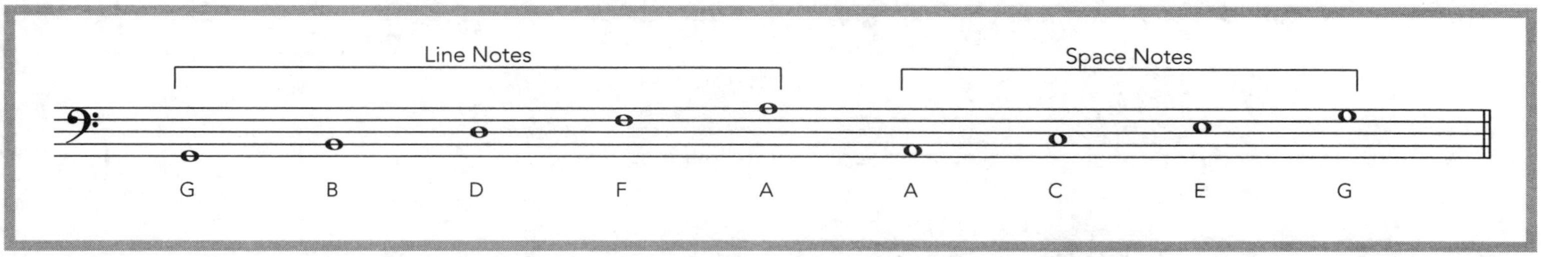

Notice that each line or space note is two letter names away from the last. For example, in the case of the 1st-line G and the 2nd-line B, B is two letters away from G: G–A–B. In the case of the 1st-space A and the 2nd-space C, C is two letters away from A: A–B–C. This will help you recognize notes more quickly.

Let's look at the staff in another way. Notice on the staff below that if you start from the bottom space and ascend, reading every line and space up to the top space, the staff simply reads in alphabetical order: A–B–C–D–E–F–G.

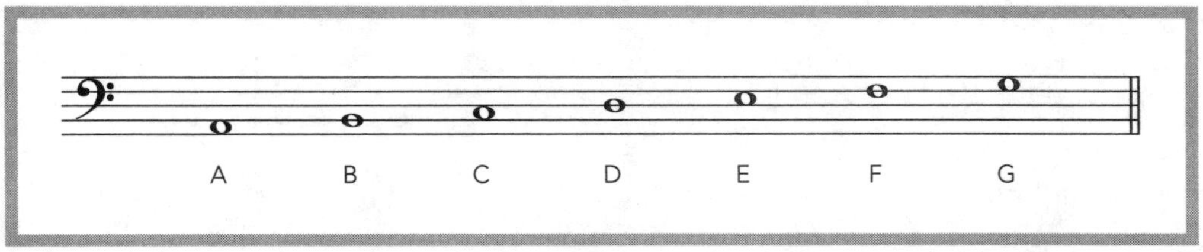

There is an easy way to remember the names of the lines and spaces. Starting with the first letter of the lines, we can form the following phrase: **G**ood **B**oys **D**o **F**ine **A**lways.

For the spaces, use this phrase: **A**ll **C**ows **E**at **G**rass.

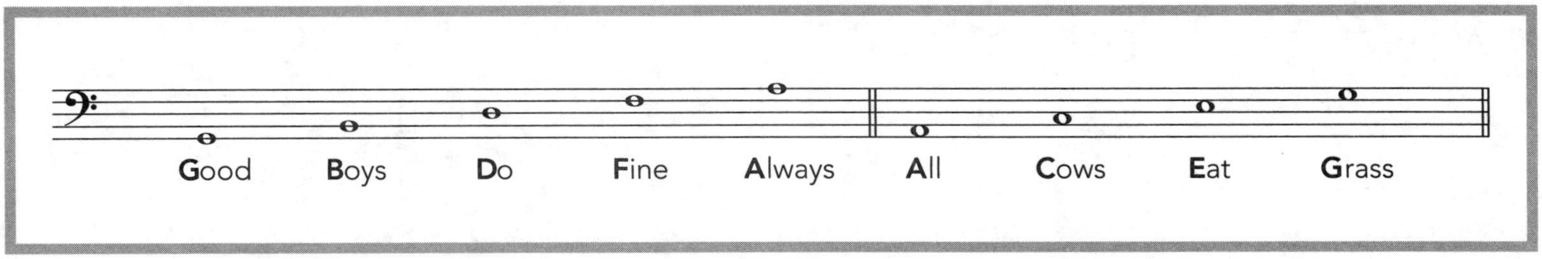

ACCIDENTALS

The natural notes separated by a whole step have notes between them called *accidentals.* An accidental changes a natural note, making it either higher or lower.

SHARPS

A *sharp* is notated by placing a ♯ symbol before a note.

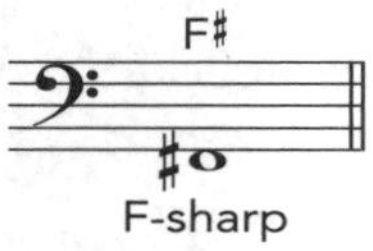

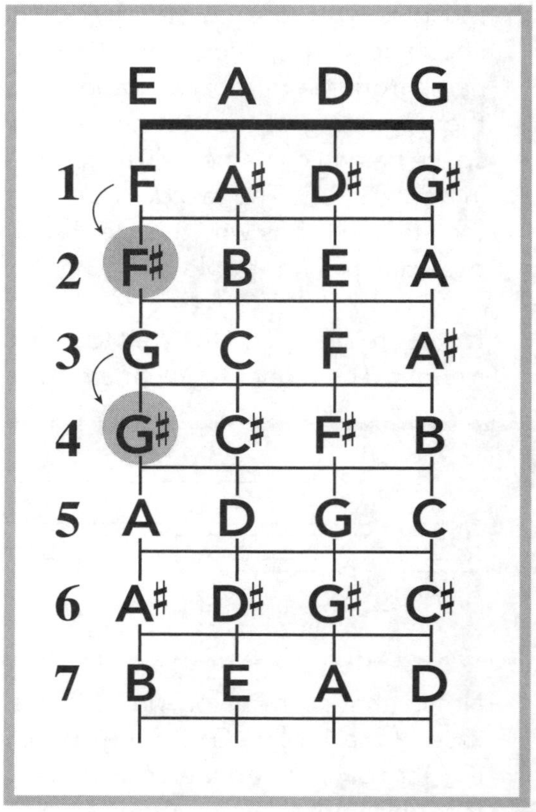

A sharp raises a note by one half step (or one fret). Let's look at the E string for some examples of sharps.

Notice the 2nd fret is an F♯ because it is one step higher than the 1st-fret F.

The 4th fret is called G♯ because it is one half step higher than the 3rd-fret G.

The full musical alphabet consists of twelve notes. Ascending from A using sharps, it reads:

A–A♯–B–C–C♯–D–D♯–E–F–F♯–G–G♯

FLATS

A *flat* is notated by placing a ♭ symbol before a note.

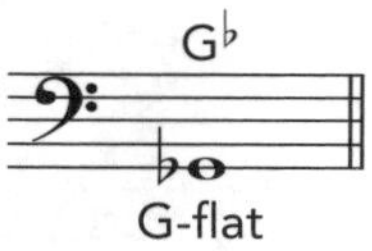

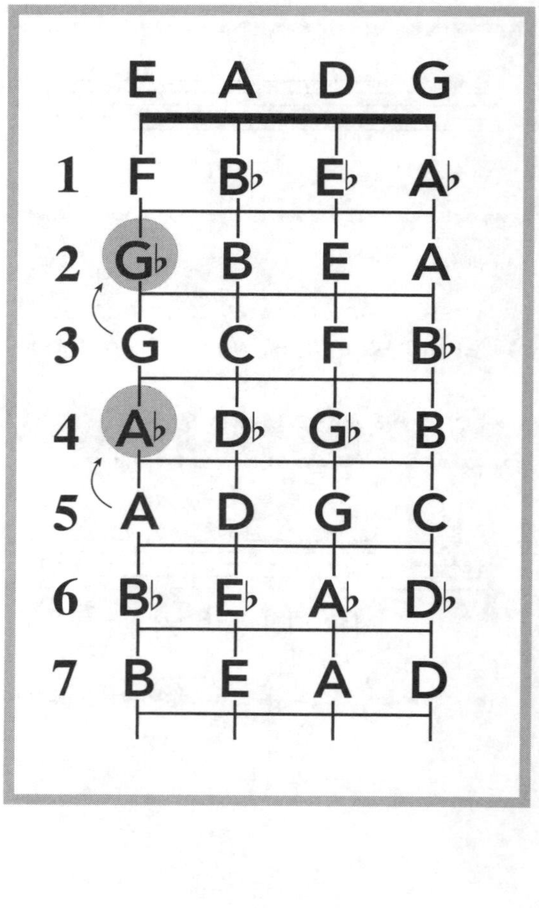

A flat lowers a note by one half step.

Let's look at the E string for some examples of flats.

The 2nd fret is a G♭ because it is one half step lower than the 3rd-fret G.

The 4th fret is called A♭ because it is one half step lower than the 5th-fret A.

Descending from A using flats, the musical alphabet reads:

A–A♭–G–G♭–F–E–E♭–D–D♭–C–B–B♭

Enharmonic Equivalents

Every accidental has two possible names. Two different note names that have the same pitch are known as *enharmonic equivalents*. You might have noticed on page 8 that the E string, 2nd fret was called both F♯ and G♭. F♯ and G♭ are enharmonic equivalents.

One factor to consider when deciding which enharmonic equivalent to use is the direction of the bass line. Let's look at the notes between E and A as an example. If a bass line is descending from A to E, it makes more sense to spell the line A–A♭–G–G♭–F–E. These notes can be played on the E string by starting from the 5th fret and playing every fret down to the open E. Each note in this line is a half step lower than the last.

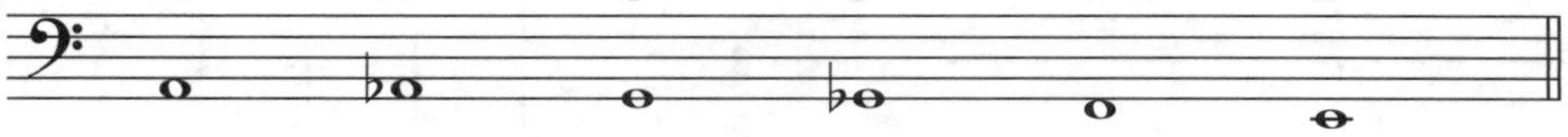

If the same notes are played ascending from E, it makes more sense to spell the line E–F–F♯–G–G♯–A. This line can be played on the E string starting on the open string and playing every fret up to the 5th fret.

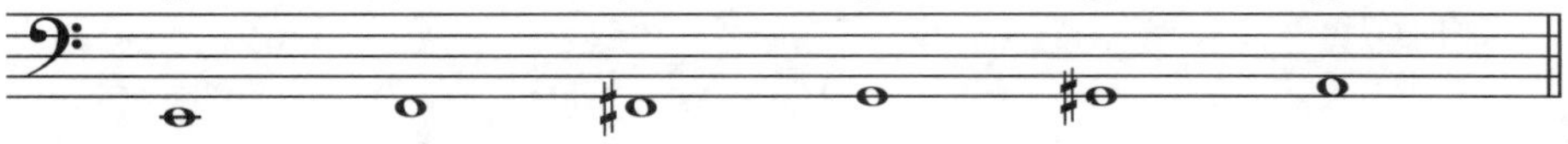

Continue to work on memorizing the notes. Once you have a good grasp on the naturals of the first five frets, begin to work on the accidentals. The worksheet on page 11 should help you along.

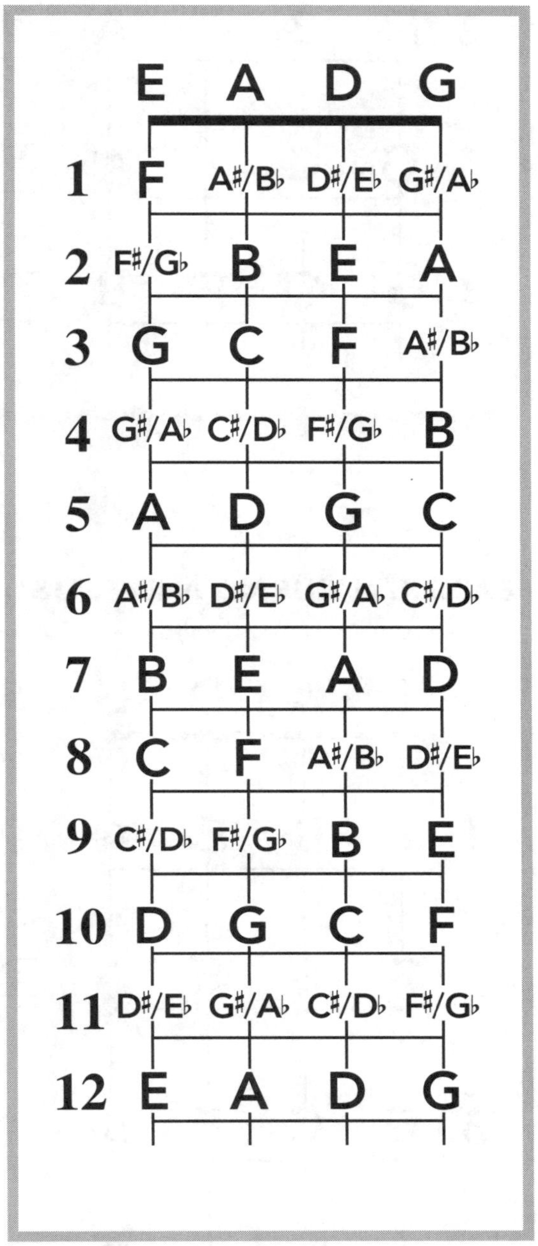

READING NATURALS AND SHARPS

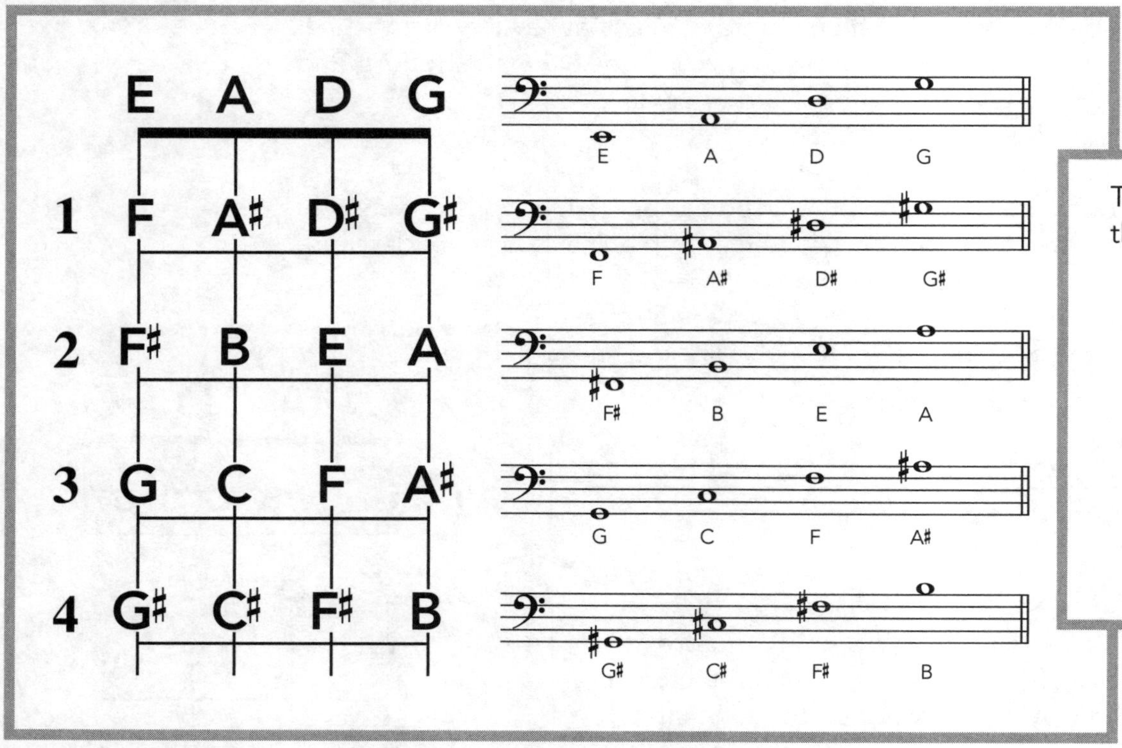

To sharp an open string, go to the 1st fret of that string.

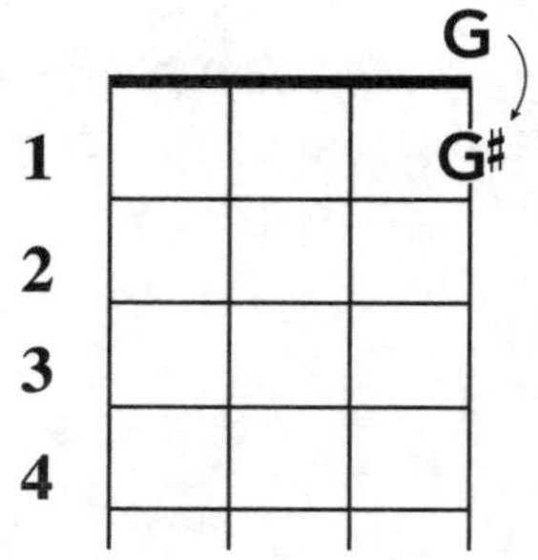

READING NATURALS AND FLATS

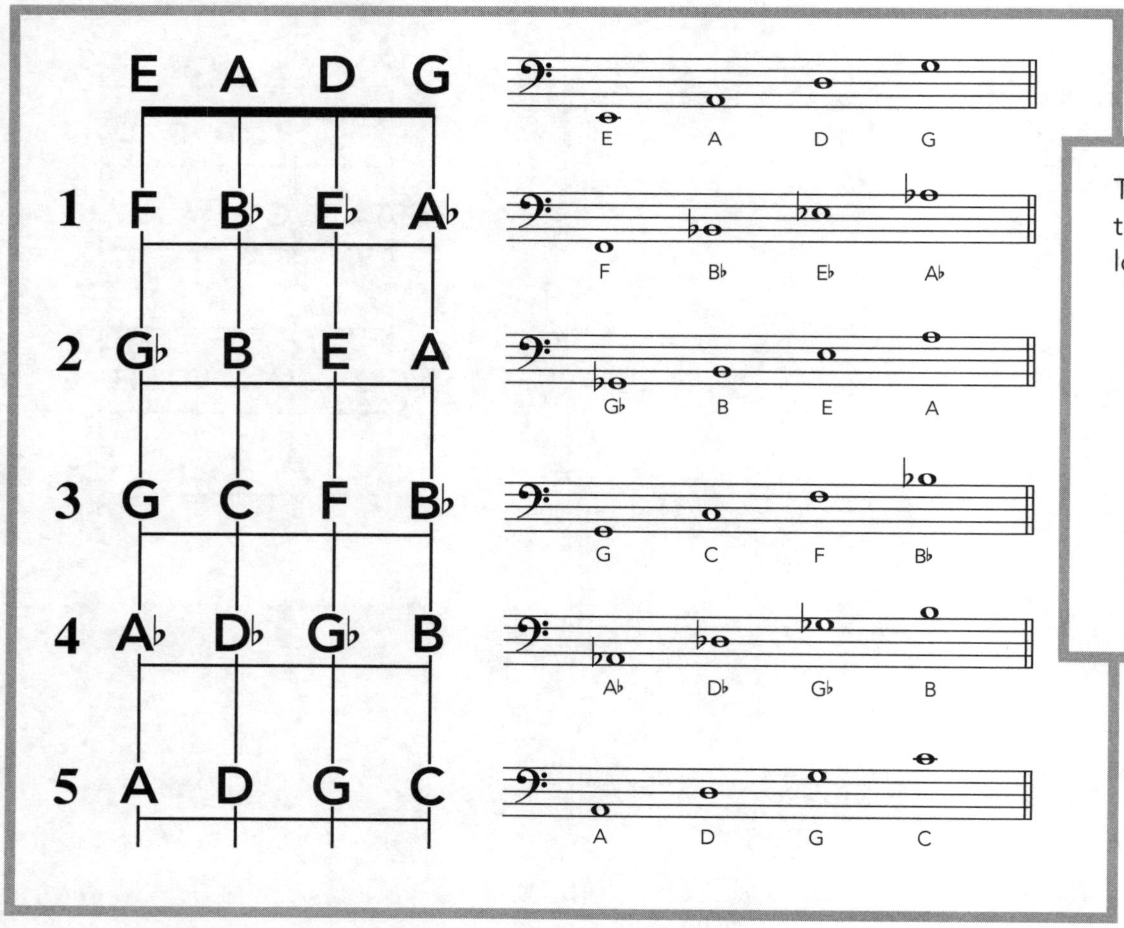

To flat an open string, go to the 4th fret of the adjacent lower string.

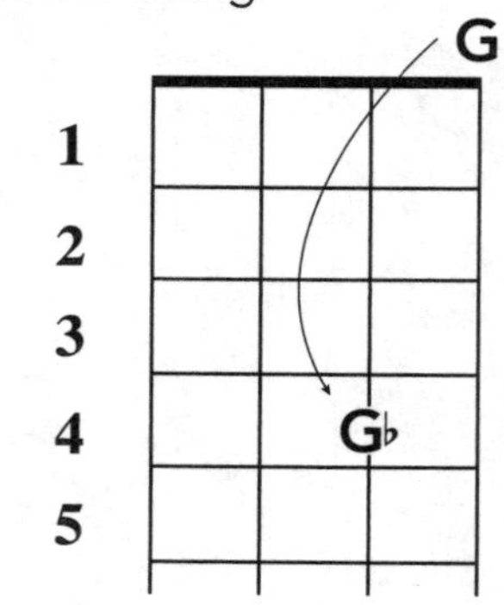

WORKSHEET 1: FRETBOARD KNOWLEDGE, NATURAL NOTES AND ACCIDENTALS

Throughout the book there will be worksheets to help you monitor your progress. It is a good idea to keep some scrap paper available on which to write your answers so you can reuse these worksheets. You should also have your bass in hand for reference. The answers to all of the questions will be found upside down below each worksheet.

1. Give the note name of the following frets.

   a. 1st fret, E string ______________

   b. 5th fret, G string ______________

   c. 4th fret, A string ______________

   d. 2nd fret, D string ______________

   e. 7th fret, A string ______________

   f. 3rd fret, G string ______________

2. Name the enharmonic equivalent of the following notes.

   a. B♭ ______ b. G♯ ______ c. G♭ ______

   d. F♯ ______ e. D♭ ______ f. E♭ ______

3. Fill in the following charts.

   a. Fill in naturals only. b. Fill in naturals and sharps. c. Fill in naturals and flats.

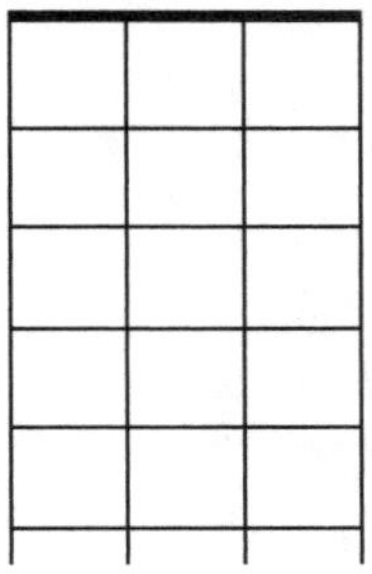

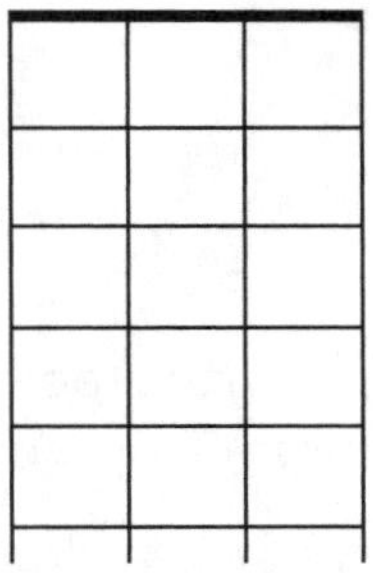

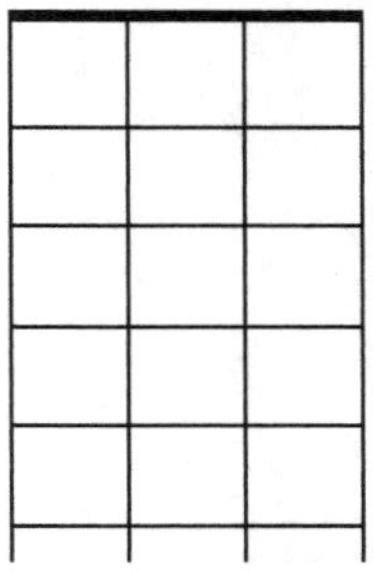

Answers

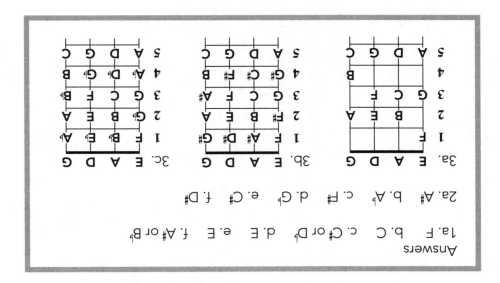

1a. F b. C c. C♯ or D♭ d. E e. E f. A♯ or B♭

2a. A♯ b. A♭ c. F♯ d. G♭ e. C♯ f. D♯

3a.

	E	A	D	G
1	F			
2		B	E	A
3	G	C	F	
4				B
5	A	D	G	C

3b.

	E	A	D	G
1	F	A♯	D♯	G♯
2	F♯	B	E	A
3	G	C	F	A♯
4	G♯	C♯	F♯	B
5	A	D	G	C

3c.

	E	A	D	G
1	F	B♭	E♭	A♭
2	G♭	B	E	A
3	G	C	F	B♭
4	A♭	D♭	G♭	B
5	A	D	G	C

Ledger Lines

Ledger lines are used to show pitches above and below the staff. The ledger lines act as an extension of the staff. The format of line, space, line, space, stays the same. The names still appear in alphabetical order.

NOTES BELOW THE STAFF

Notice that there is only one ledger line below the staff. Conveniently enough, the lowest note on a four-string bass, E, is the very first ledger line below the staff.

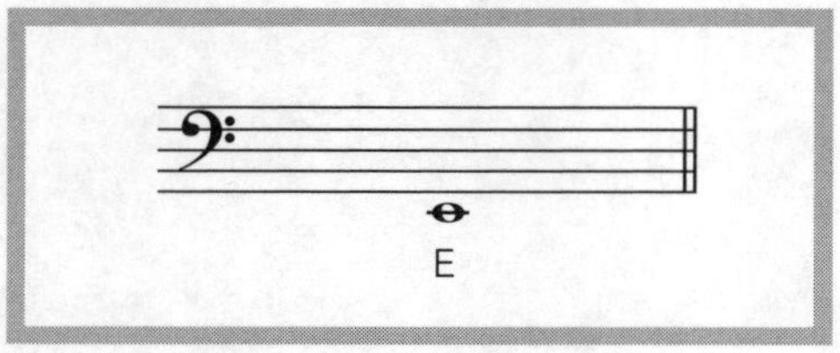

This extra line creates a space between the low E and the bottom line of the staff, G. This is the low F-note (1st fret, E string). The F-note is also easy to spot because it seems to be hanging from the bottom of the staff. There is no need to use the E ledger line when writing the low F-note.

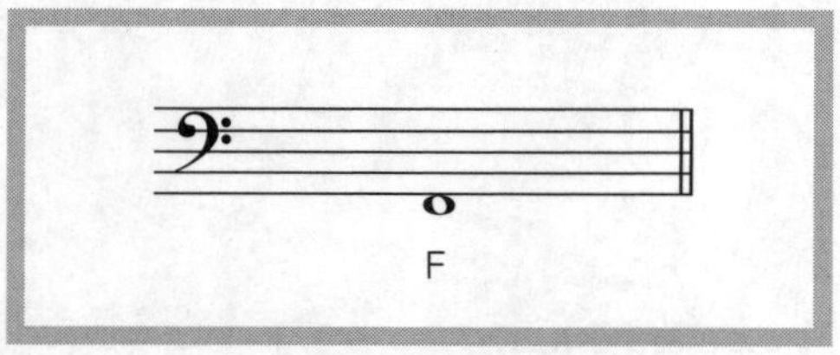

NOTES ABOVE THE STAFF

The first ledger line above the staff is C, two letter names away from the top-line A. The B-note sits on top of the staff. As with the low F, a line is not needed to make the space for the B-note.

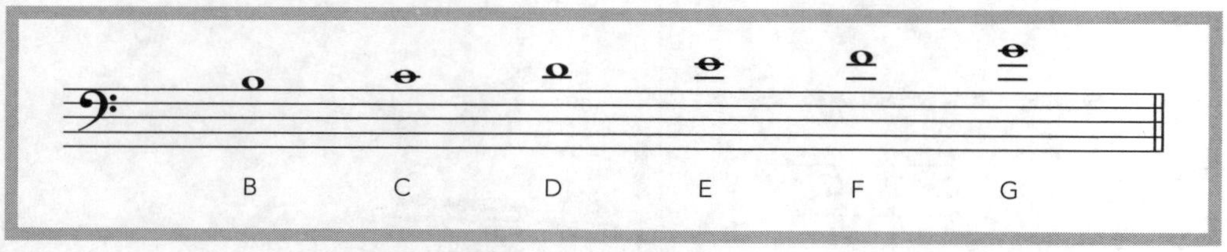

WORKSHEET 2: FRETBOARD KNOWLEDGE AND PITCH NOTATION

1. Give the note name of the fret specified.

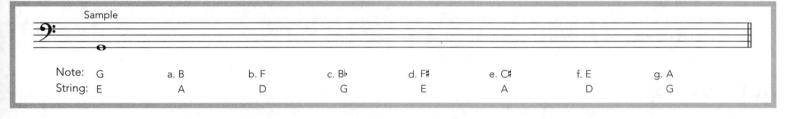

	Example						
Note	B	a. ____	b. ____	c. ____	d. ____	e. ____	f. ____
String	A	A	D	E	G	E	D
Fret	2	3	2	1	4	3	4

2. On the staff below, draw the requested note.

Sample

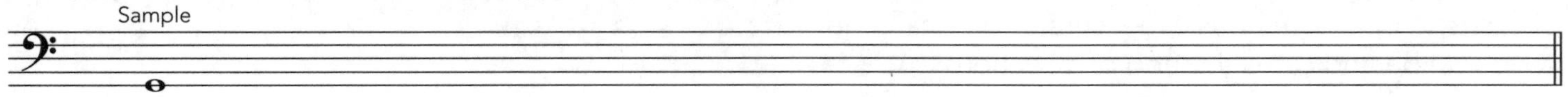

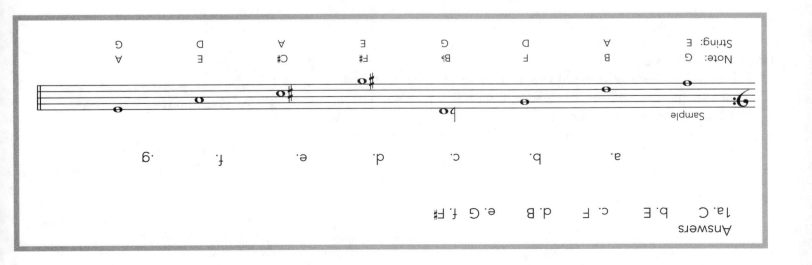

Note:	G	a. B	b. F	c. B♭	d. F♯	e. C♯	f. E	g. A
String:	E	A	D	G	E	A	D	G

Answers

1a. C b. E c. F d. B e. G f. F♯

Sample

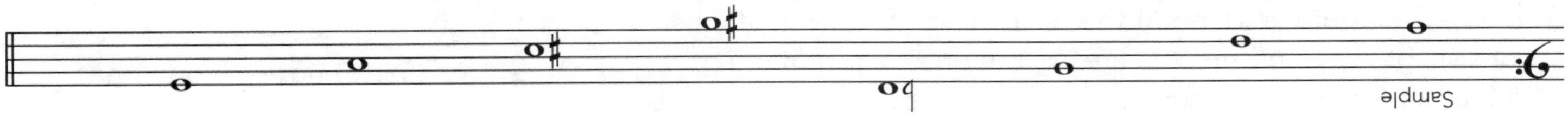

Note:	G	B	F	B♭	F♯	C♯	E	A
String:	E	A	D	G	E	A	D	G

a. b. c. d. e. f. g.

TIME NOTATION

NOTES

Differences in appearance tell us how long each note lasts. All notes have a *head*; some have a *stem*; some have a stem and *flag*. Notes with flags are *beamed* together when they appear in groups.

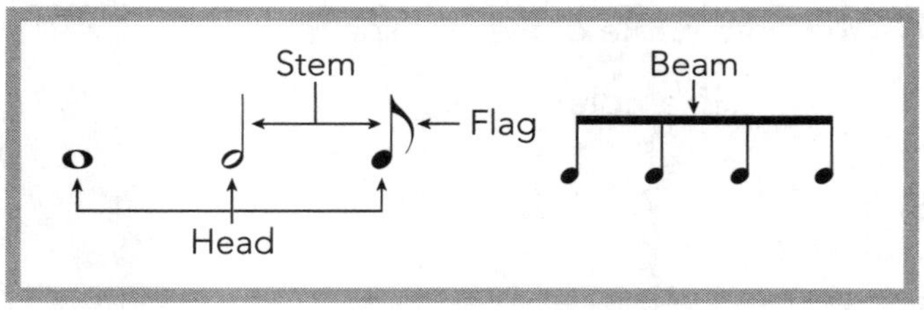

MEASURES AND BEATS

The vertical lines that run through a staff are called *bar lines*. The distance between bar lines is called a *measure*. Measures divide written music into groups of *beats*. A beat is the basic measure of musical time. A *double bar* indicates the end of a section.

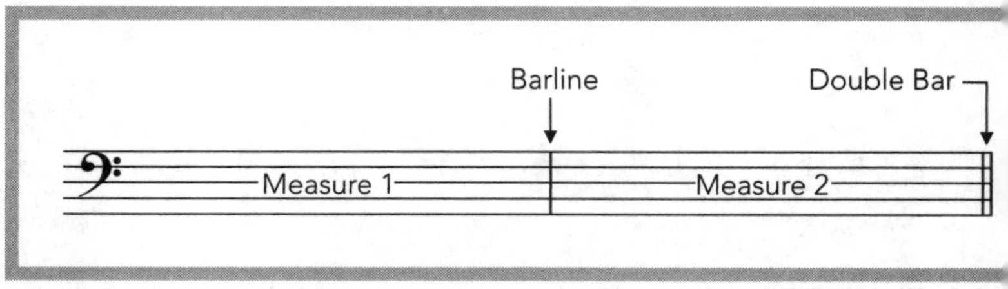

NOTE DURATION

The type of note we place on the staff signifies its duration (how many beats the note should be held). The following list shows the types of notes and their durations in beats. It should be noted that these durations assume that the *time signature* has a **4** on the bottom (see below).

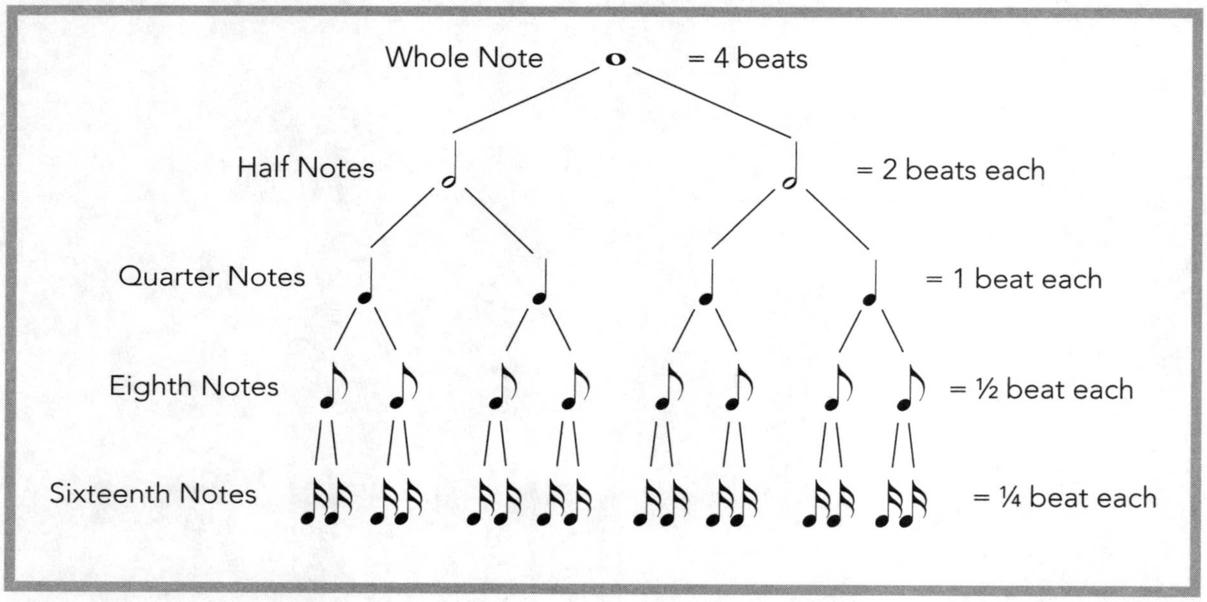

TIME SIGNATURES

The time signature is found at the beginning of a piece of music. It consists of two numbers that are written one on top of the other. The top number signifies how many beats will be in each measure. The bottom number indicates what type of note will receive one beat.

4/4 4 beats per measure
Quarter note ♩ = one beat

3/4 3 beats per measure
Quarter note ♩ = one beat

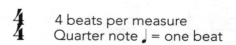

Sometimes a **C** is used in place of **4/4**. This is called *common time*.

RESTS

Rests are placed on the staff to indicate moments of silence. The name of each rest corresponds to the name of the specific note value and the duration for which they are held. A whole rest means four beats of silence (or a whole measure of rest); a half rest means two beats of silence and so forth.

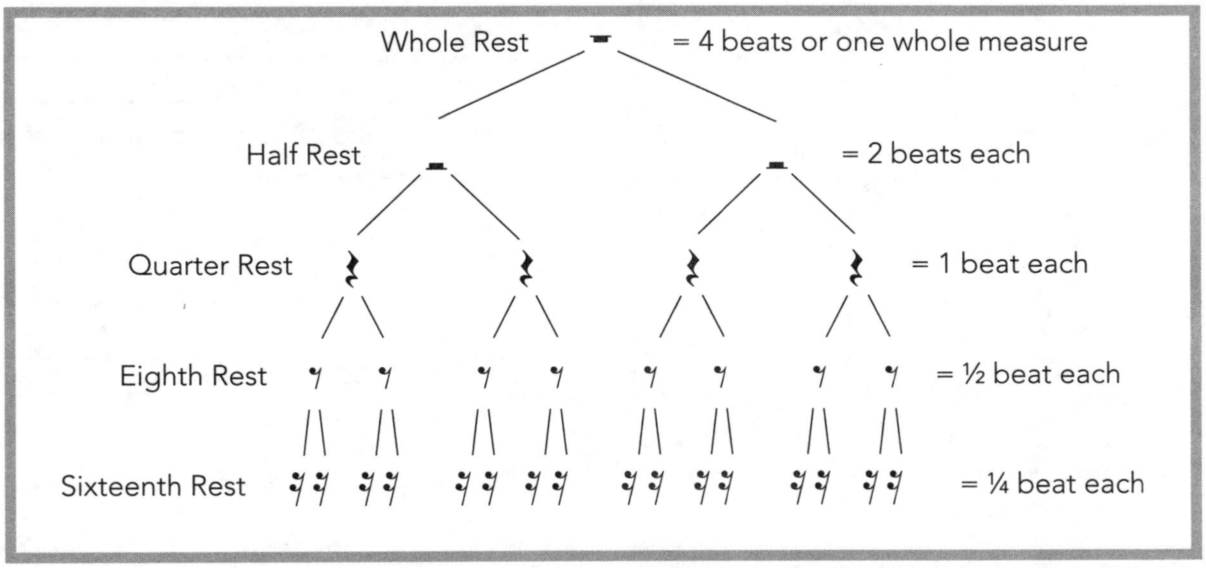

TIES

A *tie* used to increase the length of a note by linking it with another note. When two notes are tied together, the second note is not plucked. Rather, the value of the second note is simply added to that of the first.

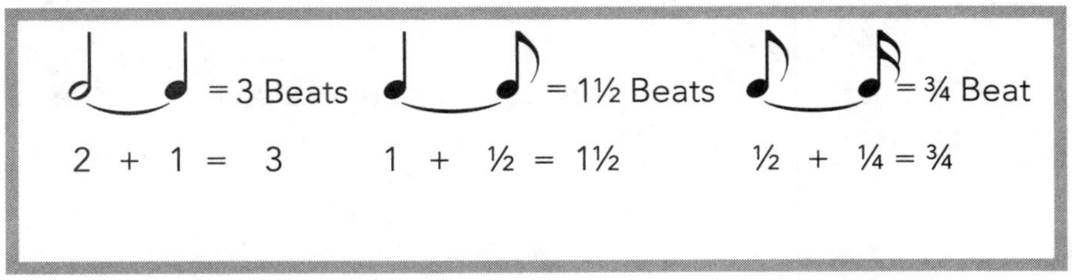

DOTS

A *dot* is placed after a note increases that note's value by one half. For example, placing a dot after a half note increases the value of the half note from two beats to three beats (2+1=3). Dotted quarter notes and dotted eighth notes work the same way.

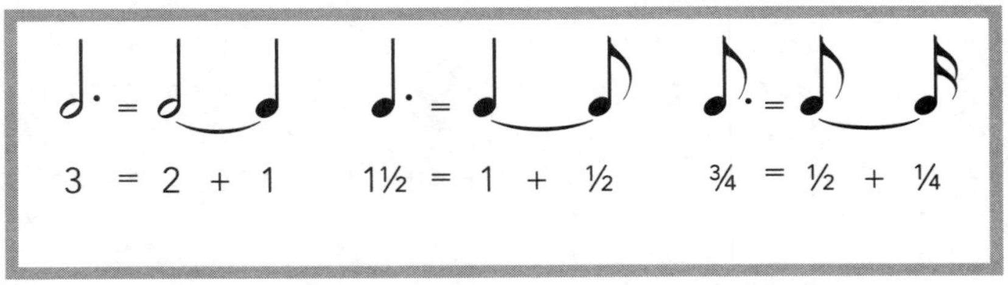

THE RULES FOR ACCIDENTALS; INTRODUCING NATURALS

Notice that in this example, measure 1 has an F♯ on beat 3 followed by an F on beat 4. The F on beat 4 will still be played as an F♯. Once a note has been sharped or flatted, each time that same note occurs in that measure it is played as a sharp or a flat. When you cross a bar line, the note automatically returns to its natural position unless it is sharped or flatted again.

A *natural* sign ♮ is used to return a note to its original position after it has been changed with an accidental. Notice that in measure 2, the F♯ is returned to F♮.

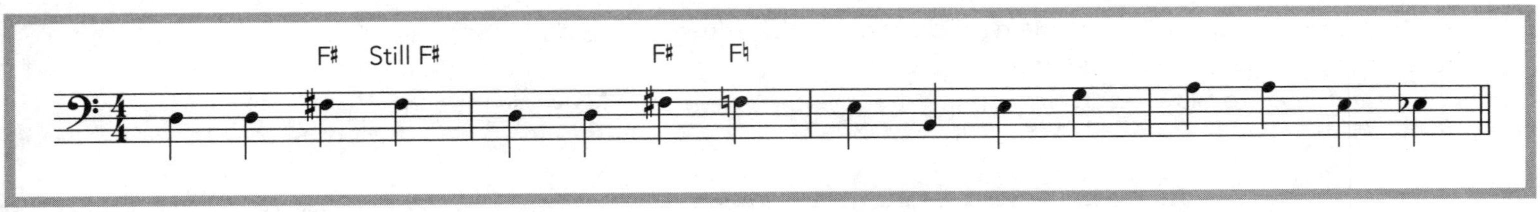

Triplets

A *triplet* is three notes played in the time of two. Thus, an eighth-note triplet is played in the same time as two eighth notes.

THE EIGHTH-NOTE TRIPLET

The *eighth-note triplet*, being equal to two eighth notes, is also equal to one quarter note. The example to the right is a measure in $\frac{4}{4}$ time with four eighth-note triplets. Notice that the numeral three placed below the beam (or above, if the notes are stemmed upward). Count "1–&–a, 2–&–a, 3–&–a, 4–&–a."

THE QUARTER-NOTE TRIPLET

The quarter-note triplet is equal to two quarter notes or one half note. To execute the quarter note triplet, count as you did for eighth-note triplets and simply play on every other count. The example to the right is a measure in $\frac{4}{4}$ time with two quarter-note triplets. Counts that are not played are gray.

THE HALF-NOTE TRIPLET

The half-note triplet is equal to two half notes or one whole note. Once again, count as you did for eighth-note triplets. The notes will fall on beat "1," the "&" of beat "2" and the "a" of beat "3."

RHYTHM CHART

The following chart shows all of the note values that have been discussed thus far. Notice that all of the ideas take up one measure of $\frac{4}{4}$ time, and the note values become smaller as you read from top to bottom.

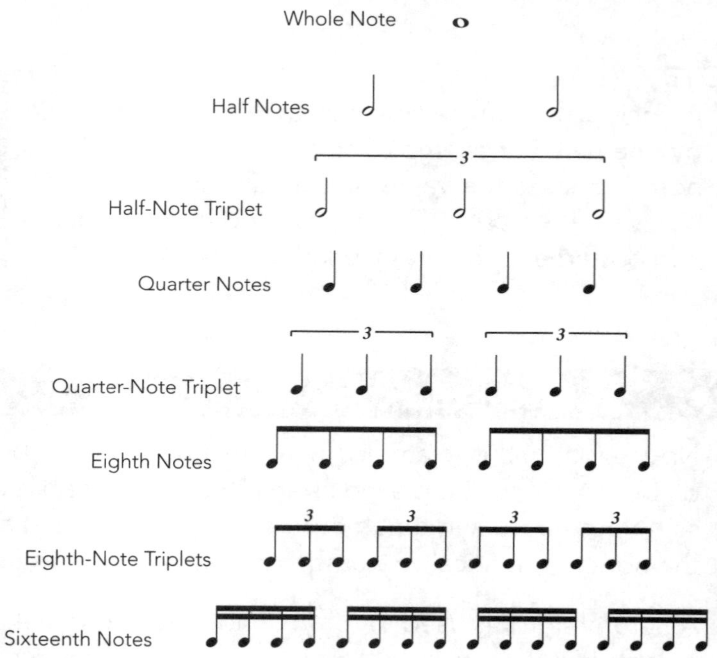

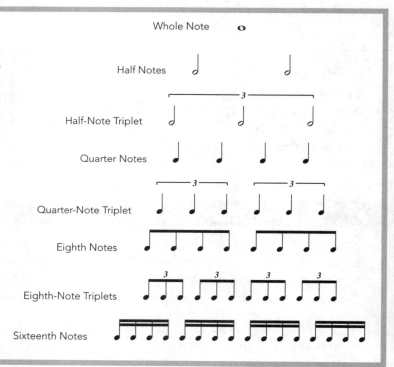

Sometimes the music will have a *swing* indication, which means the eighth notes are played unevenly, rather than as written (*straight*). Swing eighth notes are written the same as normal eighth notes but are played a lot like an eighth note triplet with the first two notes tied.

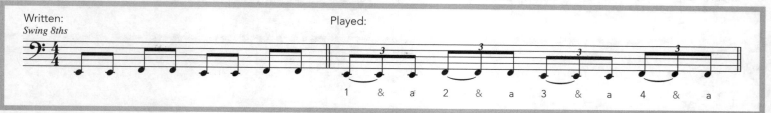

Meter

Meter is the pattern of beats in a piece of music. Time signatures fall into two basic categories of meters: *simple* meters, in which each pulse is divisible by two; and *compound* meters, in which each pulse is divisible by three.

SIMPLE METERS

In 2/4, 3/4 and 4/4, the quarter note is the basic pulse. The quarter note subdivides into two eighth notes.

In 2/2, 3/2 and 4/2, the half note is the basic pulse. The half note subdivides into two quarter notes.

COMPOUND METERS

In 6/8, 9/8, and 12/8, the eighth notes are grouped in threes, making the pulse a dotted quarter note. You can feel each dotted quarter note as a triplet. Think of it this way, 6/8 time feels like 2/4 with a triplet on every beat.

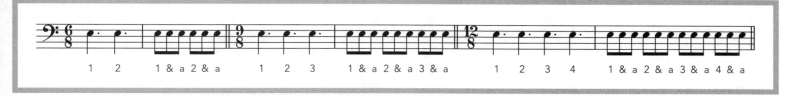

In 6/4, 9/4 and 12/4, the basic pulse can be felt as a dotted half note, which subdivides into three quarter notes.

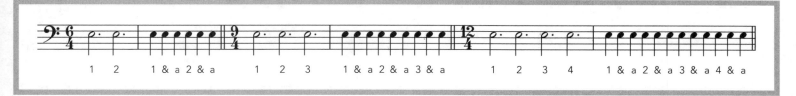

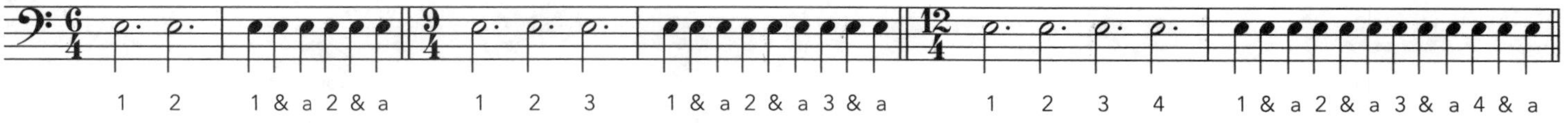

Let's look at 12/8 a little more closely. Notice that in measure 1, there is a dotted quarter note followed by three quarter-note/eighth-note groups. If you tap your foot to the pulse of the dotted quarter, the measure will feel like a quarter note followed by three swing eighth notes. Apply this concept to the next three measures.

ODD TIME

Some time signatures are referred to as being *odd time*. The most common examples of odd time are $\frac{5}{4}$ and $\frac{7}{4}$.

$\frac{5}{4}$ TIME

In $\frac{5}{4}$ time, there are five beats per measure. This can be counted simply as 1, 2, 3, 4, 5, although it is usually easier to break down odd times into more manageable groups of two, three or four beats. $\frac{5}{4}$ can be thought of as a group of three followed by a group of two (1–2–3, 1–2), or a group of two followed by a group of three (1–2, 1–2–3).

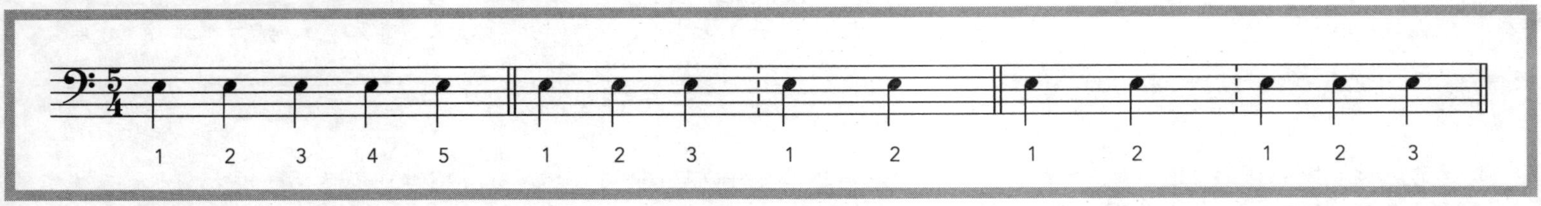

$\frac{7}{4}$ TIME

In $\frac{7}{4}$ time, there are seven beats per measure. To make this time signature more manageable, it is usually counted as a group of four beats followed by a group of three beats (1–2–3–4, 1–2–3), or a group of three beats followed by a group of four beats (1–2–3, 1–2–3–4).

The following piece is in $\frac{7}{4}$. Each measure starts with two half notes. You can count every measure as a group of four beats followed by a group of three beats.

WORKSHEET 3: TIME NOTATION

1. Give the name of the following notes and rests.

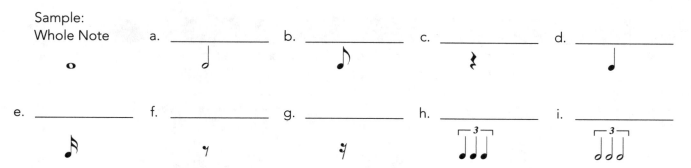

Sample: Whole Note a. ____________ b. ____________ c. ____________ d. ____________

e. ____________ f. ____________ g. ____________ h. ____________ i. ____________

2. Draw the following notes and rests on the staff.

Sample

Whole Note a. Half Note b. Quarter Note c. Eighth Note d. Half Rest e. Quarter Rest

3. What type of note receives one count in $\frac{4}{4}$ time? ____________

4. How many beats do the following notes receive in $\frac{4}{4}$ time?

a. = ______ b. = ______ c. = ______ d. = ______ e. = ______

5. Name the meter of the following time signatures, simple or compound.

a. $\frac{4}{4}$ ____________ b. $\frac{12}{8}$ ____________

Answers

1a. half note b. eighth note c. quarter rest d. quarter note e. sixteenth note

f. eighth rest g. sixteenth rest h. quarter-note triplet i. half-note triplet

Sample 2a. b. c. d. e.

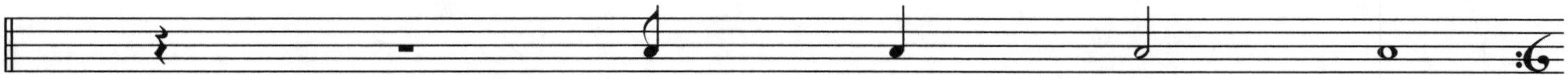

Whole Note, Half Note, Quarter Note, Eighth Note, Half Rest, Quarter Rest

3. Quarter note 4. a. 4 b. 3 c. 1 ½ d. 1 ½ e. 3

5a. simple b. compound

Scales, Keys and Key Signatures

A *scale* is a group of notes arranged in a specific pattern of half steps and whole steps.

The Major Scale

The *major scale* is the most commonly used scale in the popular music of Western culture and is the foundation of music theory. Therefore, a thorough understanding of this scale is a must. Below is a major scale starting on the note C, called the C Major scale.

C Major Scale

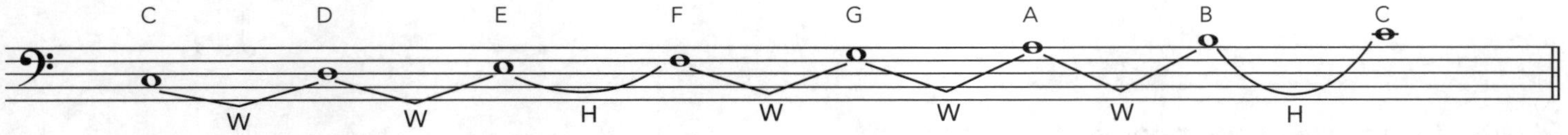

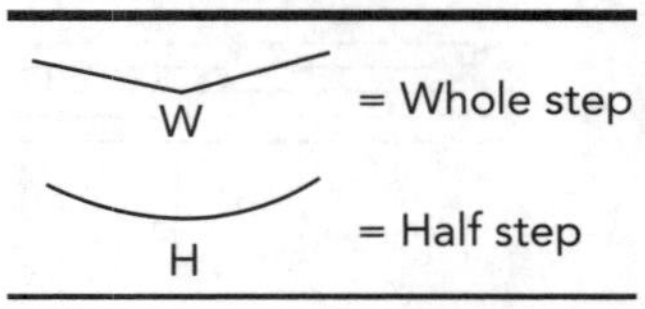

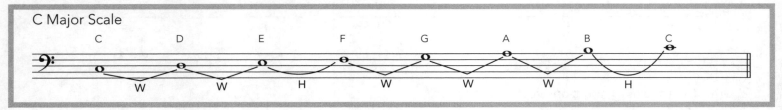

The C Major scale has no sharps or flats and contains all seven natural notes. The last note of the scale repeats the first a *perfect octave* higher. A perfect octave is a distance of 12 half steps. Notice the whole-step/half-step formula shown below the staff. This formula holds true for every major scale.

There are 12 major scales, one for each note of the musical alphabet.

Each note in a major scale is also referred to as a *scale degree* and assigned a number. This will help when starting the scale from notes other than C. It will also help when comparing the major scale to other scales.

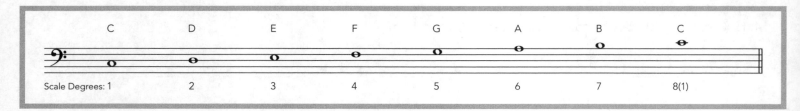

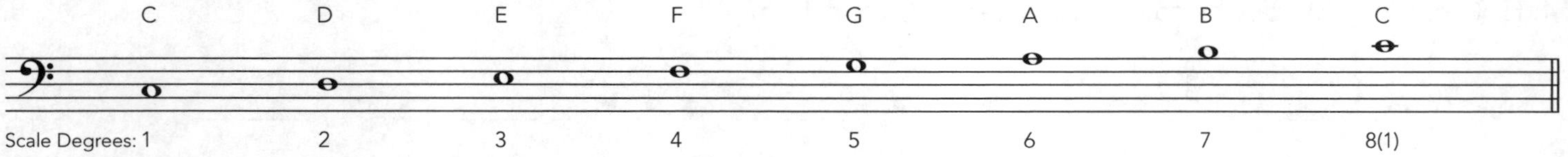

Here are two common fingerings for a major scale. Simply start the fingering on the desired root. The numbers in the circles are left-hand fingers:

1 = index finger
2 = middle finger
3 = ring finger
4 = pinky

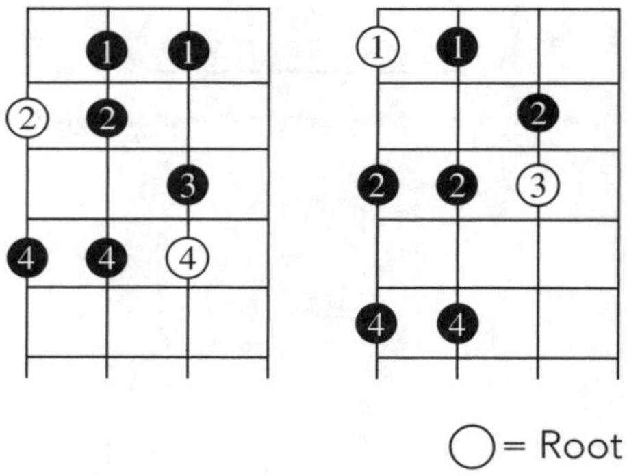

The white circles are the first scale degree, also called the *tonic.*

Most people agree that the major scale has a very happy sound. You may know the song "Do Re Mi," from the Rodgers and Hammerstein musical, *The Sound of Music.* This song is based on the sound of the major scale. Play a C Major scale and listen to the sound.

THE SHARP KEYS

Each key is made up of seven of the 12 possible pitches. The specific notes of the 12 keys are found by playing a major scale from each root. As discussed on page 20, the key of C has no sharps or flats. All of the other key signatures have at least one accidental. The accidentals in a key are either sharp or flat, never both. The following are the sharp keys.

Using the whole-step/half-step formula, a G Major scale is constructed as follows:

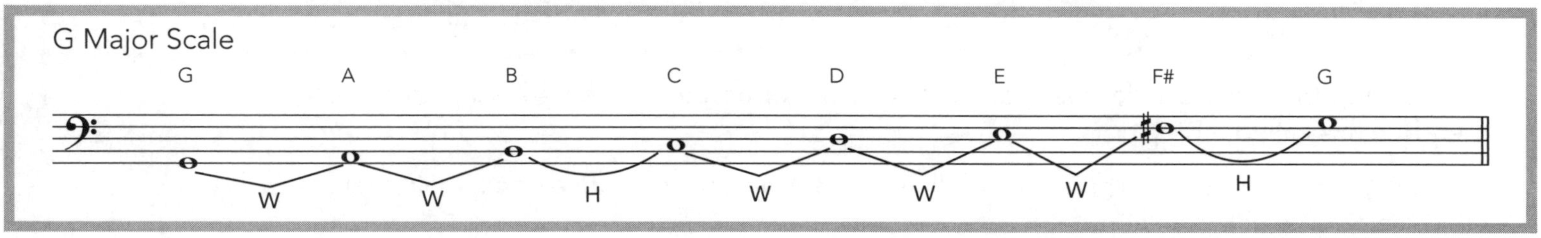

Notice the F♯ on the 7th scale degree. In a G Major scale, the F must be raised to F♯ to satisfy the whole-step/half-step formula. E to F♯ is a whole step. F♯ to G is a half step. Therefore, the key of G has an F♯. The 7th scale degree in G must be referred to as F♯ and not G♭ because every letter name in the musical alphabet must be used to spell a major scale.

The sharp keys are shown below. Notice that each new sharp key contains the sharp or sharps from the previous key. Notice also that each new key has one more sharp than its predecessor. This new sharp is found one half step below the root of the scale. For example, the D Major scale has an F♯ in it as does the previous key of G. The D Major scale also has one new sharp (C♯), which is found one half step below the root (D).

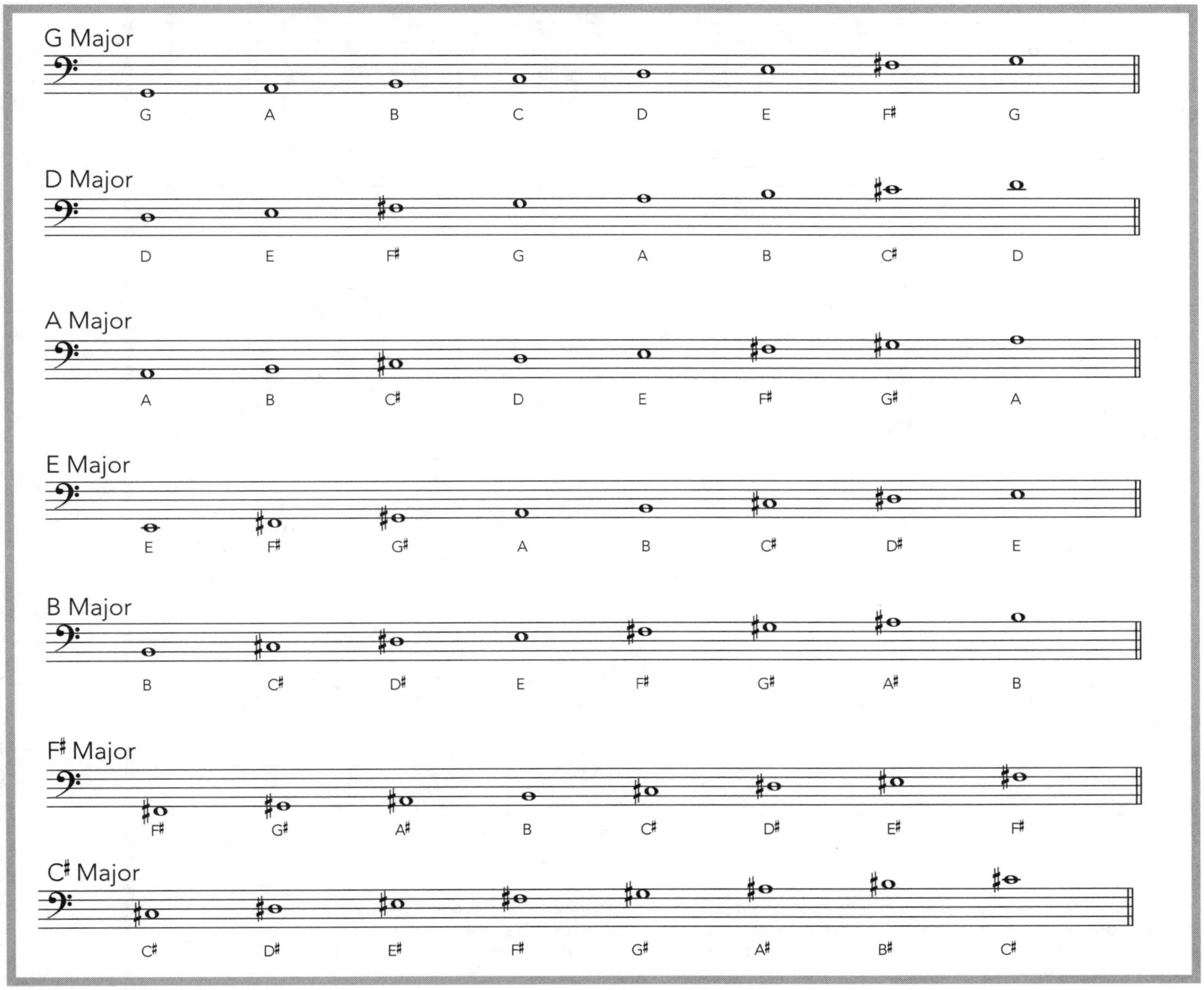

THE FLAT KEYS

The flat keys are also found using the whole-step/half-step formula. The following is an F Major scale.

F Major Scale

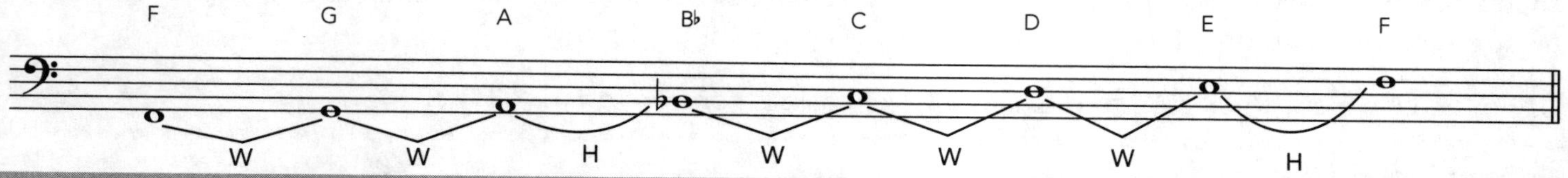

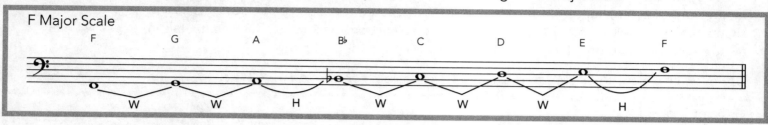

Considering the 3rd scale degree is an A, it is not an option to call the 4th scale degree A♯, therefore it is called a B♭.

Below is the B♭ Major scale. There are two flats in a B♭ Major scale. Notice once again that the 4th scale degree (E♭), is a flat note.

B♭ Major Scale

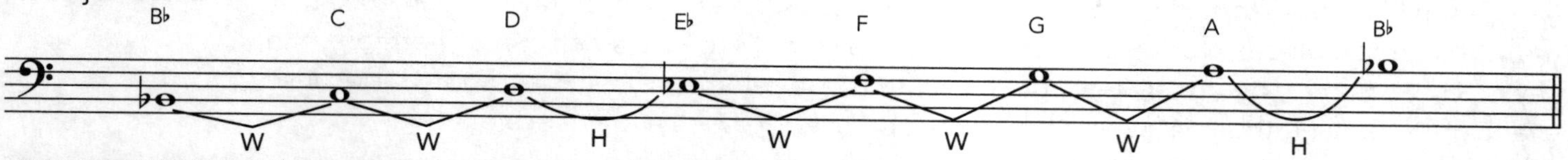

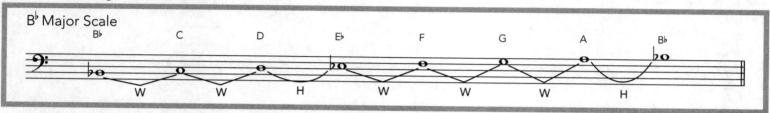

Below are all seven flat keys. Each new key has one new flat. The new flat is always found on the 4th scale degree of the new scale. For example, an E♭ Major scale has two flats from the B♭ Major scale (B♭ and E♭). It also has one new flat (A♭), which is the 4th scale degree of the E♭ Major scale.

F Major

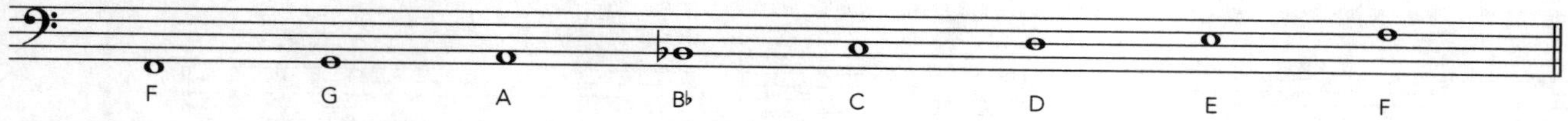

B♭ Major

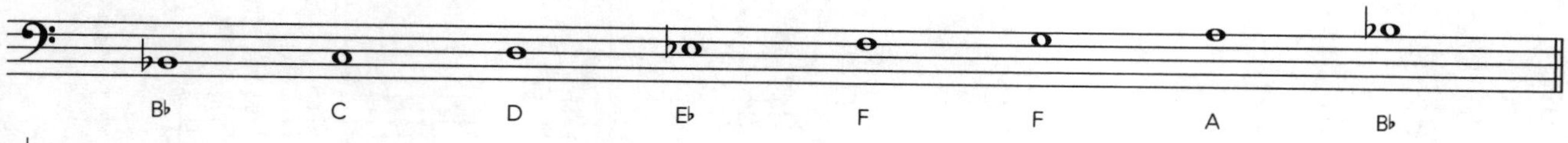

E♭ Major

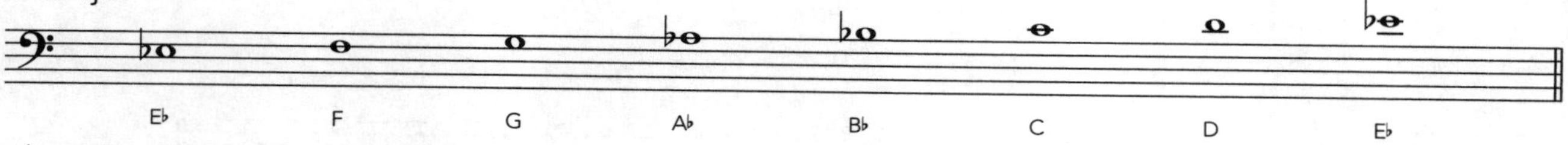

A♭ Major

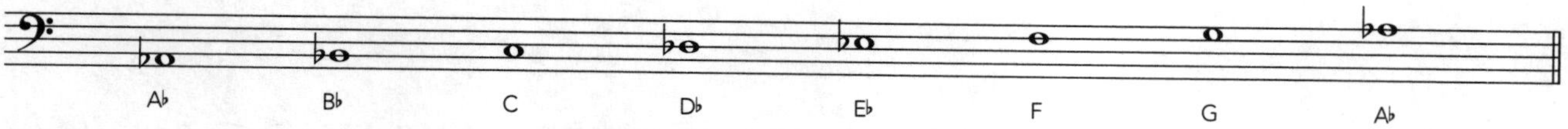

D♭ Major

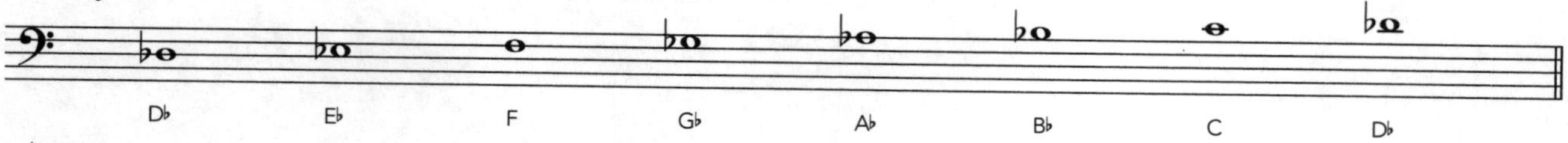

G♭ Major

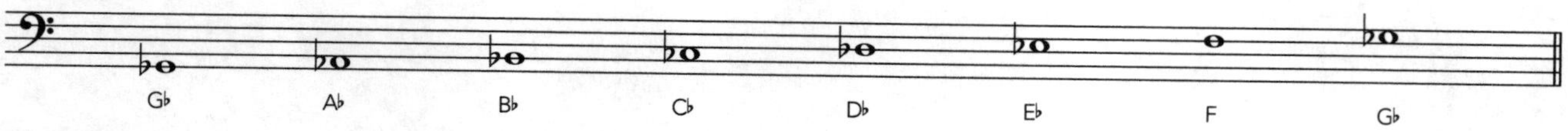

C♭ Major *

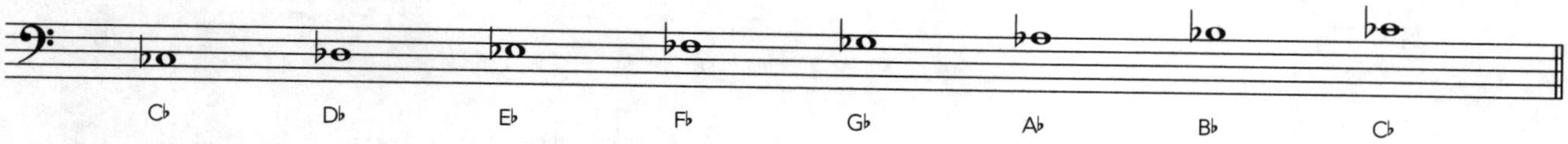

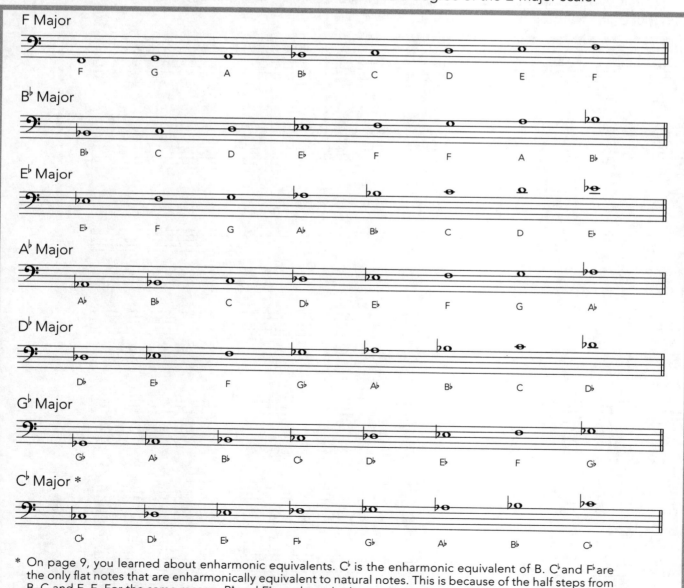

* On page 9, you learned about enharmonic equivalents. C♭ is the enharmonic equivalent of B. C♭ and F♭ are the only flat notes that are enharmonically equivalent to natural notes. This is because of the half steps from B–C and E–F. For the same reason, B♯ and E♯ are the only sharp notes enharmonically equivalent to natural notes (C and F, respectively).

Key Signatures

To make music easier to read and write, the accidentals that occur in a key are placed at the beginning of every line of music. This grouping of accidentals is referred to as a *key signature*.

Following are the key signatures for all of the major keys.

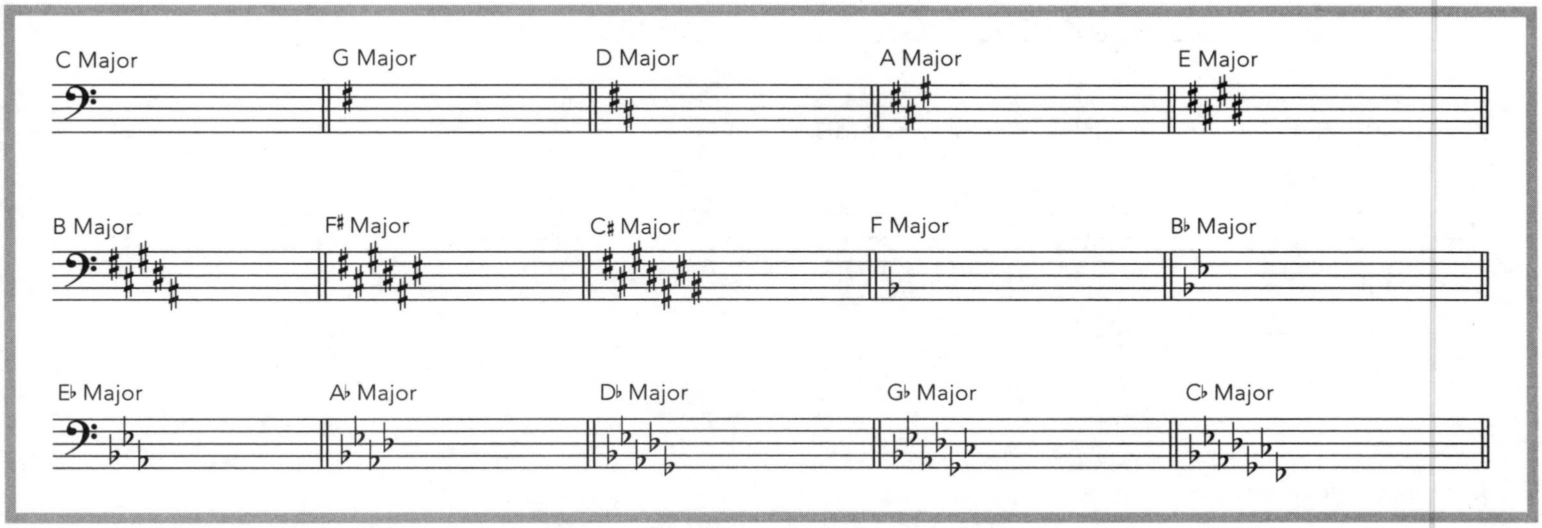

Notice that for the sharp keys, the root note is always the next higher note above the last sharp. For example, the key signature for A Major has three sharps: F♯, C♯ and G♯. A is the next higher note above the last sharp, G♯. For the flat keys, the root of the key is always the next to last flat (except for the key of F, which has only one flat). For example, the key signature for E♭ Major has three flats, B♭, E♭ and A♭. The next to last flat is E♭.

The Cycle of 4ths and 5ths

Notice that as you go through the sharp keys starting from C, each new key is five scale steps away from the previous key. This is known as the *cycle of 5ths*.

Notice also that each new flat key is four scale steps away from the previous key. This is known as the *cycle of 4ths*. The chart at the right illustrates both cycles.

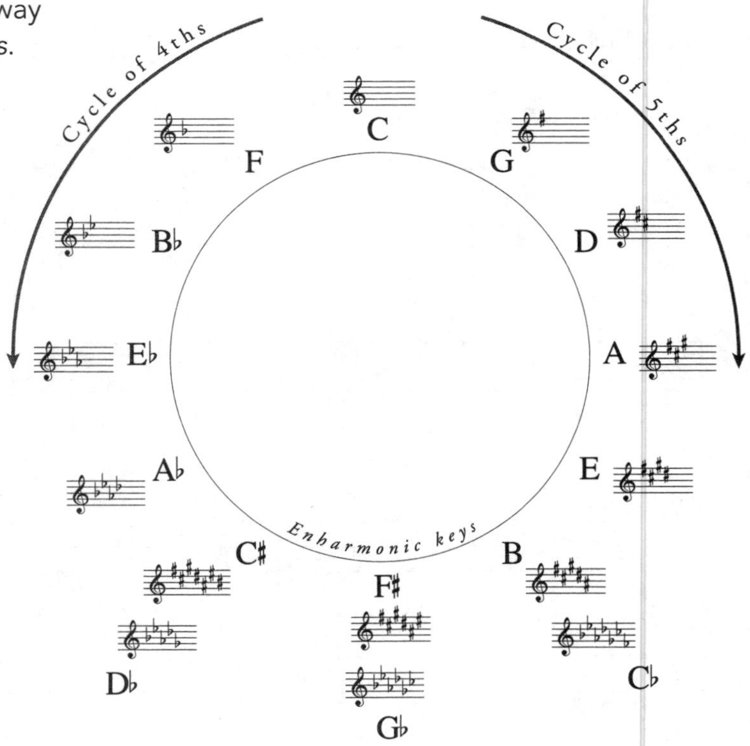

These cycles will help you memorize key signatures quickly. Just remember that C Major has no sharps or flats and both cycles add one sharp or flat respectively as you go through them.

You should have an easy time memorizing your first four sharp keys. They are the open strings from highest to lowest: G, D, A, E.

Notice that the order of sharps of the key signatures is a cycle of 5ths. Starting from the F♯ in the key of G Major. Each new sharp is a 5th away: F♯, C♯, G♯, D♯, A♯, E♯.

The order of flats in the flat key signatures are a cycle of 4ths: B♭, E♭, A♭, D♭, G♭, C♭.

WORKSHEET 4: MAJOR SCALES AND KEY SIGNATURES

1. Using W for "whole step" and H for "half step," write the whole-step/half-step formula for a major scale.

____

2. Write the following major scales using accidentals.

a. G Major b. B♭ Major

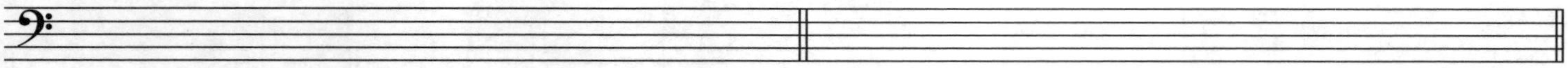

c. A Major d. F Major

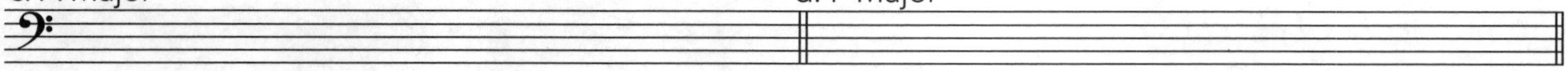

3. Write the following key signatures.

a. E Major b. A♭ Major c. D Major d. D♭ Major

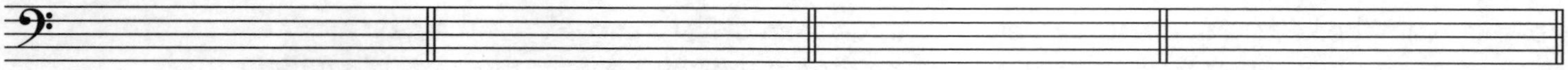

4. Name the key that coincides with the following number of sharps or flats.

a. Four flats ___________

b. Two sharps ___________

c. No sharps or flats ___________

d. Five sharps ___________

e. Two flats ___________

Answers

1 W W H W W W H

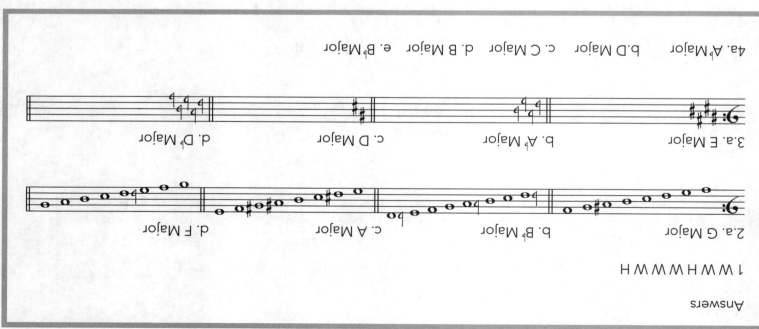

2.a. G Major b. B♭ Major c. A Major d. F Major

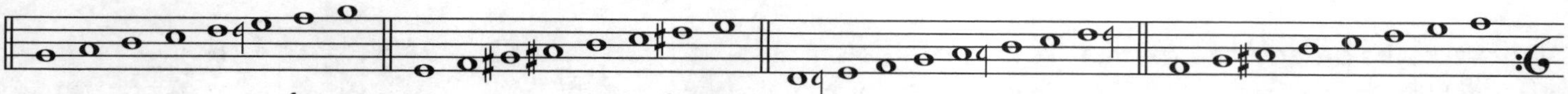

3.a. E Major b. A♭ Major c. D Major d. D♭ Major

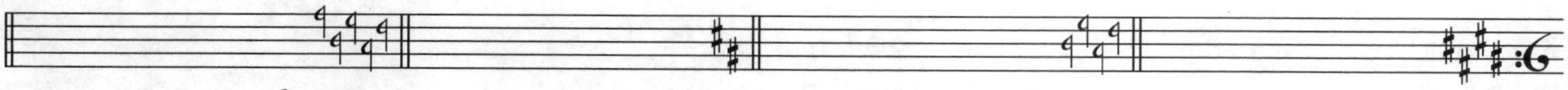

4a. A♭ Major b. D Major c. C Major d. B Major e. B♭ Major

Relative Minor Keys

Each major key has a *relative minor key.* The relative minor and major keys share the same key signature. In other words, the two scales have the same seven notes, the difference being that they start on different tonics.

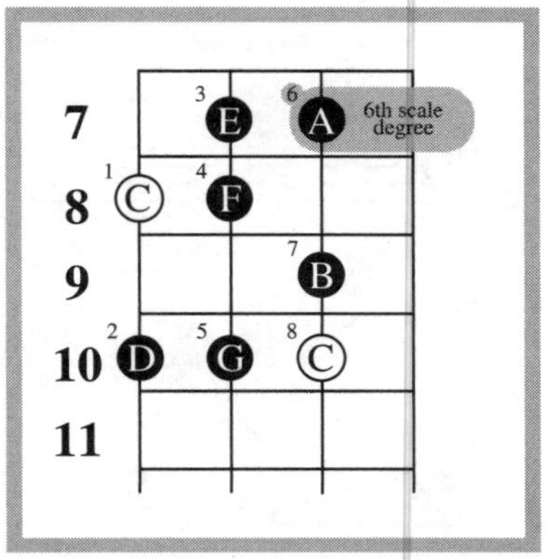

The relative minor scale is always found on the sixth degree of a major scale. The 6th scale degree of C Major is A (C, D, E, F, G, A). Therefore the relative minor of C Major is A Minor.

The relative minor key is also found three half steps below the root of the major scale (C, B, B♭, A).

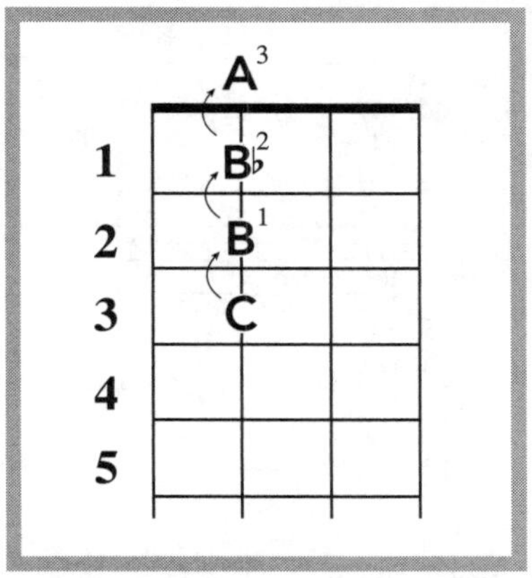

The Natural Minor Scale

The seven notes of a relative minor key are referred to as the *natural minor* scale. The natural minor scale is found by starting on the root of the relative minor key and ascending through the notes of the relative major key until you reach the octave. Remember to play the appropriate accidentals in relation to the major key.

Here is the A Natural Minor scale, which is derived from the C Major scale.

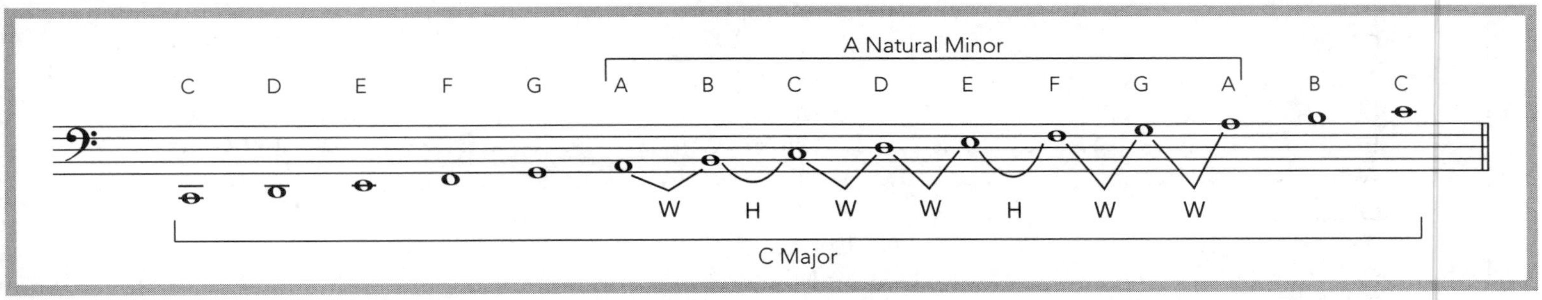

Notice that the pattern of whole steps and half steps is different from that of the major scale. The half steps of a natural minor scale occur between the 2nd and 3rd scale degrees and the 5th and 6th scale degrees.

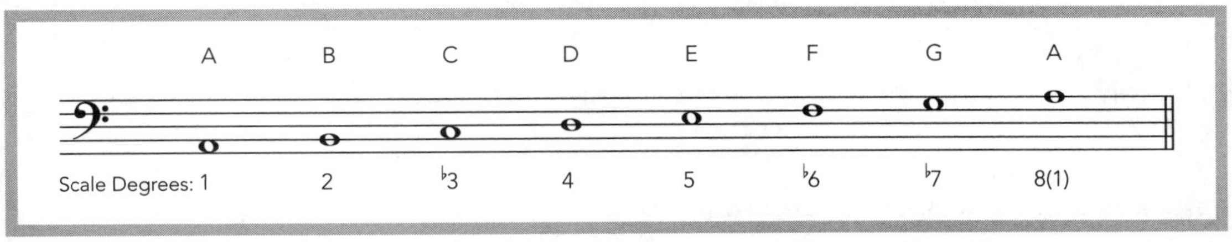

Each natural minor scale has a *relative major* key. It is found three half steps above the root of the natural minor scale. Just as A Minor is the relative minor to the key of C Major, C Major is the relative major to the key of A Minor.

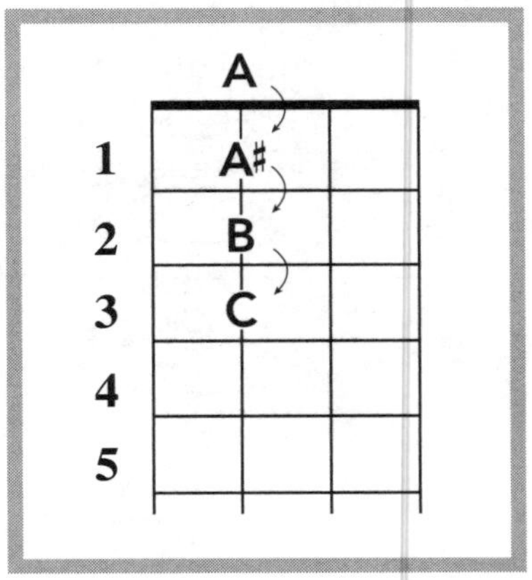

Parallel Minor Keys

A *parallel minor* key is found by playing a natural minor scale starting on the same root as the major scale. The parallel minor of C Major is C Minor. A parallel minor scale can be found by lowering the 3rd, 6th, and 7th scale degrees of a major scale.

The following is a chart summarizing the idea of relative and parallel minor keys.

Major Key	Relative Minor Key	Parallel Minor Key
C	A Minor	C Minor
G	E Minor	G Minor
D	B Minor	D Minor
A	F♯ Minor	A Minor
E	C♯ Minor	E Minor
B	G♯ MInor	B Minor
F♯	D♯ Minor	F♯ Minor
C♯	A♯ Minor	C♯ Minor
F	D Minor	F Minor
B♭	G Minor	B♭ Minor
E♭	C Minor	E♭ Minor
A♭	F Minor	A♭ Minor
D♭	B♭ Minor	D♭ Minor
G♭	E♭ Minor	G♭ Minor
C♭	A♭ Minor	C♭ Minor

Here are three ways to think of a natural minor scale.

1. As a relative minor scale. Simply play all the notes of a major scale starting and ending on the sixth scale degree.

2. As a formula of whole steps and half steps: W–H–W–W–H–W–W.

3. As a parallel minor scale of a major scale. Lower the 3rd, 6th and 7th scale degrees of the major scale.

WORKSHEET 5: RELATIVE MAJOR AND MINOR; PARALLEL MINOR

1. Give the relative minor of the following major keys:

   a. C Major ____________

   b. B♭ Major ____________

   c. G Major ____________

   d. D Major ____________

   e. A♭ Major ____________

2. Give the relative major of the following minor keys:

   a. D Minor ____________

   b. A Minor ____________

   c. B♭ Minor ____________

   d. F# Minor ____________

   e. C Minor ____________

3. Write the following key signatures.

a. A Minor b. D Minor c. C Minor d. D# Minor e. F Minor

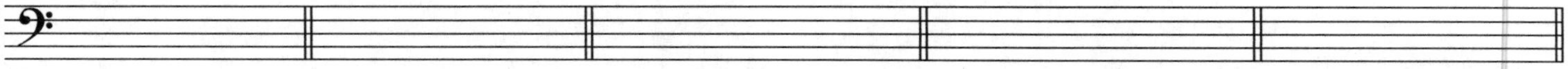

4. Write the following scales using accidentals.

a. C Minor b. E Minor c. F Minor

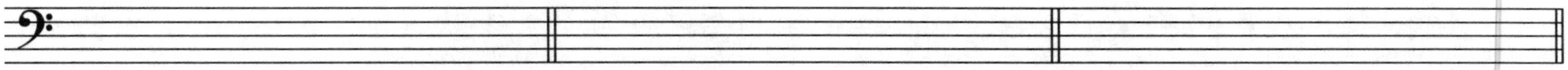

Answers

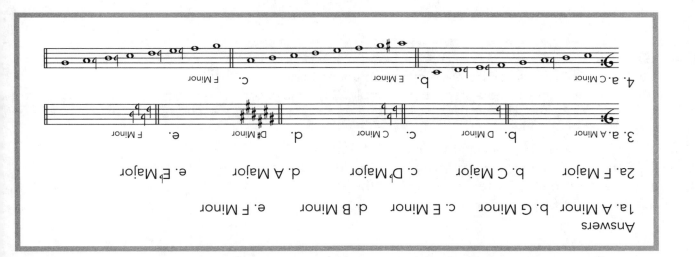

1a. A Minor b. G Minor c. E Minor d. B Minor e. F Minor

2a. F Major b. C Major c. D♭ Major d. A Major e. E♭ Major

3. a. A Minor b. D Minor c. C Minor d. D# Minor e. F Minor

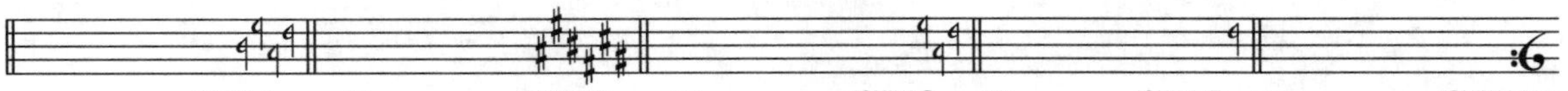

4. a. C Minor b. E Minor c. F Minor

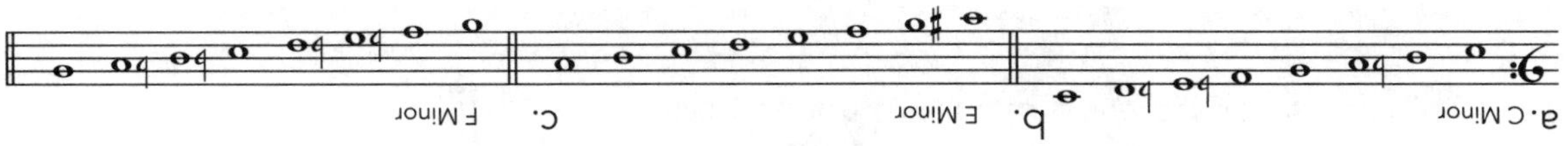

Intervals

An *interval* is the distance between two notes. Each interval is given a number that refers to its distance from a given root. Play each interval *melodically* (one after another) and *harmonically* (simultaneously). A tip for learning the sound of each interval will be provided.

Listen closely to the distinct sound of each interval. Being able to hear intervals is important for a bass player. It enables us to hear and respond to what is happening in the music. It is good to have a specific melody with which you can associate any melodic interval. There will be a suggestion for hearing every interval in this section. While there are many more options than those given, you should settle on one song or bass line for each interval.

It will also be noted whether an interval sounds *consonant* (harmonious, settled) or *dissonant* (harsh, clashing) when played harmonically.

Major and Perfect Intervals

All of the scale steps in a major scale are referred to as *major* or *perfect* intervals. The number of the scale step agrees with the number of the interval. Let's look at each interval in close detail.

PERFECT UNISON

A note that is in *perfect unison* with another is the exact same note. For example C is in unison with C.

A perfect unison is the most consonant interval. An example of two notes in unison is found on the first two notes of the bass line to "Sunshine of Your Love" by Cream.

The diagram at the right shows a common fingering for a unison.

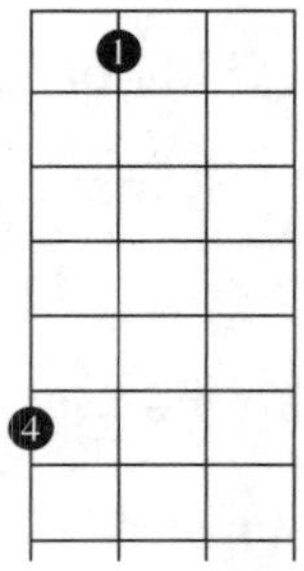

MAJOR 2ND

The second scale degree of a major scale is a *major 2nd* above the tonic. A major 2nd is a distance of one whole step. D is a major 2nd above C. A is a major 2nd above G.

The harmonic major 2nd sounds somewhat dissonant. The distance between the second and third notes of "Happy Birthday" is a major 2nd. A major 2nd can also be heard as the first two notes of a major scale.

The diagram at the right shows two common fingerings for a major 2nd.

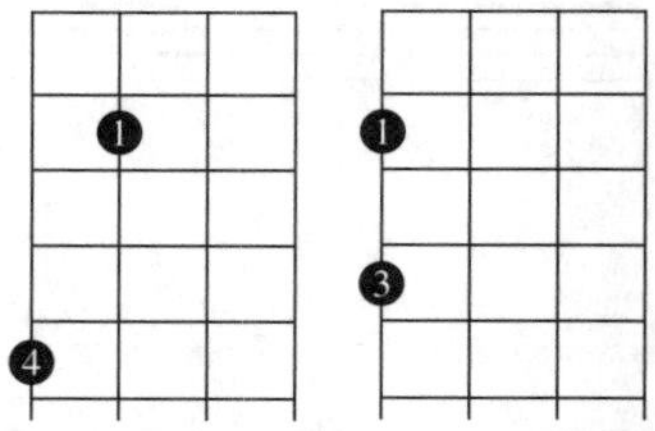

MAJOR 3RD

The third scale degree of a major scale is a *major 3rd* above the tonic. A major 3rd is a distance of two whole steps. For example, E is a major 3rd above C.

The harmonic major 3rd is very consonant sounding. The first two notes of "When the Saints Come Marching In" are a major 3rd apart. Also, the first two notes of the bass line to "Blister in the Sun" by the Violent Femmes are a major 3rd apart.

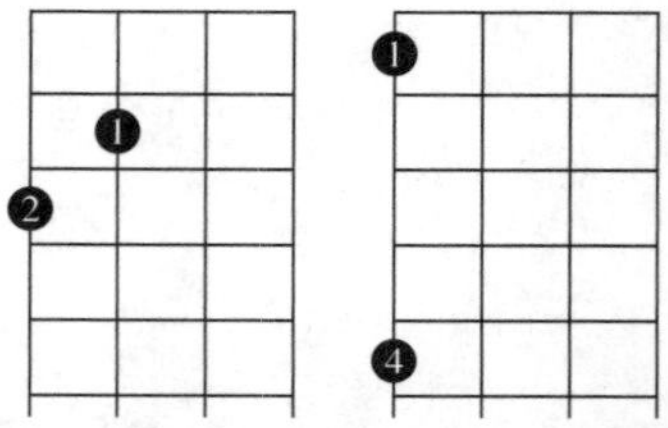

PERFECT 4TH

Perfect 4th

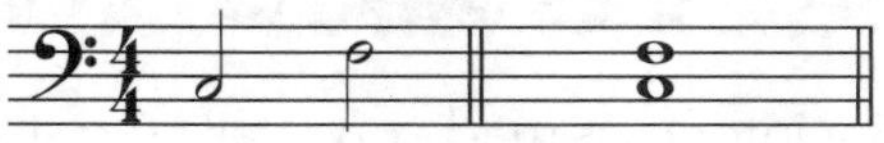

The fourth scale degree of a major scale is a *perfect 4th* above the tonic. A perfect 4th is a distance of two and a half steps. For example, F is a perfect 4th above C.

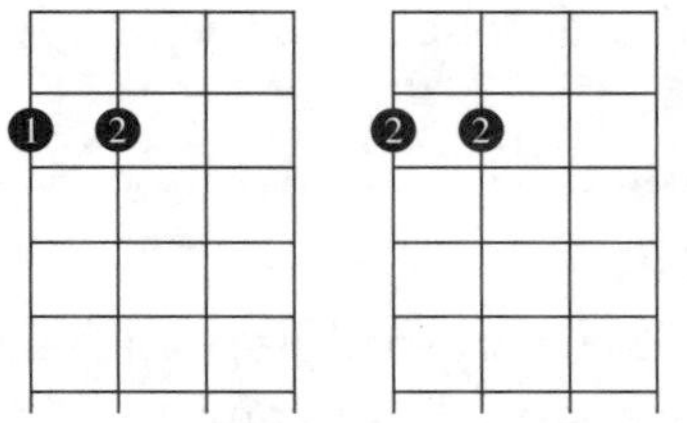

The harmonic perfect 4th is consonant sounding, yet can be heard as *unresolved* or unsettled. The first two notes of "Here Comes the Bride" are a perfect 4th apart.

PERFECT 5TH

Perfect 5th

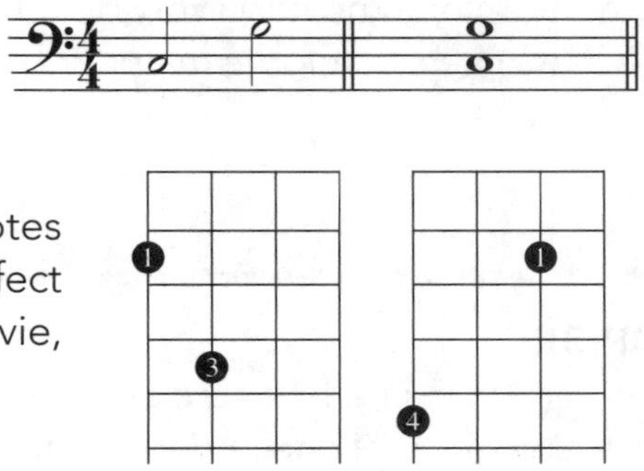

The fifth scale degree of a major scale is a *perfect 5th* above the tonic. The perfect 5th is the distance of three and a half steps. For example, G is a perfect 5th above C.

The harmonic perfect 5th sounds very consonant. The first two notes of the bass line from the Led Zeppelin song "Ramble On" are a perfect 5th apart, as are the first two long notes of the theme from the movie, *Star Wars*.

MAJOR 6TH

Major 6th

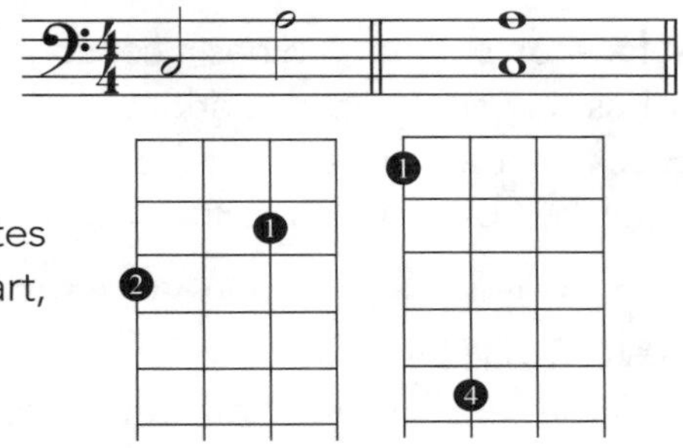

The sixth scale degree of a major scale is a *major 6th* above the tonic. The major 6th is a distance of four and a half steps. For example, A is a major 6th above C.

The harmonic major 6th is very consonant sounding. The first two notes of the theme for NBC, the television network, are a major 6th apart, as are the first two notes of "My Bonnie Lies Over the Ocean."

MAJOR 7TH

Major 7th

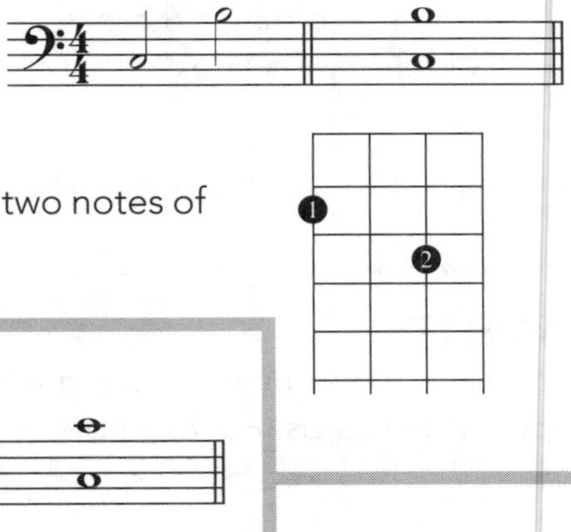

The seventh scale degree of a major scale is a *major 7th* above the tonic. It is a distance of five and a half steps. For example, B is a major 7th above C.

The harmonic major 7th interval sounds very dissonant. The first two notes of "Ceora" by Lee Morgan are a major 7th apart.

PERFECT OCTAVE

Perfect Octave

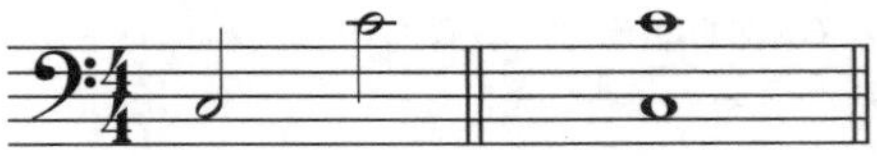

A perfect octave was first explained on page 20. The eighth scale degree of a major scale is a perfect octave above the tonic. Other than the perfect unison, it is the closest distance between any two notes with the same name. The perfect octave is a distance of six whole steps or 12 half steps. For example, C on the 5th fret of the G string is a perfect octave above the C on the 3rd fret of the A string.

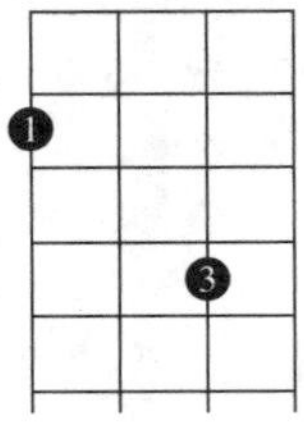

The harmonic perfect octave sounds extremely consonant. The first two notes of "Somewhere Over the Rainbow" from *The Wizard of Oz* are an octave apart.

Minor Intervals

When a major interval is made one half step smaller, the quality becomes *minor*. The easiest way to reduce the distance of a major interval is by lowering the top note with a flat or natural sign.

MINOR 2ND

A *minor 2nd* is one half step smaller than a major 2nd. It is a distance of one half step. For example, D♭ is a minor 2nd above C.

Minor 2nd

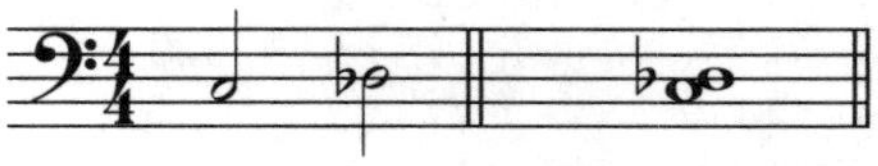

A harmonic minor 2nd has a very dissonant sound. The theme from the movie *Jaws* uses a melodic minor 2nd.

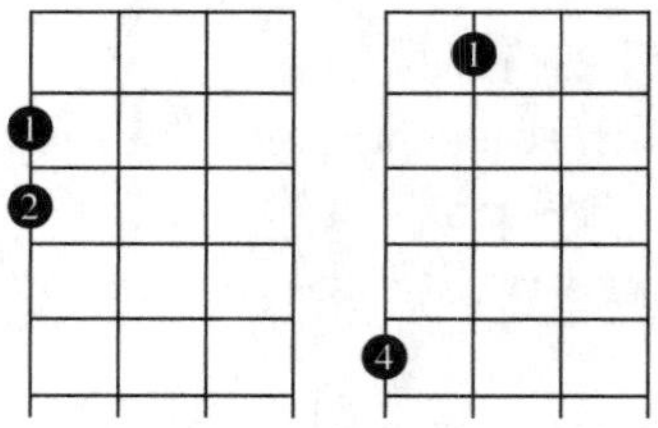

MINOR 3RD

A *minor 3rd* is one half step smaller than a major 3rd. The minor 3rd is a distance of one and a half steps. For example, E♭ is a minor 3rd above C.

Minor 3rd

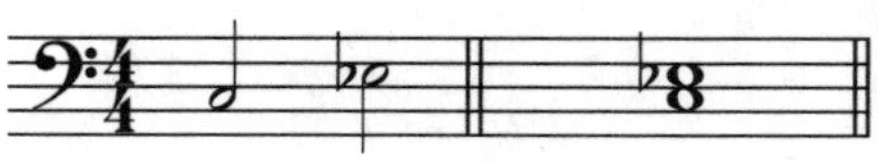

A harmonic minor 3rd has a consonant sound, and many listeners describe it has having a sad or dark quality. The first two notes of "Iron Man" by Black Sabbath are a minor 3rd apart, as are the first two notes of the famous "Lullaby" by Johannes Brahms.

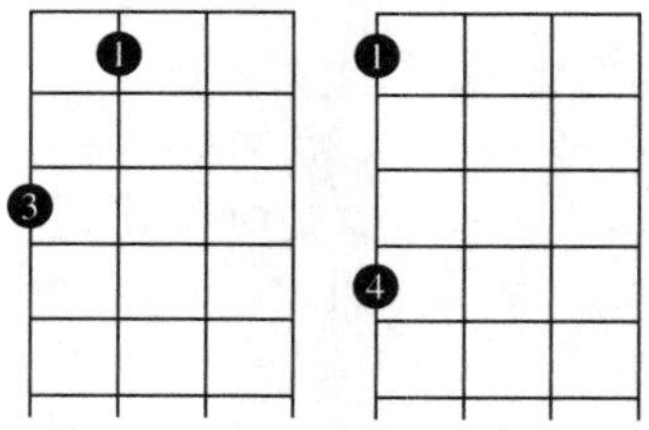

MINOR 6TH

A *minor 6th* is one half step smaller than a major 6th. It is a distance of four whole steps. For example, A♭ is a minor 6th above C.

Minor 6th

A harmonic minor 6th has a consonant sound. The first two notes of John Coltrane's "Equinox" are a minor 6th apart.

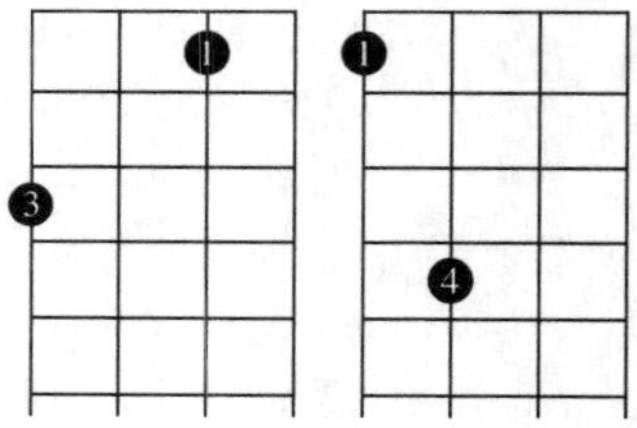

MINOR 7TH

A *minor 7th* is one half step smaller than a major 7th. It is a distance of five whole steps. For example, B♭ is a minor 7th above C.

Minor 7th

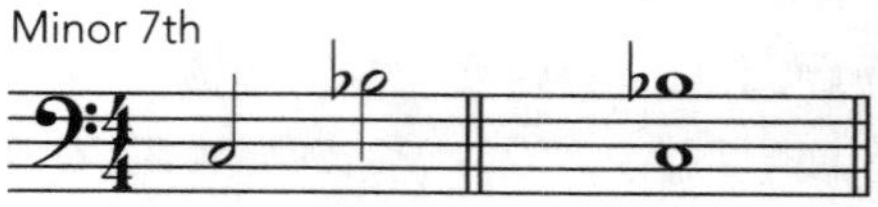

The harmonic minor 7th sounds somewhat dissonant. The first two notes of the theme of the original television series of *Star Trek* are a minor 7th apart.

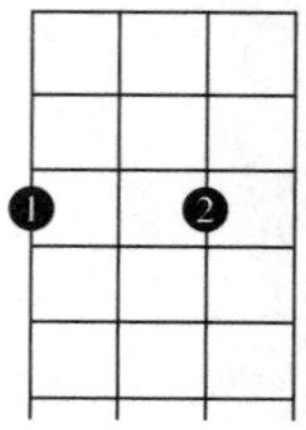

Diminished and Augmented Intervals

When a perfect interval is made smaller, the quality becomes *diminished*. The easiest way to reduce a perfect interval is to lower the top note with a flat or a natural. When a perfect or a major interval is made larger, the quality becomes *augmented*. The best way to make a perfect or major interval larger is to raise the top note with a sharp or a natural.

AUGMENTED 4TH/DIMINISHED 5TH

When a perfect 4th is made larger it becomes an *augmented 4th*. When a perfect 5th is made smaller it becomes a *diminished 5th*. These two intervals are enharmonically equivalent (see page 9). Both are a distance of three whole steps, which is why we often call it a *tritone*. For example, F♯ is an augmented 4th above C, and G♭ is a diminished 5th above C.

Augmented 4th

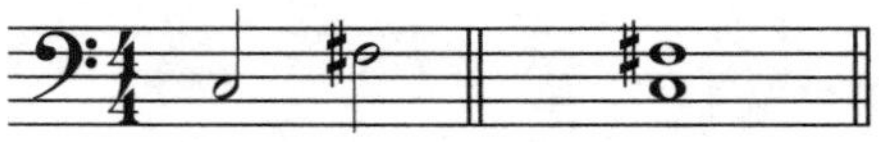

Diminished 5th

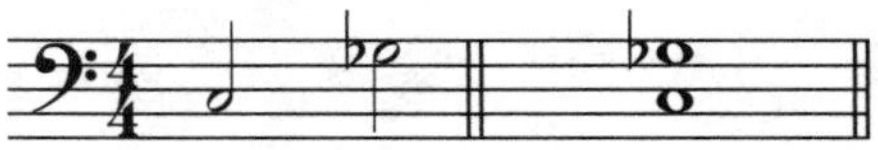

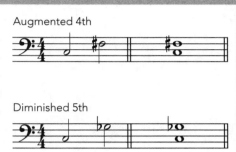

A harmonic tritone is very dissonant and harsh sounding. The first two notes of "The Beautiful People" by Marilyn Manson are a tritone apart.

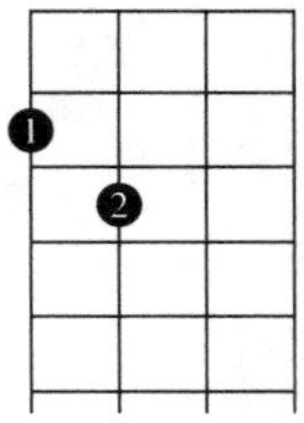

The tritone is the most commonly used augmented or diminished interval. Here is a list of others you might see, with brief explanations.

AUGMENTED 2ND
An *augmented 2nd* is one half step larger than a major 2nd. It is the enharmonic equivalent of a minor 3rd. D♯ is an augmented 2nd above C.

AUGMENTED 5TH
An *augmented 5th* is one half step larger than a perfect 5th. It is the enharmonic equivalent of a minor 6th. G♯ is an augmented 5th above C.

AUGMENTED 6TH
An *augmented 6th* is one half step larger than a major 6th. It is the enharmonic equivalent of a minor 7th. A♯ is an augmented 6th above C.

DIMINISHED 4TH
A *diminished 4th* is one half step smaller than a perfect 4th. It is the enharmonic equivalent of a major 3rd. F♭ is a diminished 4th above C.

Interval Abbreviations

Perfect Unison ..... PU
Minor 2nd............ m2
Major 2nd............ M2
Minor 3rd............. m3
Major 3rd............. M3
Perfect 4th........... P4
Augmented 4th ... A4
Diminished 5th d5
Perfect 5th........... P5
Minor 6th............. m6
Major 6th............. M6
Minor 7th............. m7
Major 7th............. M7
Perfect Octave..... P8

INVERTING INTERVALS

To *invert* an interval is to raise the lower note, or lower the upper note, one octave. When an interval is inverted, the number and quality name change.

The sum of the original interval name and the inverted interval name must equal nine. For example, a 2nd becomes a 7th and a 3rd becomes a 6th.

The following chart shows all of the numbered intervals and their inversions.

Interval		Inversion		
Unison (1)	+	Octave (8)	=	9
2nd	+	7th	=	9
3rd	+	6th	=	9
4th	+	5th	=	9
5th	+	4th	=	9
6th	+	3rd	=	9
7th	+	2nd	=	9
Octave (8)	+	Unison (1)	=	9

When a perfect interval is inverted it remains perfect. All other interval qualities reverse when inverted: major becomes minor, minor becomes major, augmented becomes diminished and diminished becomes augmented.

Interval Quality		Inversion Quality
Perfect	→	Perfect
Major	→	Minor
Minor	→	Major
Augmented	→	Diminished
Diminished	→	Augmented

Let's apply both of these rules to invert a major 2nd. When inverted, a major 2nd becomes a minor 7th (see the third measure below). Remember, a major interval becomes minor when inverted, and the sum of the intervals must equal nine (2+7=9).

The following are some examples of intervals and their inversions.

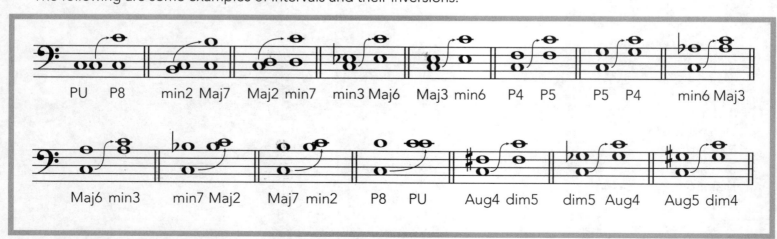

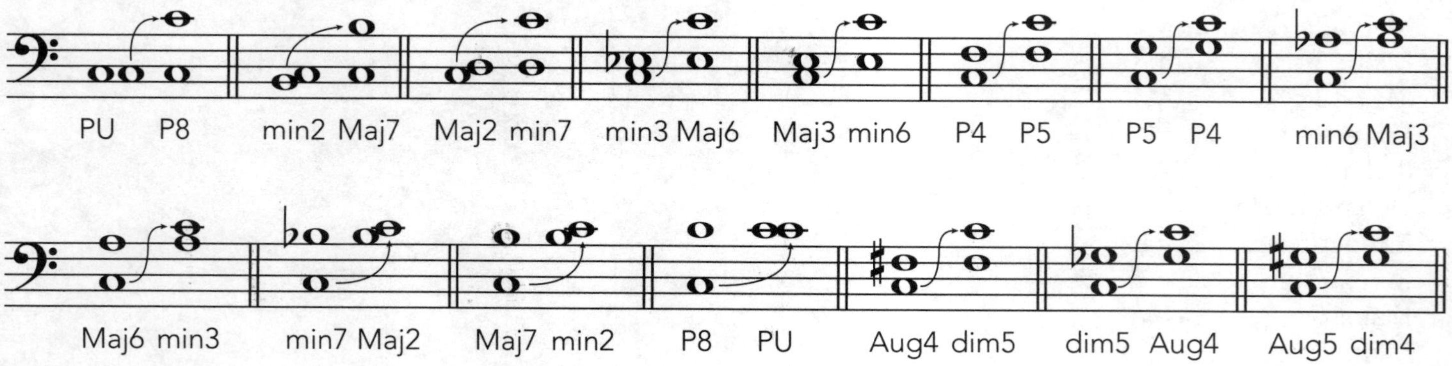

WORKSHEET 6: INTERVALS AND INTERVAL INVERSIONS

1. Name the following intervals.

a. b. c. d. e.

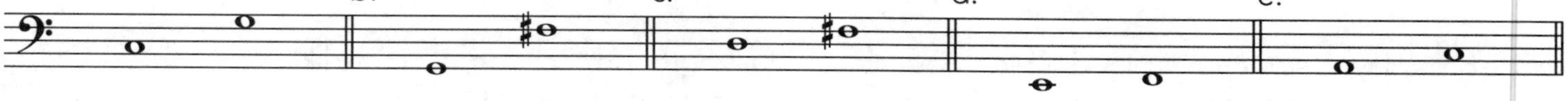

2. Using the following starting notes, write the requested intervals on the staff.

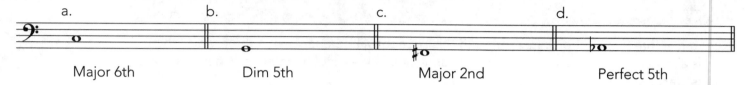

a. b. c. d.

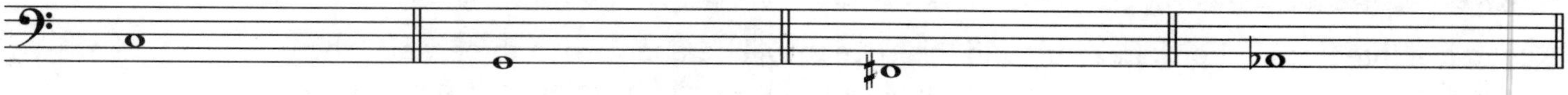

Major 6th Dim 5th Major 2nd Perfect 5th

3. Give the note names of the following intervals in relation to the given note.

a. A minor 2nd above E ____________

b. A perfect 5th above G ____________

c. A major 6th above A ____________

d. A minor 3rd above D ____________

e. A major 7th above E♭ ____________

4. Name the inversion of the following intervals.

a. Perfect 4th ____________

b. Minor 7th ____________

c. Major 3rd ____________

d. Diminished 5th ____________

e. Minor 2nd ____________

Answers

1. a. b. c. d. e.

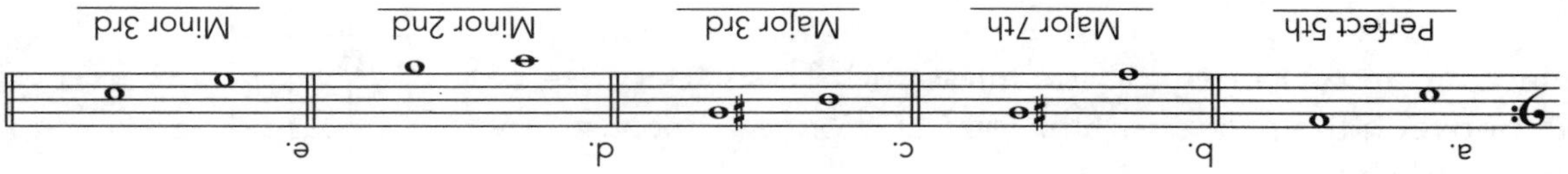

Perfect 5th Major 7th Major 3rd Minor 2nd Minor 3rd

2. a. b. c. d.

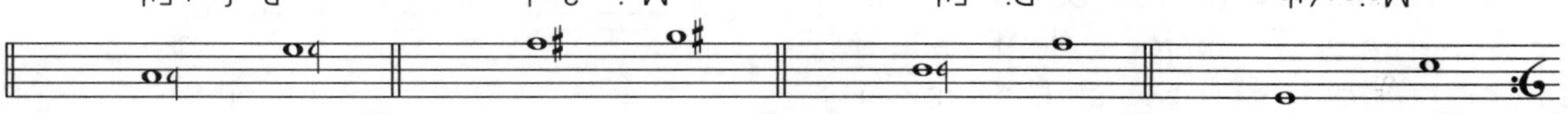

Major 6th Dim 5th Major 2nd Perfect 5th

3a. F b. D c. F♯ d. F e. D

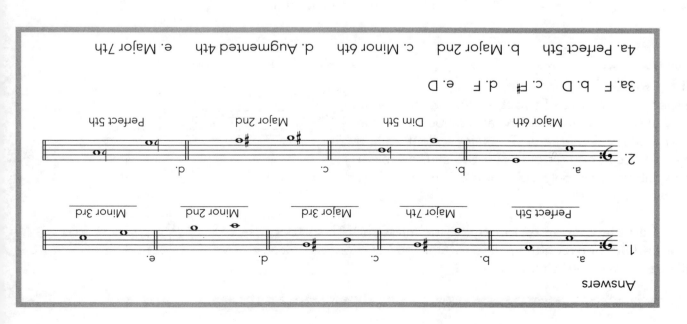

4a. Perfect 5th b. Major 2nd c. Minor 6th d. Augmented 4th e. Major 7th

Introducing Chords

Two notes played together are referred to as an interval or a *double stop*. Three or more notes played at the same time make a *chord*.

While bass players sometimes play double stops and even full chords on occasion, it is more likely that we will be play the *arpeggios* (broken chords, played one note at a time). A bass player must constantly interpret the chords that are played by the guitar or piano player. Only with a full understanding of chords is a bass player able to fluently create complimenting bass lines.

Triads

A *triad* is a three-note chord. Each triad in this section will be analyzed in three ways: the intervals above the *root* (the lowest note and namesake of the triad); in relation to a major scale; and as stacked 3rds.

MAJOR TRIAD

A *major* triad consists of a root, a major 3rd and a perfect 5th. A major triad can also be built from the 1st, 3rd and 5th scale degrees of a major scale. Finally, a major triad can be built by stacking two 3rds: a major 3rd under a minor 3rd. For example, a C Major triad has a major 3rd from C to E and a minor 3rd from E to G. The symbol for a major triad is just the note name. C Major is "C."

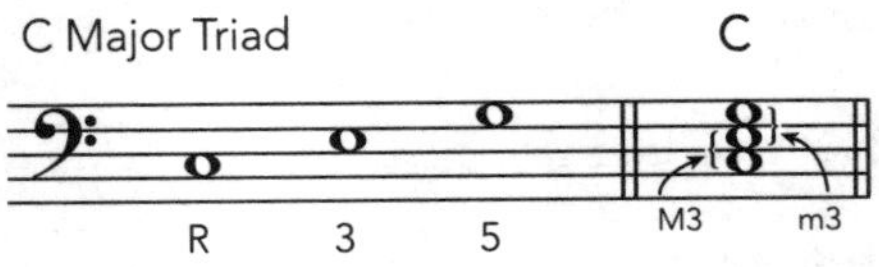

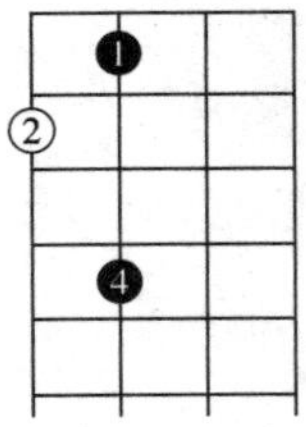

A major triad has a consonant, happy sound. Major triads are used in the bass line to The Beatles' "Ob-la-di, Ob-la-da."

○= Root

MINOR TRIAD

A *minor* triad consists of a root, a minor 3rd and a perfect 5th. A minor triad can also be built from the 1st, ♭3rd and 5th scale degrees of a major scale. Finally, it can be thought of as a minor 3rd under a major 3rd. The symbols commonly used for a C Minor triad are Cmin, Cm or C-. In this book, we will use Cmin.

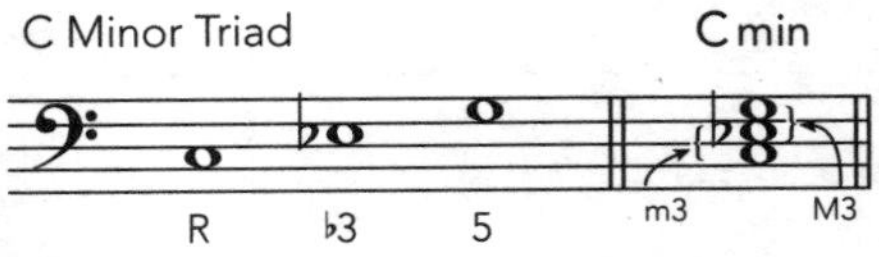

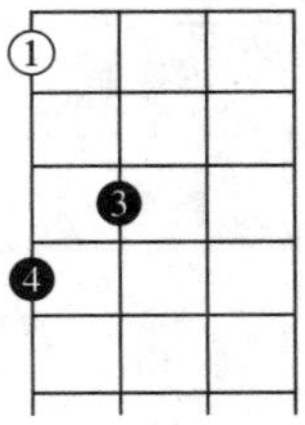

A minor triad sounds consonant, yet sad. The repetitive riff in Cliff Burton's (Metallica) bass solo, "(Anesthesia) Pulling Teeth," starts with a minor triad.

DIMINISHED TRIAD

A *diminished* triad consists of a root, a minor 3rd and a diminished 5th. A diminished triad can also be built from the 1st, ♭3rd, and ♭5th scale degrees of a major scale. Finally, a diminished triad can be thought of as two stacked minor 3rds. The symbols commonly used for a C Diminished triad are Cdim or C°. In this book, we will use Cdim.

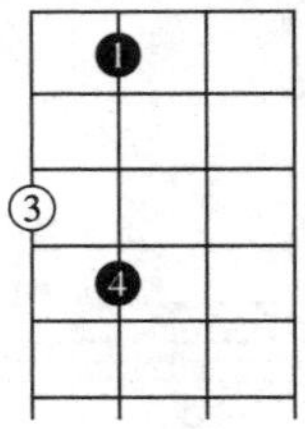

The diminished triad has an extremely dissonant sound. This is because of the diminished 5th between the root and ♭5th. The last chord of "Because" by the Beatles is a diminished chord.

AUGMENTED TRIAD

The *augmented* triad consists of a root, a major 3rd and an ♯5th. An augmented triad can also be built from the 1st, 3rd and ♯5th scale degrees of a major scale. Finally an augmented triad can be thought of as two stacked major 3rds. The first chord of "Oh! Darling" by the Beatles is an augmented triad.

The augmented triad has a dissonant sound.

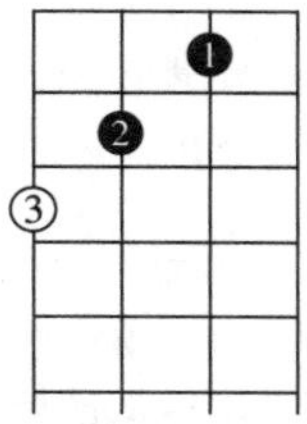

The following is a summary of triads.

Triad	Scale Degrees	Intervals Above the Root	Stacked 3rds
Major	1–3–5	Root, M3, P5	M3, m3
Minor	1–♭3–5	Root, m3, P5	m3, M3
Diminished	1–♭3–♭5	Root, m3, d5	m3, m3
Augmented	1–3–♯5	Root, M3, A5	M3, M3

WORKSHEET 7: TRIADS

1. Name the intervals above the roots of the following triads.
   a. diminished triad ______________________
   b. major triad ______________________
   c. minor triad ______________________
   d. augmented triad ______________________

2. Complete the following triads from the given root.

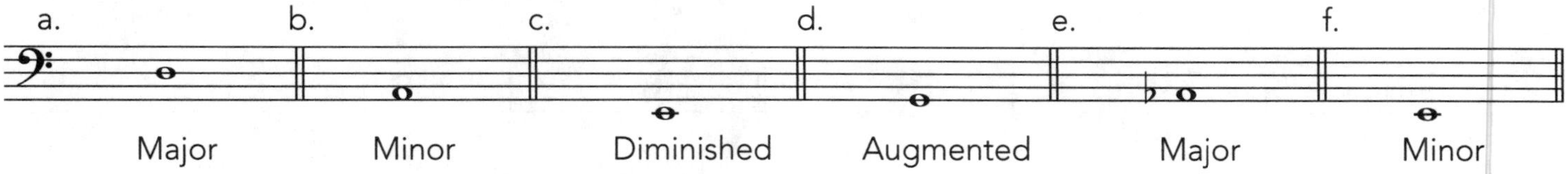

3. Identify the following triads.

_________ _________ _________ _________ _________ _________ _________ _________

Answers

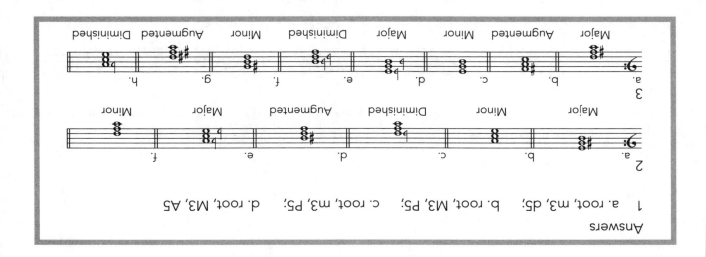

1 a. root, m3, d5; b. root, M3, P5; c. root, m3, P5; d. root, M3, A5

2

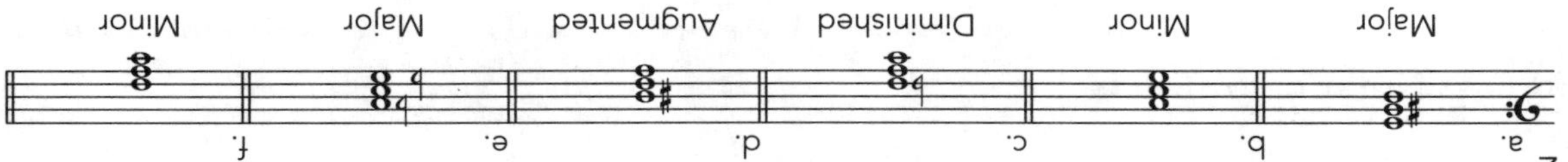

3

Inverting Triads

An *inverted* triad is one in which a chord tone other than the root is in the *bass* (or the lowest note). Each of the four triad qualities can be inverted. There are three basic ways to *voice* (arrange the notes of) a triad: root position, 1st inversion and 2nd inversion. All of the triads covered thus far have been shown in root position.

A **root position** triad has its **root in the bass**.
A **1st inversion** triad has its **3rd in the bass**.
A **2nd inversion** triad has its **5th in the bass**.

For example, a C Major triad has C in the bass; in 1st inversion, a C Major triad has E in the bass; in 2nd inversion, a C Major triad has G in the bass.

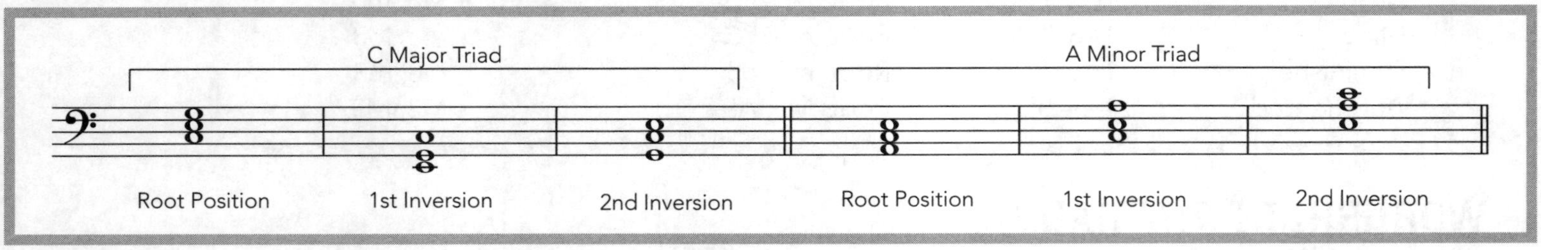

SLASH CHORDS

Slash chords can be used to write chord symbols for inverted chords. In slash chord notation, the chord symbol is written to the left of the slash and the note to be played in the bass is written to the right. A C Major triad in 1st inversion is written "C/E" (C Major with E in the bass). A C Major triad in 2nd inversion is written "C/G" (C Major with G in the bass).

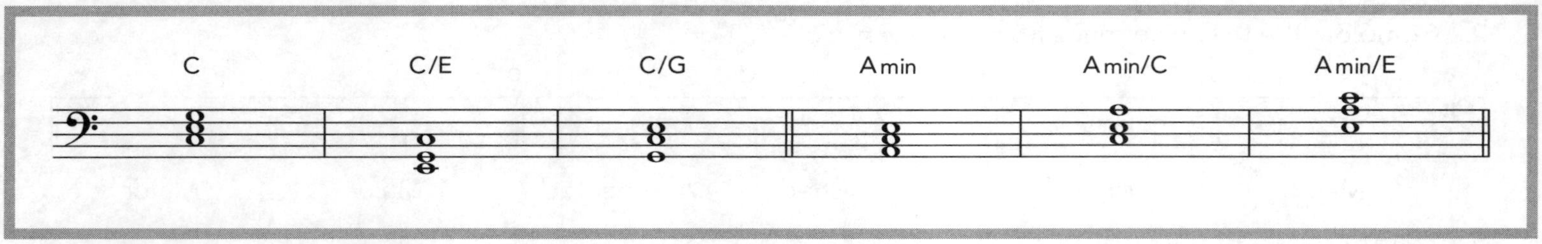

FIGURED BASS NOTATION

Another way to notate inversions is called *figured bass*. In figured bass, numbers are used to indicate the intervals above the bass of the chord. Let's look at the C Major triad and A Minor triad and see how figured bass is used for root position and inverted voicings.

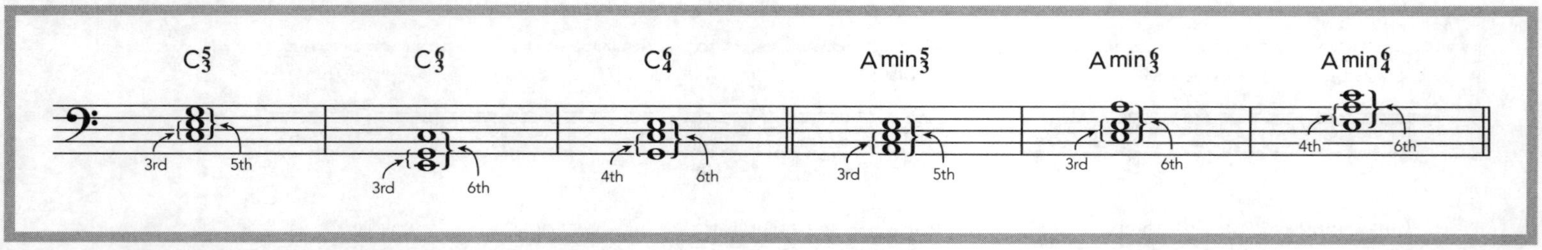

Summary of Figured Bass Notation of Triads

Root position = $^{5}_{3}$ (Figured bass is usually not written for root position chords.)

1st inversion = $^{6}_{3}$

2nd inversion = $^{6}_{4}$

WORKSHEET 8: INVERTED TRIADS

1. Write the triads for the indicated inversions.

a. G$^{5}_{3}$ b. Emin $^{6}_{3}$ c. F$^{6}_{4}$ d. A♭$^{6}_{3}$ e. Dmin $^{5}_{3}$ f. C$^{6}_{4}$

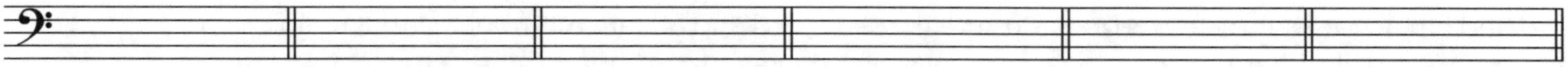

2. Write the indicated inverted triads.

a. G/B b. EAug/G♯ c. Fmin/C d. E♭/B♭ e. F♯/C♯ f. Adim/E♭ g. D/F♯ h. B♭/D

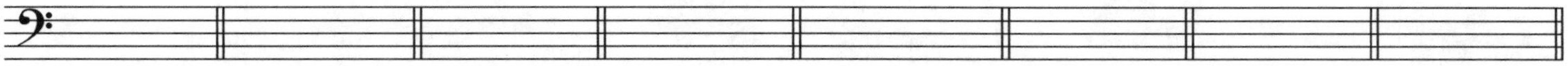

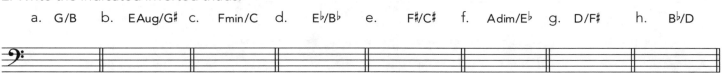

3. Identify the following inverted triads using slash chords.

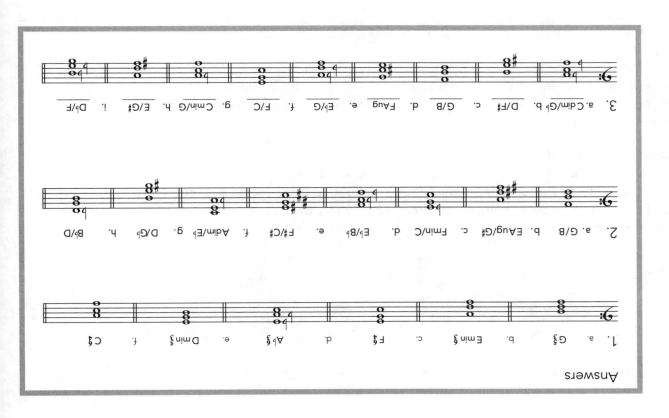

a.______ b.______ c.______ d.______ e.______ f.______ g.______ h.______ i.______

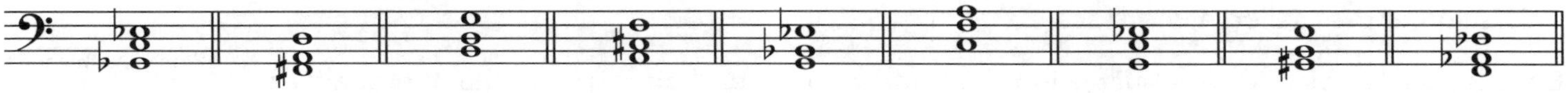

Answers

1. a. G$^{5}_{3}$ b. Emin$^{6}_{3}$ c. F$^{6}_{4}$ d. A♭$^{6}_{3}$ e. Dmin$^{5}_{3}$ f. C$^{6}_{4}$

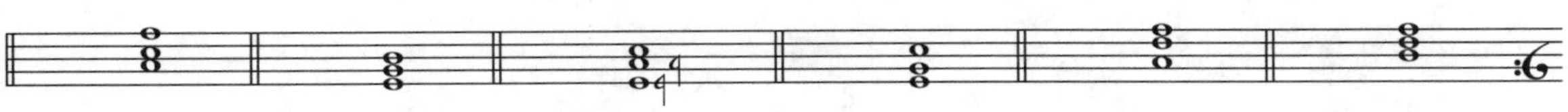

2. a. G/B b. EAug/G♯ c. Fmin/C d. E♭/B♭ e. F♯/C♯ f. Adim/E♭ g. D/G♭ h. B♭/D

3. a. Cdim/G♭ b. D/F♯ c. G/B d. FAug e. E♭/G f. F/C g. Cmin/G h. E/G♯ i. D♭/F

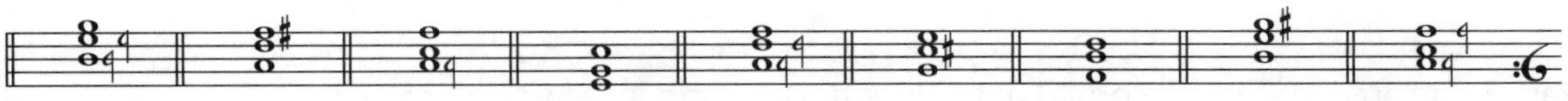

Diatonic Triads in Major Keys

Each major key has seven *diatonic* triads. Diatonic means "belonging to the key." The diatonic triads for each key are found by building a triad from each of the seven scale degrees of a major scale.

To build diatonic triads in a major key, start with the seven notes of the given key. Then add a 3rd and 5th above each scale degree. Be sure that each 3rd and 5th are members of that major scale. This is called *harmonizing the scale*. Let's use the key of C Major as an example.

First, spell a C Major scale.

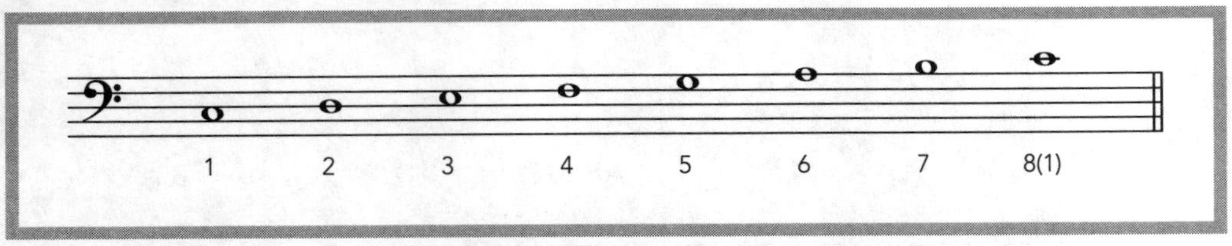

Next, build a triad using the 3rd and 5th above each scale degree. Notice that every triad consists of every other note of the major scale above that root. Finally check the quality of each triad to see if it is major, minor or diminished (there is no augmented triad in a major key).

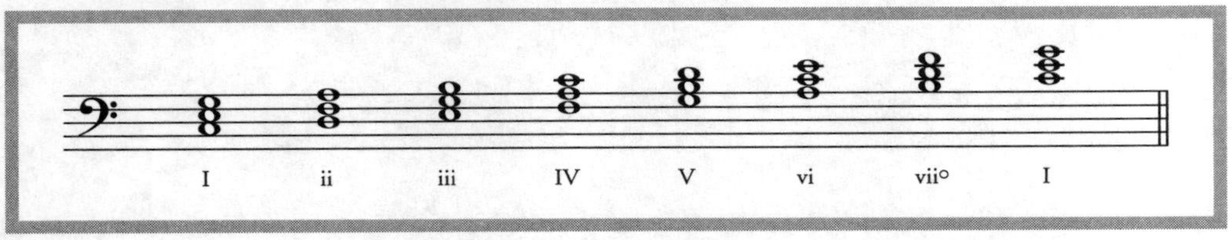

This is sometimes called a *chord scale*.

Because each major scale is built using the same whole-step/half-step formula, the qualities of the diatonic triads will remain consistent for every key. For this reason, Roman numerals are used to analyze the triads in a given key. The Roman numerals agree with the number of the scale step. There is a quick review of Roman numerals and their Arabic equivalents at the right. Notice that this symbol ° is used to indicate a diminished triad.

Roman Numeral Review	
I, i	1
II, ii	2
III, iii	3
IV, iv	4
V, v	5
VI, vi	6
VII, vii	7

I, IV and V are major
ii, iii, and vi are minor
vii° is diminished

Memorizing the qualities of diatonic triads is essential to understanding and interpreting chord progressions. Here's another tip: Saying that a chord is "diatonic to the key of C Major" is the same as saying that it is "in the key of C Major."

SCALE DEGREE FUNCTION NAMES

The *function* or behavior of each chord becomes important as we consider them in relation to one another in the context of a song or piece of music. Each triad in a key has a function name that should be learned, as these names are commonly used by musicians.

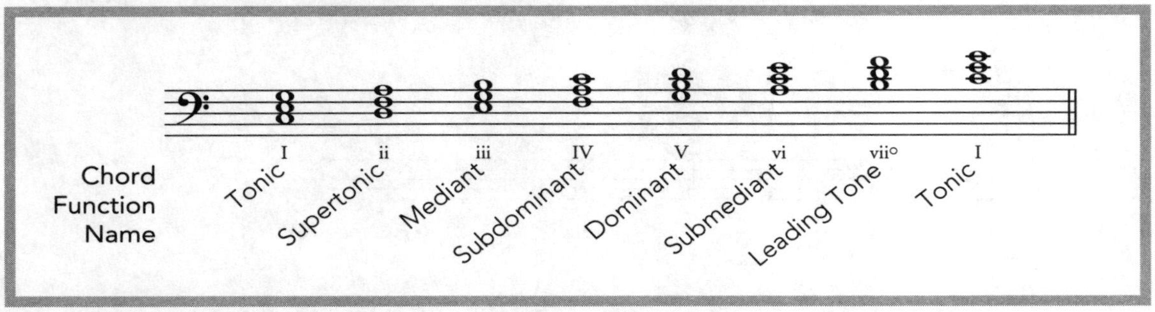

Diatonic Triads in Minor Keys (Natural Minor Scale)

The same method used to generate diatonic triads in major keys is used for minor keys. The difference in this case being that a minor scale is used to generate the triads, therefore the scale steps and qualities will change. Let's use they key of A Minor as an example.

Start with an A Natural Minor scale (other types of minor scales can be used, too, and they will be covered on page 63.

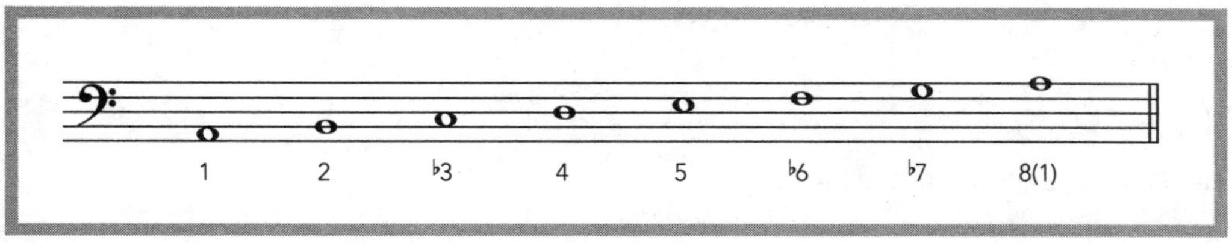

Next, add a diatonic 3rd and 5th above each scale degree and analyze the resulting triads with Roman numerals. Notice that as with scale degrees, the triads of the minor scale are analyzed as parallel to those of the major scale. So, a triad built on the third note of the scale, which we think of as being ♭3 when compared to 3 of a parallel major scale, is thought of as being ♭III when compared to the iii in a major key.

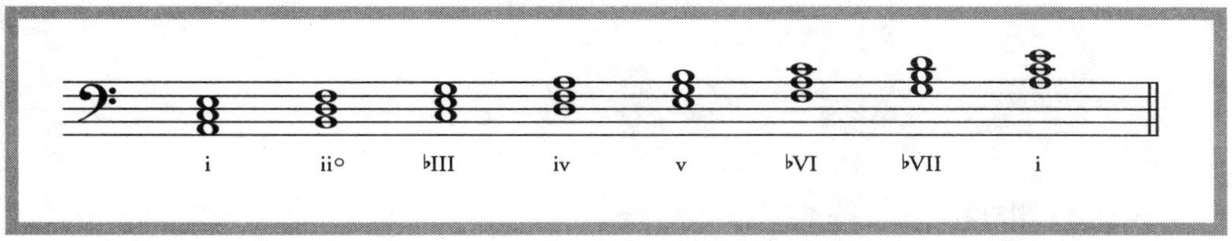

The chord qualities will remain the same for every minor key harmonized with the natural minor scale.

i, iv and v are minor
♭III, ♭VI, and ♭VII are major
ii° is diminished

WORKSHEET 9: DIATONIC TRIADS

1. Give the Roman numerals of a major key.

____

2. Give the Roman numerals of a minor key.

____

3. Give the specific note name and quality of the indicated triad.
   a. The V of C Major ______________
   b. The ii of G Major______________
   c. The vi of E Major ______________
   d. The iv of F Minor ______________
   e. The vii° of E♭ Major______________
   f. The i of D Minor ______________
   g. The iii of B♭ Major______________

4. Name all of the diatonic triads in the key of G Major.

____

5. Analyze the following triads using Roman numerals. All of the triads are in the key of F Major.

a. b. c. d. e. f.

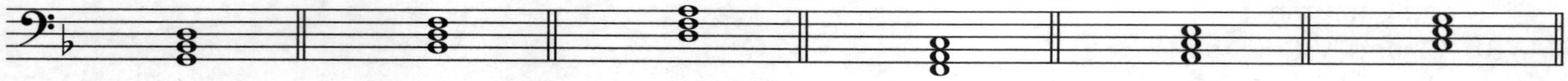

____ ____ ____ ____ ____ ____

Answers

1. I ii iii IV V vi vii°

2. i ii° ♭III iv v ♭VI ♭VII

3a. G b. Amin c. C♯min d. B♭min e. Ddim f. Dmin g. Dmin

4. G, Amin, Bmin, C, D, Emin, F♯dim

5 a. b. c. d. e. f.

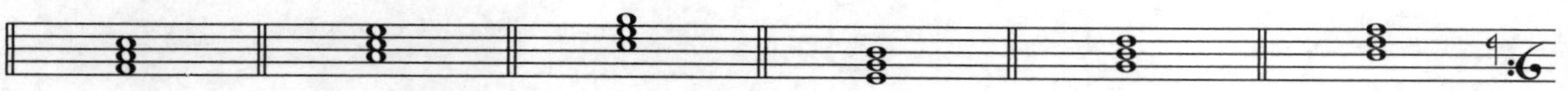

ii IV vi I iii V

7th Chords

A *7th chord* consists of four notes: a root and three notes above that root stacked in 3rds. There are four 7th chords covered in this section. Each will be analyzed in three ways: in relation to a triad; in relation to a major scale; and as stacked 3rds.

MAJOR 7TH

C Major 7th

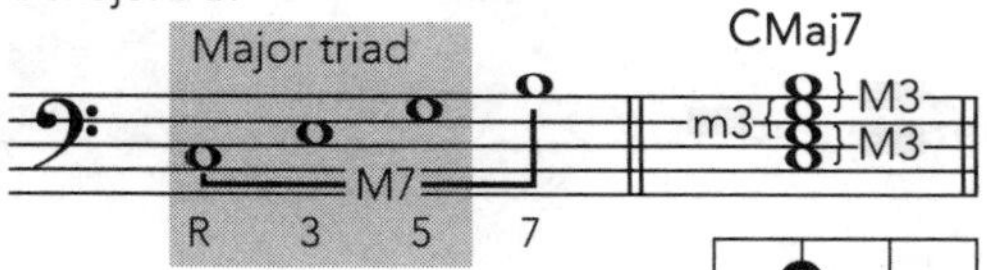

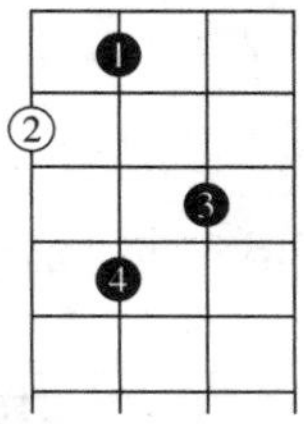

A *major 7th* chord consists of a major triad with a major 7th added above the root. It can also be built from the 1st, 3rd, 5th and 7th scale degrees of a major scale. Finally, it can be built by stacking a major 3rd, minor 3rd and a major 3rd. Common chord symbols for a C Major 7th chord are CMaj7, CM7 and C△7. In this book, we'll use CMaj7.

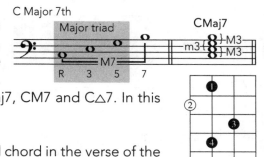

A major 7th chord sounds very open and jazzy. The second chord in the verse of the Beatles' song, "Something," is a major 7th chord.

DOMINANT 7TH

C Dominant 7

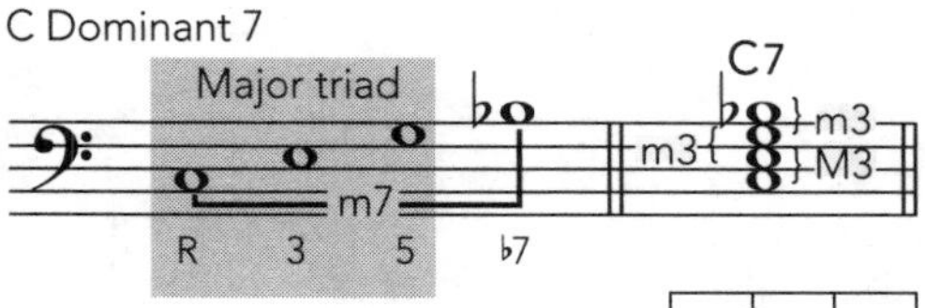

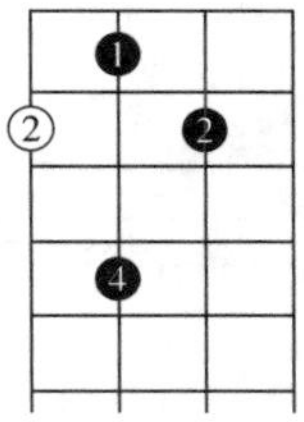

A *dominant 7th* chord is a major triad with a minor 7th added above the root. It can also be built from the 1st, 3rd, 5th and ♭7th scale degrees of a major scale. Finally, it can be built by stacking a major 3rd, minor 3rd and a minor 3rd. The chord symbol for a C Dominant 7th chord is C7.

A dominant 7th chord can be perceived as having a fair amount of tension and sounds as if it requires resolution to a more consonant sound (usually a chord whose root is a perfect 5th below). The sound is also closely associated with the blues, in which context dominant 7th chords are sometimes so prevalent as to negate any feeling of tension. The third chord in the verse of the Beatles' song, "Something," is a dominant 7th chord.

MINOR 7TH

C Minor 7

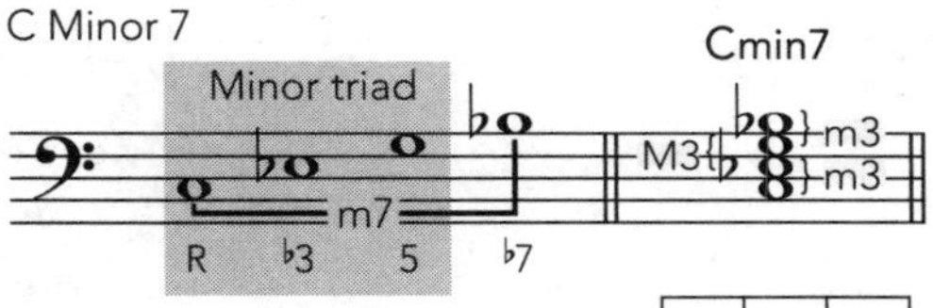

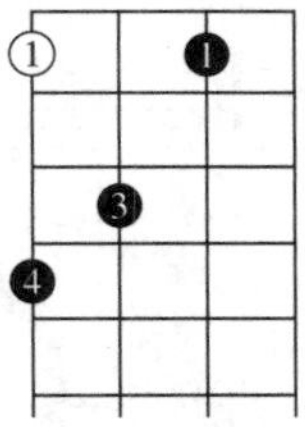

A *minor 7th* chord is a minor triad with a minor 7th added above the root. It can also be built using the 1st, ♭3rd, 5th and ♭7th scale degrees of a major scale (or, you can think of it as coming from every other note of the natural minor scale, starting on the tonic). Finally, it can be built by stacking a minor 3rd, major 3rd and a minor 3rd. Common chord symbols for C Minor 7th are Cmin7 and C-7. In this book, we'll use Cmin7.

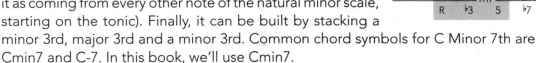

A minor 7th chord also has a slightly jazzy sound, but is more dark or sad. The first two chords in the verses of Santana's "Evil Ways" are minor 7th chords.

MINOR 7♭5

Cmin7♭5

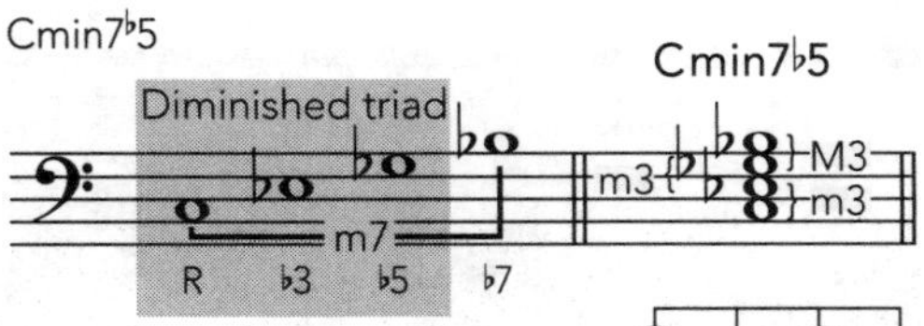

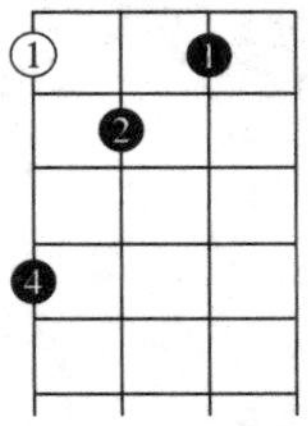

A *minor7♭5* chord is a diminished triad with a minor 7th added above the root. It can also be built using the 1st, ♭3rd, ♭5th and ♭7th scale degrees of a major scale. Finally, it can be built by stacking a minor 3rd, minor 3rd and a major 3rd. The minor 7♭5 is sometimes called *half diminished*. Common chord symbols for C Minor 7♭5 are Cmin7♭5 and Cø7. In this book, we'll use Cmin7♭5.

A minor 7♭5 chord has a dissonant, unsettled sound. The fifth chord in "Autumn Leaves" is a minor 7♭5 chord.

ø = This symbol is sometimes used for min7♭5, or half-diminished 7th.

WORKSHEET 10: 7TH CHORDS

1. Name the intervals of the following 7th chords.

   a. Minor 7th ____________________

   b. Major 7th ____________________

   c. Dominant 7th ____________________

   d. Minor 7♭5 ____________________

2. Identify the following 7th chords.

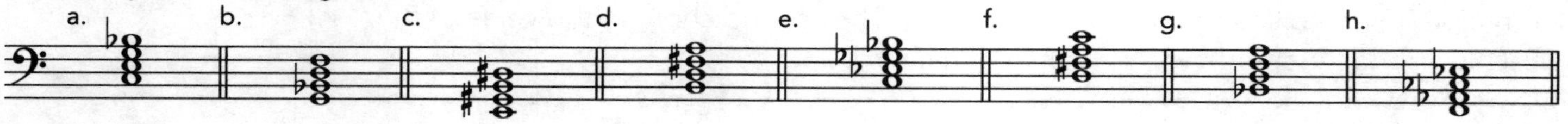

3. Write the following 7th chords.

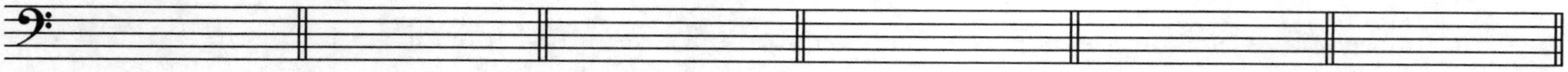

Answers

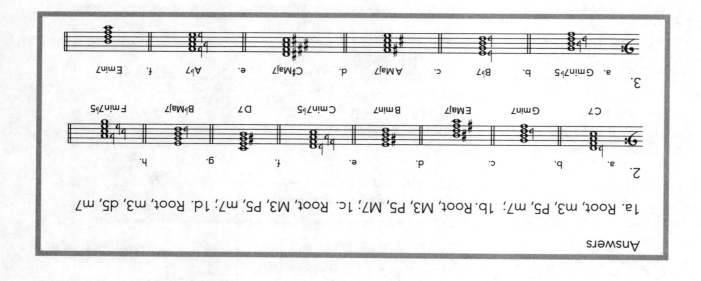

1a. Root, m3, P5, m7; 1b. Root, M3, P5, M7; 1c. Root, M3, P5, m7; 1d. Root, m3, d5, m7

2.

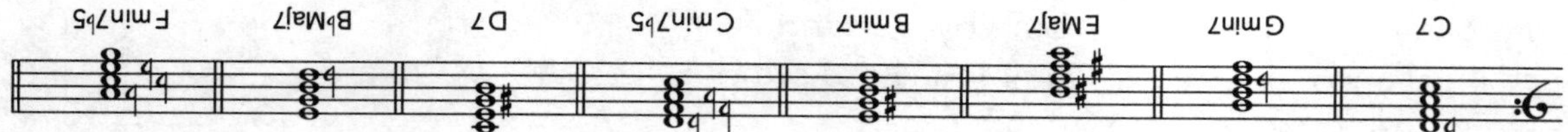

3.

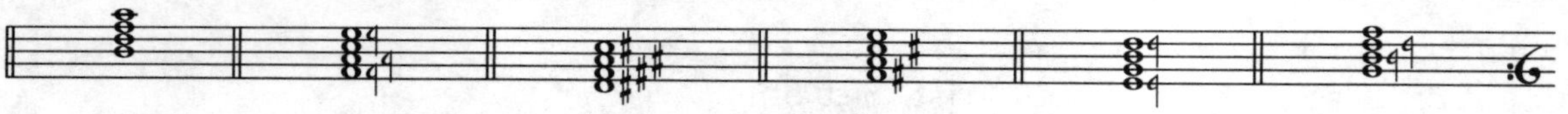

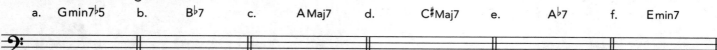

Inverting 7th Chords

Any type of 7th chord can be voiced in four basic ways: root position, 1st inversion, 2nd inversion and *3rd inversion*. Remember, an inversion is a chord with a chord tone other than the root in the bass.

7th chord inversions

Root position has the **root in the bass**.
1st inversion has the **3rd in the bass**.
2nd inversion has the **5th in the bass**.
3rd inversion has the **7th in the bass**.

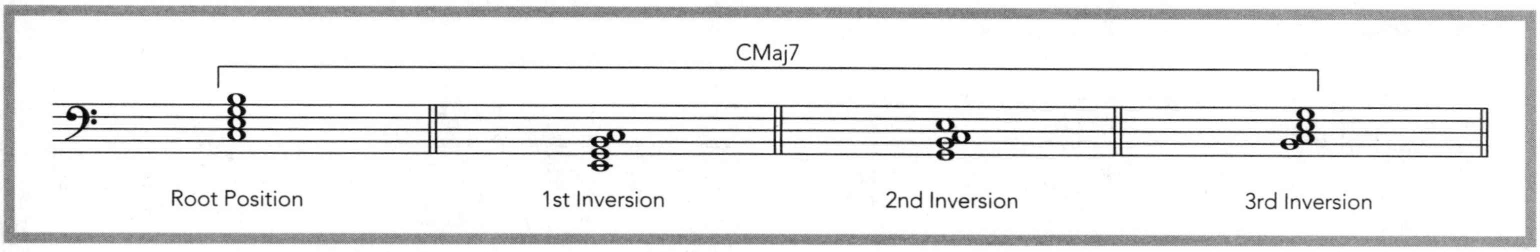

SLASH CHORD NOTATION

As with triads, 7th chord inversions are commonly notated using slash chords. Remember, a slash chord consists of the chord symbol followed by a slash and the bass note.

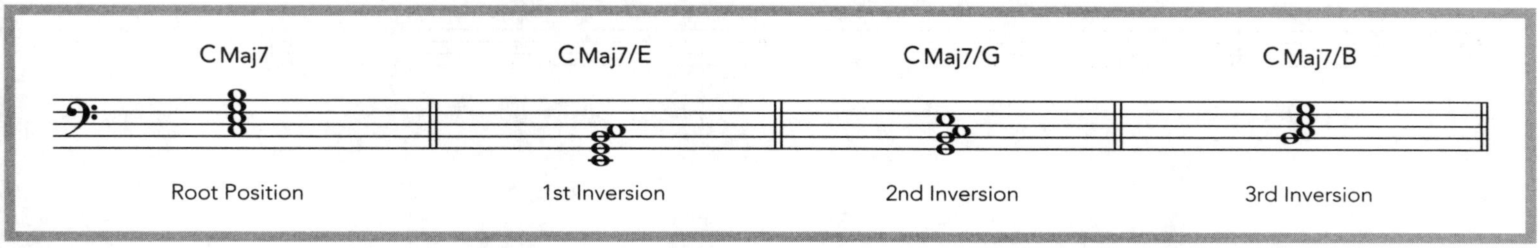

FIGURED BASS NOTATION

As with triads, figured bass notation of 7th chords is accomplished by measuring the intervals from the root. Considering the numbers for the figured bass of 7th chord inversions are always the same, memorizing them will save you the trouble of counting intervals every time.

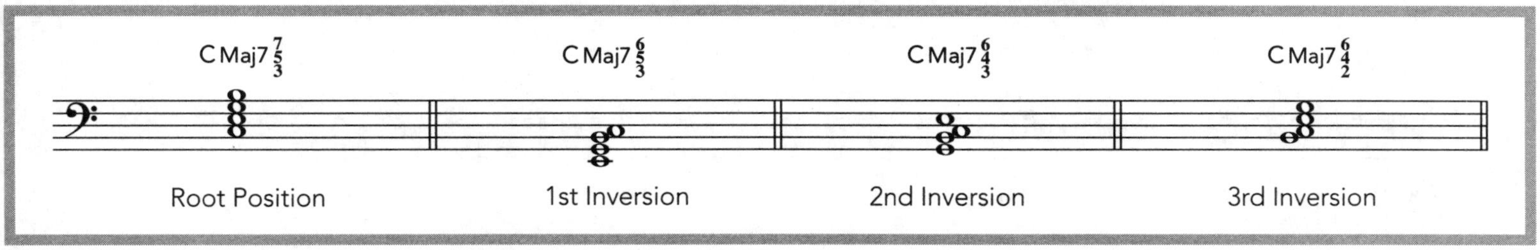

Summary of Figured Bass Notation of 7th Chords

Root position = $\begin{smallmatrix}7\\5\\3\end{smallmatrix}$ (Figured bass is usually not written for root position chords.)

1st inversion = $\begin{smallmatrix}6\\5\\3\end{smallmatrix}$

2nd inversion = $\begin{smallmatrix}6\\4\\3\end{smallmatrix}$

3rd inversion = $\begin{smallmatrix}6\\4\\2\end{smallmatrix}$

WORKSHEET 11: INVERTING 7TH CHORDS

1. Write the following inversions.

DMaj7/F♯ | GMaj7/F♯ | E7/G♯ | Amin7/G | Cmin7♭5/B♭ | Dmin7/A

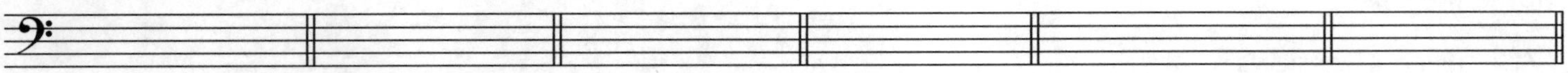

2. Identify the following inversions using slash chords.

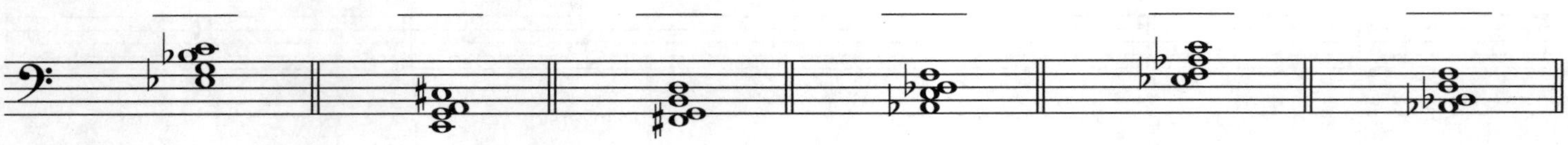

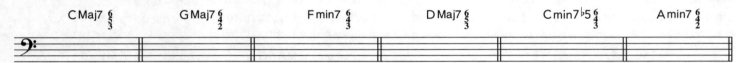

3. Write the following 7th chords.

CMaj7 $^6_5{}_3$ | GMaj7 $^6_4{}_2$ | Fmin7 $^6_4{}_3$ | DMaj7 $^6_5{}_3$ | Cmin7♭5 $^6_4{}_3$ | Amin7 $^6_4{}_2$

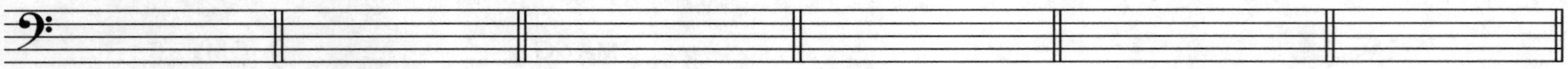

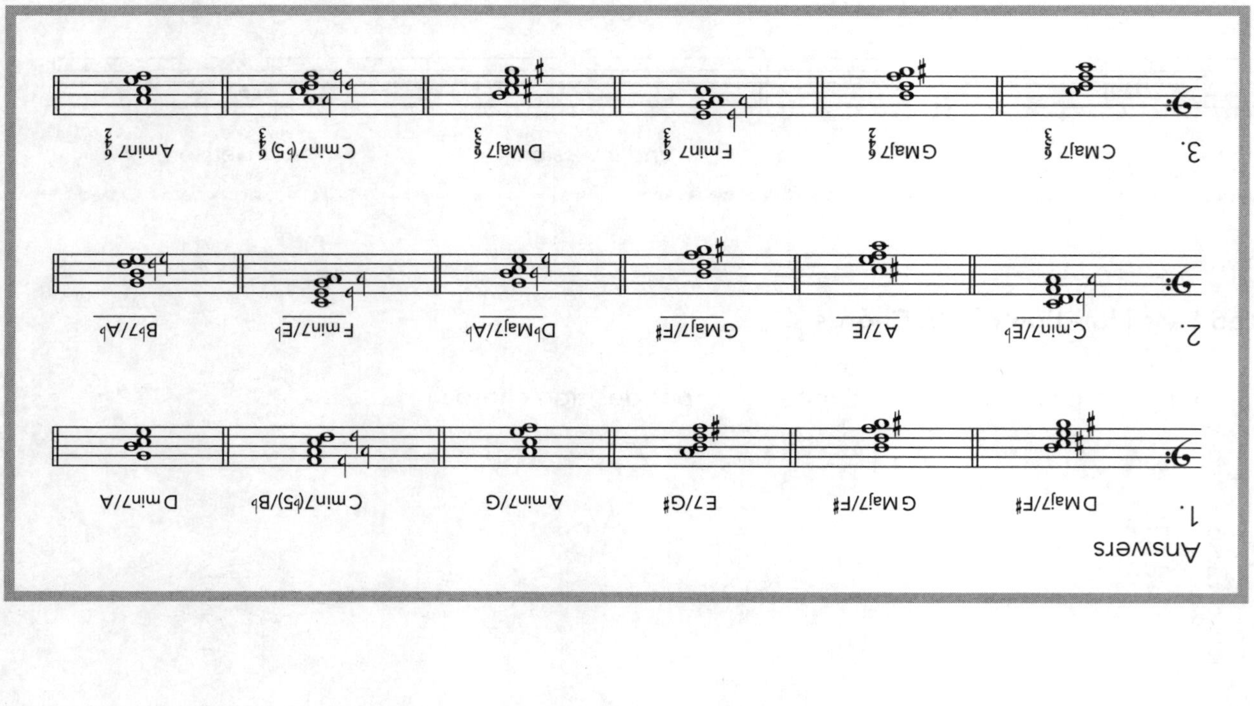

Diatonic 7th Chords in Major keys

Just as there are seven diatonic triads for every major key, there are seven diatonic 7th chords for every major key. To find the diatonic 7th chords of any major key, start with a major scale and build 7th chords above each scale degree. Let's use the key of G Major as an example.

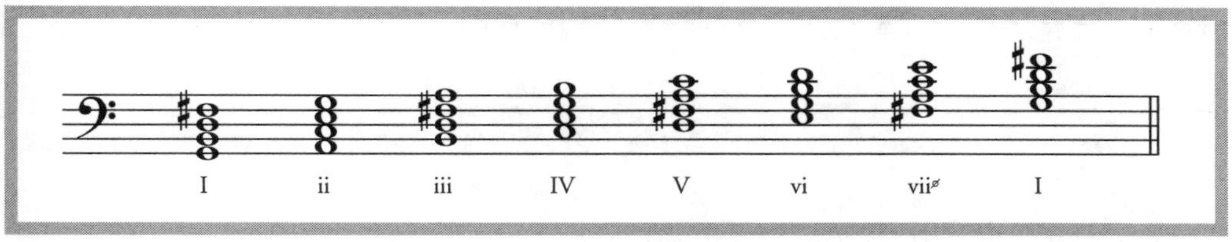

The major triads on I and IV become major 7th chords, the major triad on V becomes a dominant 7th chord, the minor triads on ii, iii and vi become minor 7th chords and the diminished triad on vii becomes a minor 7♭5 chord.

This chart shows the qualities of each Roman numeral for diatonic 7th chords. This will hold true for each major key.

I = Maj7
ii = min7
iii = min7
IV = Maj7
V = 7
vi = min7
viiø = min7♭5

Diatonic 7th Chords in Minor Keys

The same method used to generate diatonic 7th chords in major keys is used for minor keys. Simply stack 7th chords above each scale degree of a natural minor scale. Let's look at the key of A Minor.

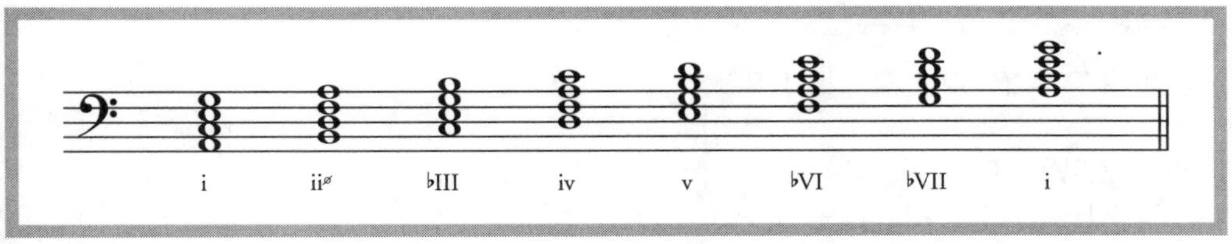

Notice that each scale degree starts with the diatonic triad and adds a 7th to form the 7th chord.

Diatonic 7th chords	i	iiø	♭III	iv	v	♭VI	♭VII
Qualities	min7	min7♭5	Maj7	min7	min7	Maj7	7

The Roman numeral formula for diatonic 7th chords in minor keys is consistent for all 12 keys.

WORKSHEET 12: DIATONIC 7TH CHORDS

1. Give the Roman numerals and qualities of diatonic 7th chords in a major key.

Roman numerals _______ _______ _______ _______ _______ _______ _______

Chord qualities _______ _______ _______ _______ _______ _______ _______

2. Give the Roman numerals and qualities of diatonic 7th chords in a minor key.

Roman numerals _______ _______ _______ _______ _______ _______ _______

Chord qualities _______ _______ _______ _______ _______ _______ _______

3. Give the names of the following diatonic 7th chords.

a. V of G Major _______________

b. ii of E Major _______________

c. iv of B Minor _______________

d. vi of C Major _______________

e. ♭III of D Minor _______________

f. viiø of B♭ Major _______________

Answers

1.	I	ii	iii	IV	V	vi	viiø
	Maj7	min7	min7	Maj7	7	min7	min7♭5
2.	i	iiø	♭III	iv	v	♭VI	♭VII
	min7	min7♭5	Maj7	min7	min7	Maj7	7

3a. D7 b. F♯min7 c. Emin7 d. Amin7 e. FMaj7 f. Amin7♭5

The Diminished 7th Chord

A *diminished 7th* chord consists of a diminished triad with a diminished 7th (or ♭♭7) added on top of the chord. A diminished 7th interval is the enharmonic equivalent of a major 6th. A diminished 7th chord is spelled R–♭3–♭5–♭♭7. To make diminished 7th chords easier to read, it is not uncommon to see the ♭♭7 notated as a 6. Each diminished 7th chord stacks three minor 3rds.

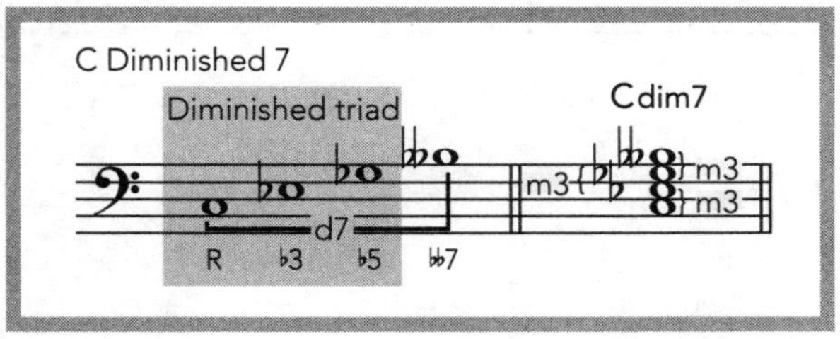

♭♭ = *Double flat.* Lower the note one whole step.

A diminished 7th chord is a *symmetrical* chord, meaning that all of the intervals are equal distances from one another. Because of its symmetrical nature, any note of a diminished 7th chord can act as the root (with a little enharmonic respelling). For example, an Edim7 (E–G–B♭–D♭) has the same four pitches as Gdim7 (G–B♭–D♭–F♭, F♭ is the same note as E). The same four pitches are found in B♭dim7 and D♭dim7. Notice that the 3rd of each chord becomes the root of the next. Also, the root is simply enharmonically respelled as the ♭♭7 of the next diminished 7th chord.

Edim7 E–G–B♭–D♭

Gdim7 G–B♭–D♭–F♭ (F♭ is the enharmonic respelling of E)

B♭dim7 B♭–D♭–F♭–A♭♭ (A♭♭ is the enharmonic respelling of G)

D♭dim7 D♭–F♭–A♭♭–C♭♭ (C♭♭ is the enharmonic respelling of B♭)

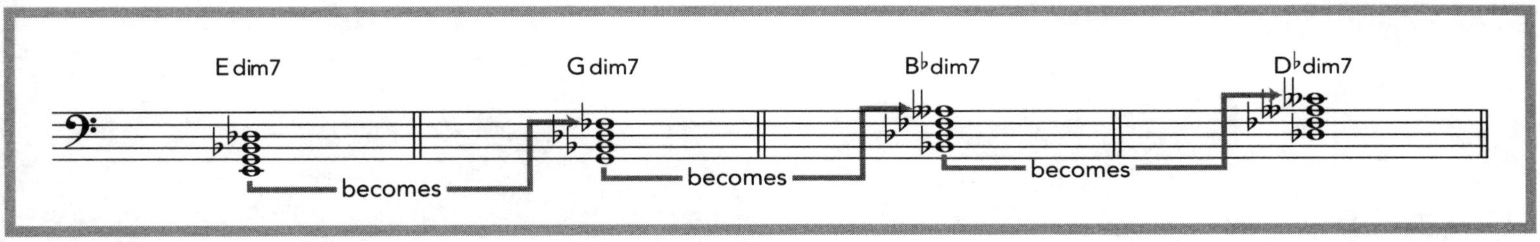

The diminished 7th chord has a very dissonant sound. Notice the sound of ascending minor 3rds as the chord is arpeggiated. The ending section of "Glass Onion" by the Beatles is composed entirely of diminished 7th chords.

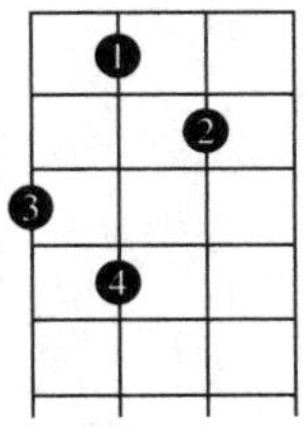

Any one of these notes could be considered the root.

WORKSHEET 13: DIMINISHED 7TH CHORDS

1. Write the following diminished 7th chords using the correct accidentals.

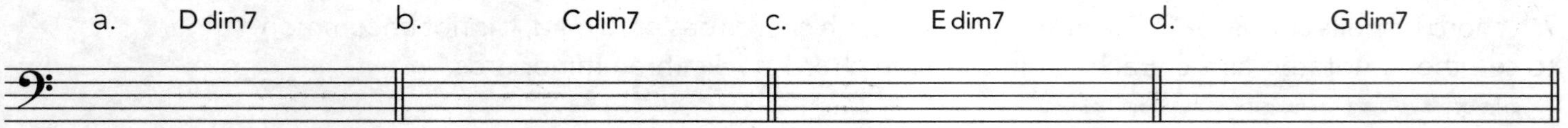

Answers

Pentatonic Scales

A *pentatonic* scale is a five-note scale. The scale name comes from the Greek word, *pente*, which means "five." Pentatonic scales are used in most musical styles. The two most common pentatonic scales are the *major pentatonic* scale and the *minor pentatonic* scale.

Major Pentatonic Scale

A major pentatonic scale is built using a root, major 2nd, major 3rd, perfect 5th and a major 6th or the 1st, 2nd, 3rd, 5th and 6th scale degrees of a major scale. Let's look at a C Major Pentatonic scale in relation to a C Major scale. Although this is a five-note scale, we usually repeat the tonic (1) at the octave (8) when we play it.

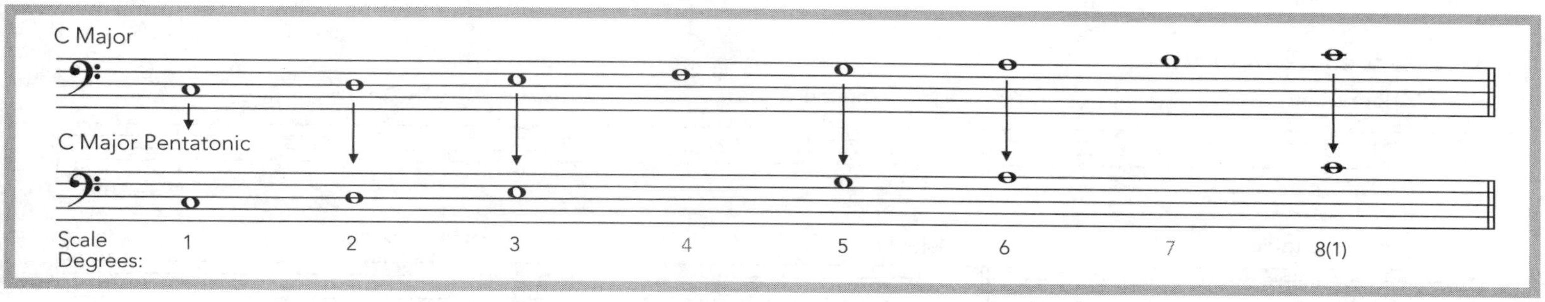

The major pentatonic scale has a very happy sound. Lines derived from this scale usually have a pop sound or country sound. The notes of the bass line to the Temptations' classic, "My Girl," played by bass master James Jamerson, are the notes of an ascending major pentatonic scale.

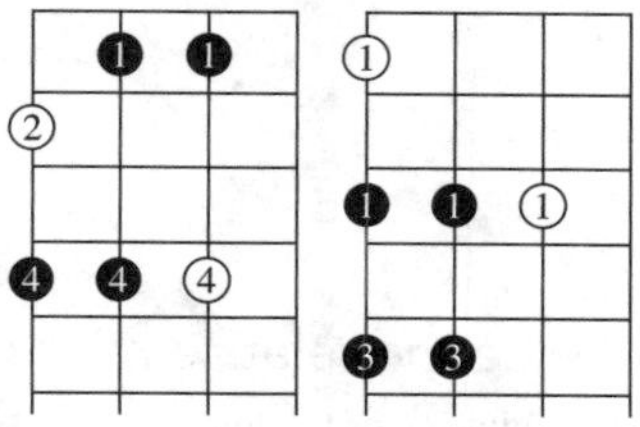

Minor Pentatonic Scale

A minor pentatonic scale is built using a root, minor 3rd, perfect 4th, perfect 5th and a minor 7th, or the 1st, ♭3rd, 4th, 5th and ♭7th scale degrees of a natural minor scale. Let's look at a C Pentatonic Minor scale in relation to a C Natural Minor scale.

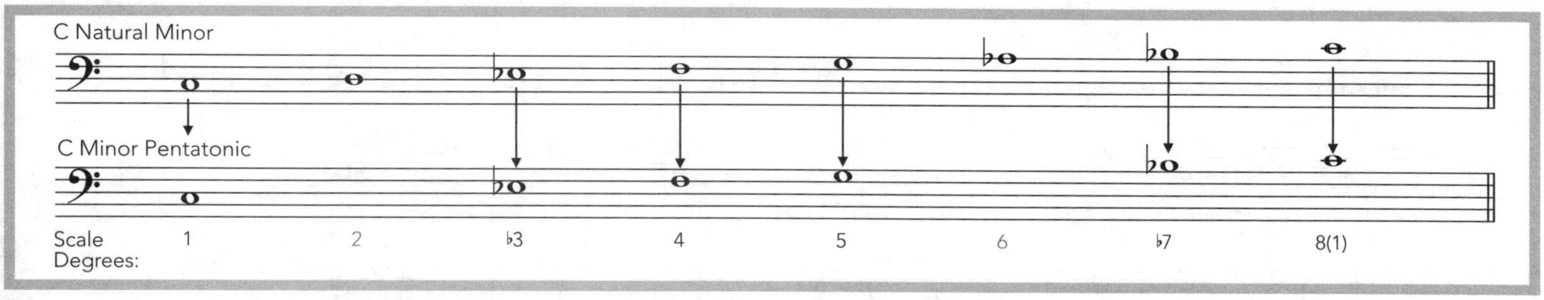

RELATIVE MAJOR AND MINOR

Just as every major scale has a relative minor, every major pentatonic scale has a relative minor pentatonic scale. As with the relative minor scale, the root of the relative minor pentatonic is found three half steps below the root of the major pentatonic scale. The A Minor Pentatonic scale is the relative minor of the C Major Pentatonic scale. The same five notes are found in both scales.

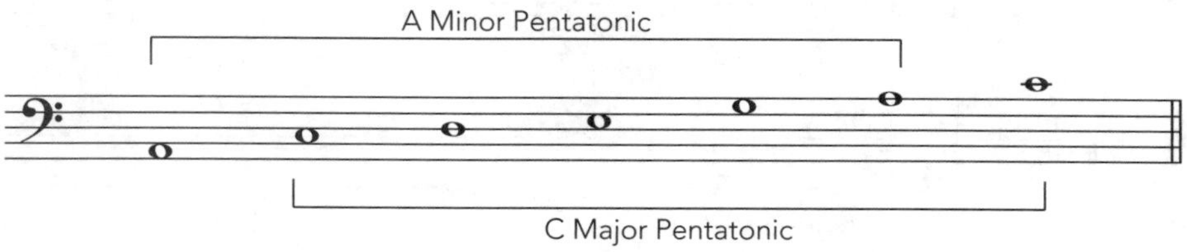

The minor pentatonic scale has a darker, bluesier sound than the major pentatonic scale. Countless riffs have been written using only notes from the minor pentatonic scale, including "Moby Dick" by Led Zeppelin.

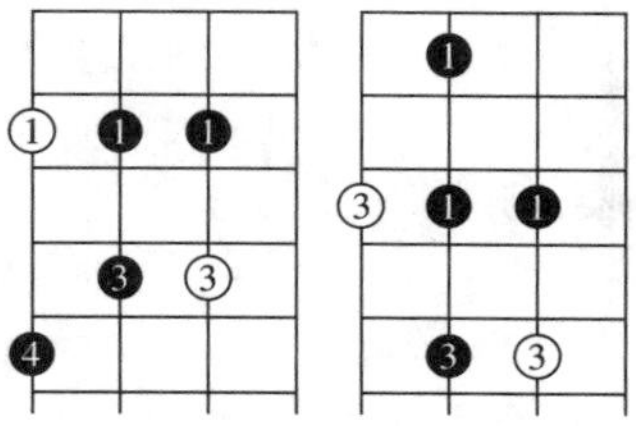

WORKSHEET 14: PENTATONIC SCALES

1. Name the intervals of a major pentatonic scale.

__________ __________ __________ __________ __________

2. Name the intervals of a minor pentatonic scale.

__________ __________ __________ __________ __________

3. Write the following scales.

G Major Pentatonic — C Minor Pentatonic — A Major Pentatonic

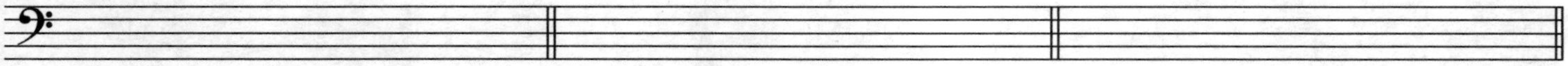

D Minor Pentatonic — B♭ Major Pentatonic — F Minor Pentatonic

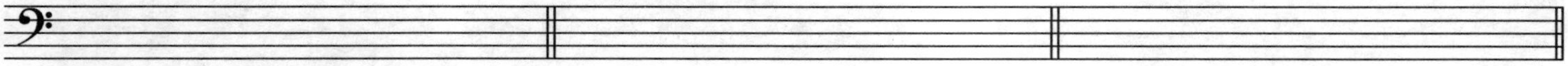

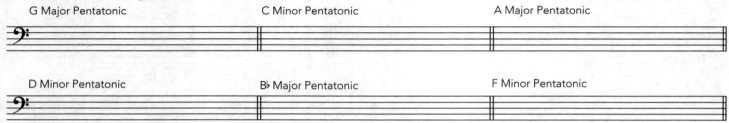

4. Write the relative minor pentatonic scale of the listed major pentatonic scales.

C Major Pentatonic — D♭ Major Pentatonic — G Major Pentatonic

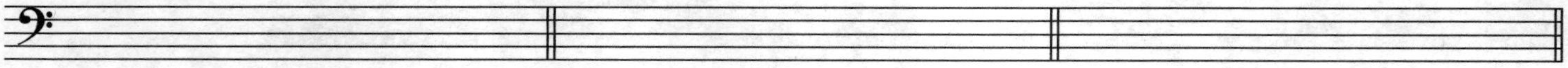

A Major Pentatonic — E♭ Major Pentatonic — F Major Pentatonic

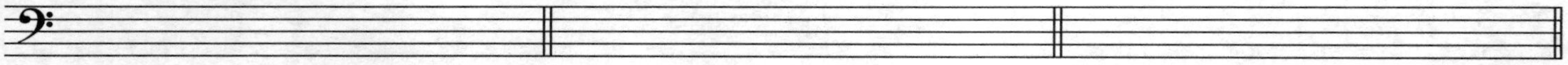

Answers

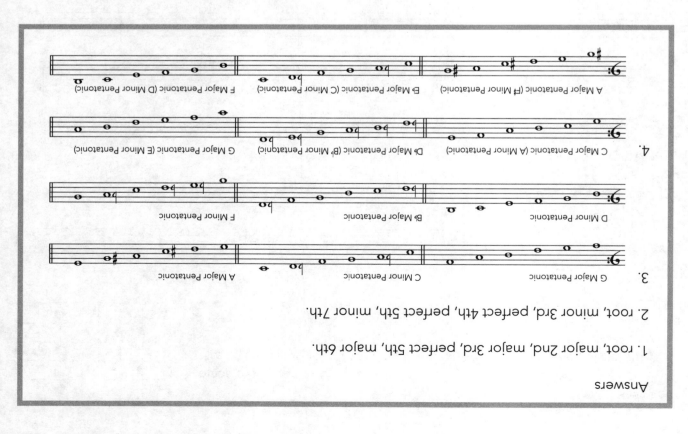

1. root, major 2nd, major 3rd, perfect 5th, major 6th.

2. root, minor 3rd, perfect 4th, perfect 5th, minor 7th.

3.

G Major Pentatonic — C Minor Pentatonic — A Major Pentatonic

D Minor Pentatonic — B♭ Major Pentatonic — F Minor Pentatonic

4.

C Major Pentatonic (A Minor Pentatonic) — D♭ Major Pentatonic (B♭ Minor Pentatonic) — G Major Pentatonic (E Minor Pentatonic)

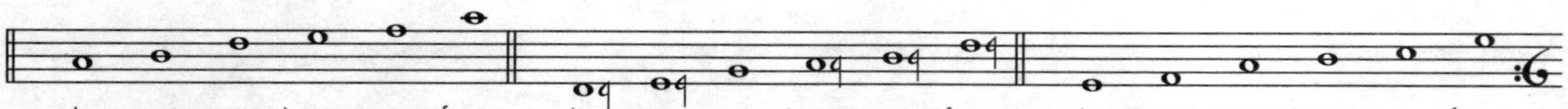

A Major Pentatonic (F♯ Minor Pentatonic) — E♭ Major Pentatonic (C Minor Pentatonic) — F Major Pentatonic (D Minor Pentatonic)

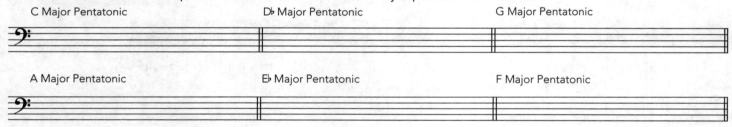

The Blues Scale

A *blues* scale is a minor pentatonic scale with an added ♭5. It is a six-note scale that is built using the 1st, ♭3rd, 4th, ♭5th, 5th and ♭7th scale degrees of the major (or natural minor) scale. As with other pentatonic scales, we usually repeat the tonic at the end.

A Blues Scale

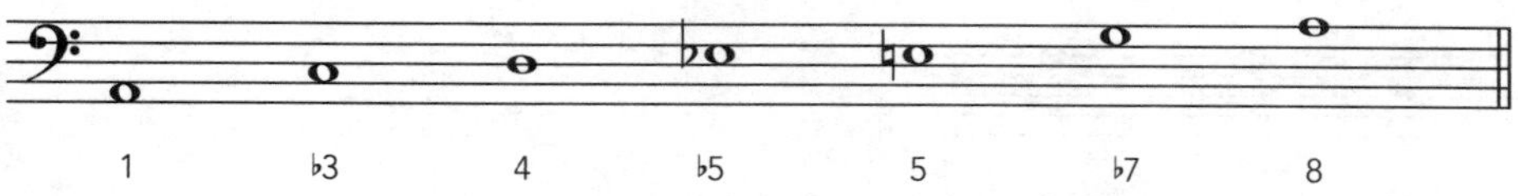

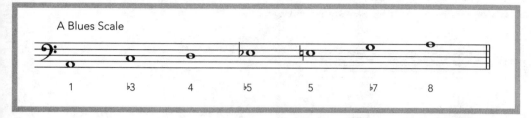

A blues scale can be used over any minor chord but is most commonly used over dominant 7th chords with the same root.

The ♭5 of the blues scale is commonly used as a passing tone from the 4th to the 5th or vice versa. When held, the ♭5 sounds very dissonant in relation to the tonic. This does not mean that you should never hold on the ♭5. If your intent is to create a sinister, disturbing sound, by all means hold on the ♭5.

Following are two simple melodies that use the blues scale. The first uses the ♭5 as a passing tone; the second resolves on the ♭5, creating a much different sound.

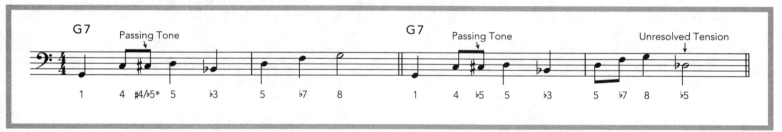

As the name implies, the blues scale has a very bluesy sound. The blues scale is fairly easy to recognize. Listen for the three chromatic notes from the 4th to the 5th (4–♭5–5). Many riffs are written using this scale, including "Walk This Way" by Aerosmith and "Heartbreaker" by Led Zeppelin.

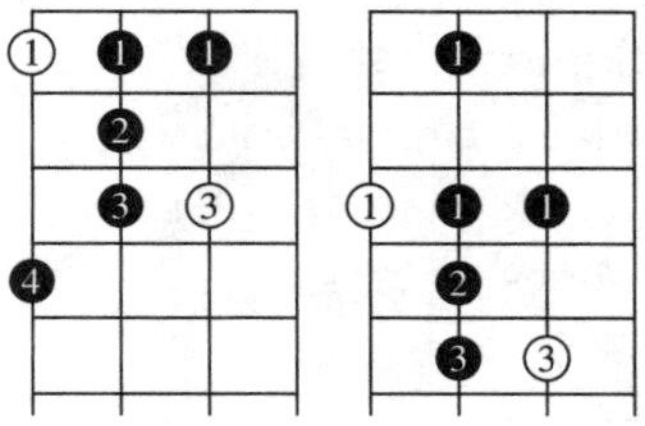

* For ease of reading, the ♭5 is often expressed as a ♯4, its enharmonic equivalent.

The Altered Blues Scale

The *altered blues* scale is a blues scale with an added major 7th (♮7). It is a seven note scale that consists of the 1st, 3rd, 4th, ♭5th, 5th, ♭7th and ♮7th of a major scale. Here is an A Altered Blues scale.

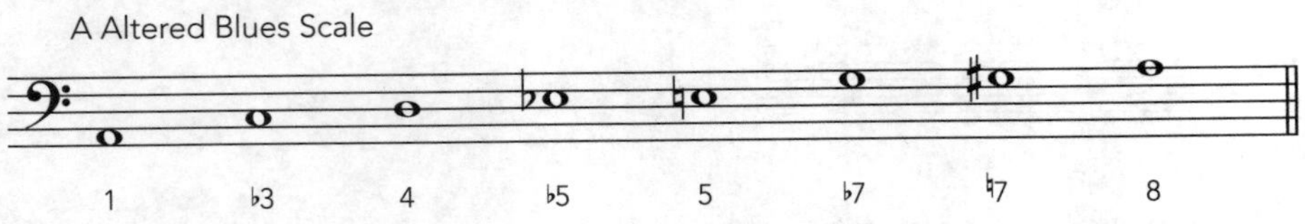

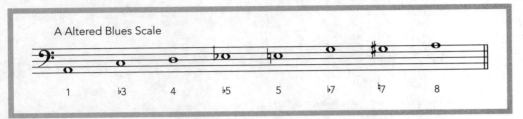

The altered blues scale can be used wherever the blues scale is applicable.

As with the blues scale, the ♭5 of the altered blues scale is most commonly used as a passing tone . The ♮7 is used as a passing tone between the ♭7 and the octave (8).

To identify an altered blues scale listen for the three chromatic tones from the 4th to 5th and the ♭7th to the octave.

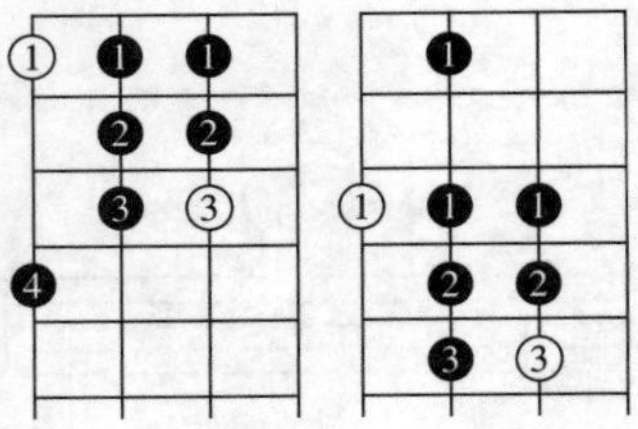

Summary of pentatonic and blues scales.

Scale	**Scale Degrees**
Major pentatonic	1–2–3–5–6
Minor pentatonic	1–♭3–4–5–♭7
Blues scale	1–♭3–4–♭5–5–♭7
Altered Blues scale	1–♭3–4–♭5–5–♭7–♮7

WORKSHEET 15: BLUES AND ALTERED BLUES SCALES

1. Name the intervals of a blues scale.

______ ______ ______ ______ ______ ______

2. Name the intervals of an altered blues scale.

______ ______ ______ ______

______ ______ ______

3. Write the following scales.

A Blues C Altered Blues E Blues

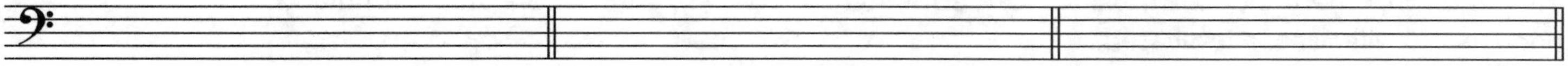

F Altered Blues G Blues D Blues

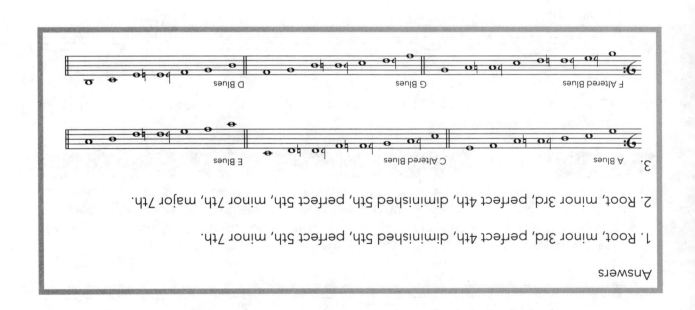

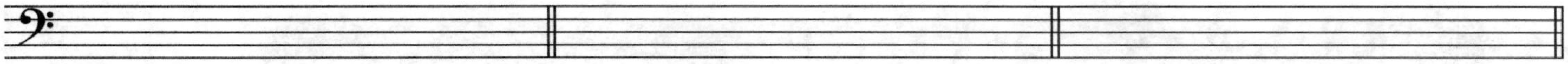

Answers

1. Root, minor 3rd, perfect 4th, diminished 5th, perfect 5th, minor 7th.

2. Root, minor 3rd, perfect 4th, diminished 5th, perfect 5th, minor 7th, major 7th.

3.

Modes of the Major Scale

A *mode* is a scale that is based on another scale. A mode can be thought of as the order in which a scale is played. If we start and end a scale on the tonic, it is in one mode; if we start and end it on the 2nd scale degree (2), treating 2 as a new tonic but not changing any of the notes, it is in another. There are seven modes of the major scale, one for each scale degree. Using the thought process just described, you can find these seven modes by starting on each scale degree, ascending through all seven notes of the scale.

The modes of the major scale fall into two categories: the major family (modes with a major 3rd) and the minor family (modes with a minor 3rd). You will notice that the quality of each mode will agree with the diatonic harmony of a major scale. In other words, if the diatonic harmony calls for a minor chord on a given scale degree, then the mode will be a minor mode.

There are two basic approaches to looking at modes: *derivative* and *parallel*. In the derivative approach, a mode is thought of as a major scale starting and ending on a specific scale degree (as explained in the first paragraph above). In the parallel approach, the scale degrees of a mode are compared to that of a major scale starting on the same note. This book will look at each mode of the major scale using both approaches. The half-step/whole-step formula for each mode will also be indicated.

Ionian

The *Ionian* mode is a major scale played from tonic to tonic. The C Major scale and the C Ionian mode are the exact same thing. The only difference is the name.

Dorian

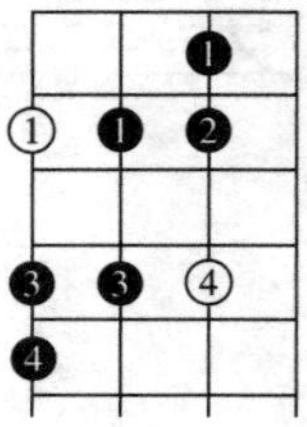

Using the derivative approach, a *Dorian* mode is found by playing a major scale starting on the 2nd scale degree and ending on the octave of the 2nd scale degree. For example, playing from D to D within a C Major scale creates the Dorian mode. Using the parallel approach, a Dorian mode is a major scale with a ♭3 and ♭7. Dorian is a minor family mode.

D Dorian

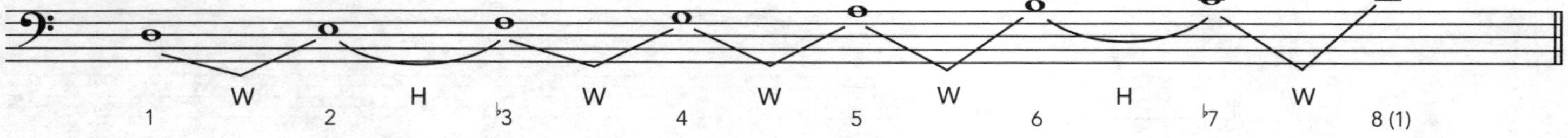

The Dorian mode has the sound of a natural minor scale with a raised 6th and is often thought of as having a "jazzy" sound.

Phrygian

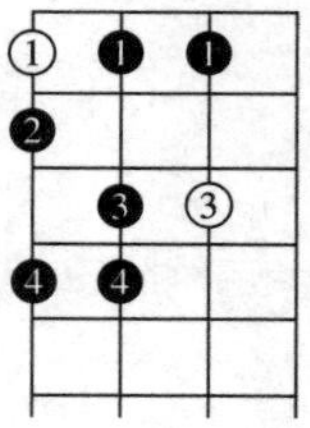

Using the derivative approach, the *Phrygian* mode is found by playing a major scale starting on the 3rd scale degree and ending on the octave of the 3rd scale degree. For example, playing E to E within a C Major scale creates the Phrygian mode. Using the parallel approach, a Phrygian mode is a major scale with a ♭2, ♭3, ♭6 and ♭7. Phrygian is a minor family mode.

E Phrygian

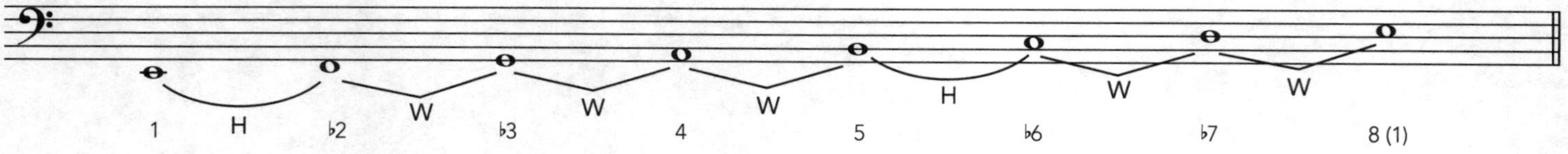

A Phrygian mode has the sound of a natural minor scale with a ♭2. The exotic character of this mode is often associated with Spanish-sounding music.

Lydian

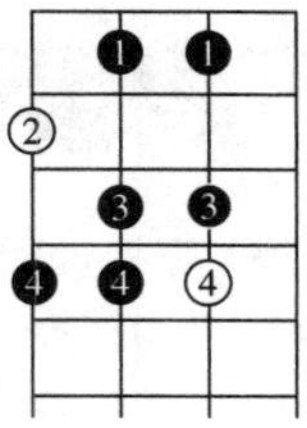

Using the derivative approach, the *Lydian* mode is found by playing a major scale starting on the 4th scale degree and ending on the octave of the 4th scale degree. For example, playing F to F within a C Major scale creates the Lydian mode. Using the parallel approach, the Lydian mode is a major scale with a ♯4. Lydian is a major family mode.

F Lydian

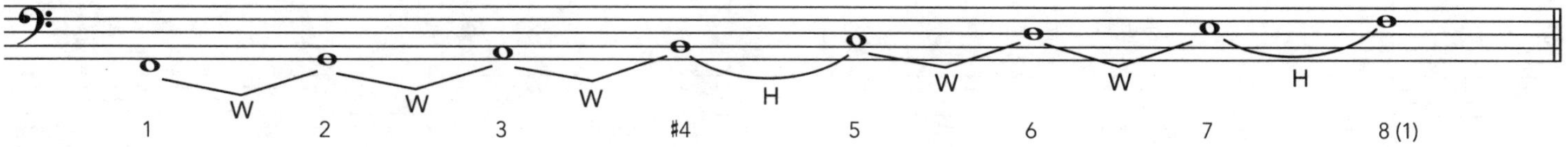

The Lydian mode has the sound of a major scale with a ♯4. This mode is often thought of as having a "bright" sound.

Mixolydian

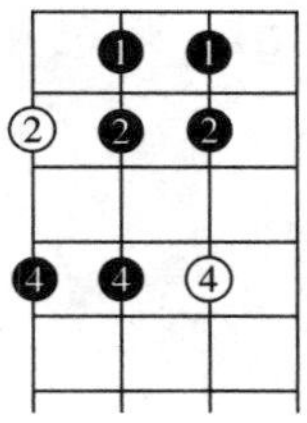

Using the derivative approach, the *Mixolydian* mode is found by playing a major scale starting on the 5th scale degree and ending on the octave of the 5th scale degree. Playing from G to G within a C Major scale creates the Mixolydian mode. Using the parallel approach, the Mixolydian mode is a major scale with a ♭7. Mixolydian is a major family mode.

G Mixolydian

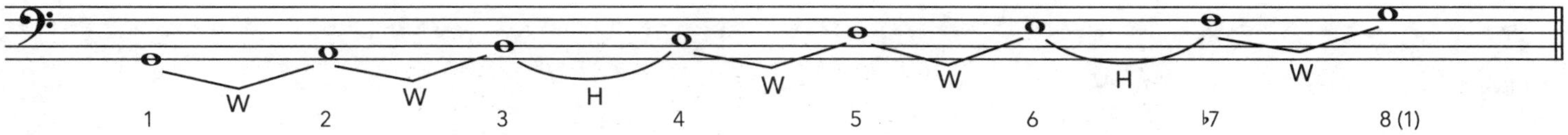

The Mixolydian mode has the sound of a major scale with a ♭7, which gives it a "bluesy" character.

Aeolian

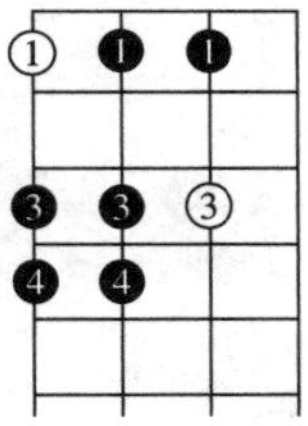

Using the derivative approach, the *Aeolian* mode is found by playing a major scale starting on the 6th scale degree and ending on the octave of the 6th scale degree. Playing from A to A within a C Major scale creates the Aeolian mode. Using the parallel approach, the Aeolian mode is a major scale with a ♭3, ♭6 and ♭7. The Aeolian mode is the same as the natural minor scale, and is therefore a minor family mode.

A Aeolian

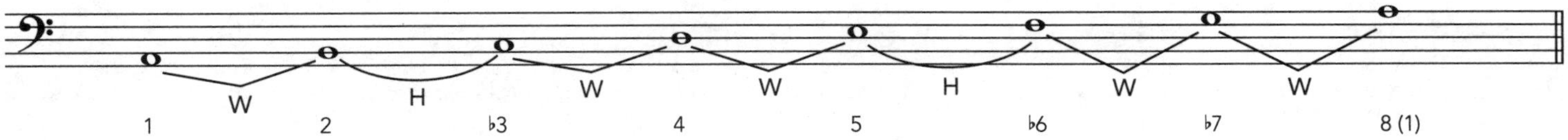

The Aeolian mode has the same sound as a natural minor scale.

Locrian

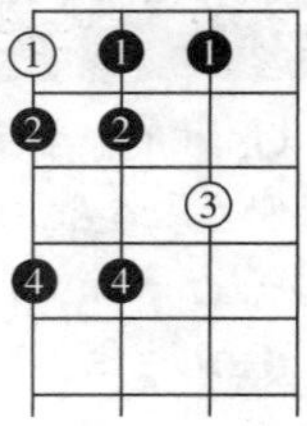

Using the derivative approach, the *Locrian* mode is found by playing a major scale from the 7th scale degree and ending on the octave of the 7th scale degree. Playing from B to B within a C Major scale creates the Locrian mode. Using the parallel approach, the Locrian mode is a major scale with a ♭2, ♭3, ♭5, ♭6 and ♭7. Locrian is a minor family mode.

B Locrian

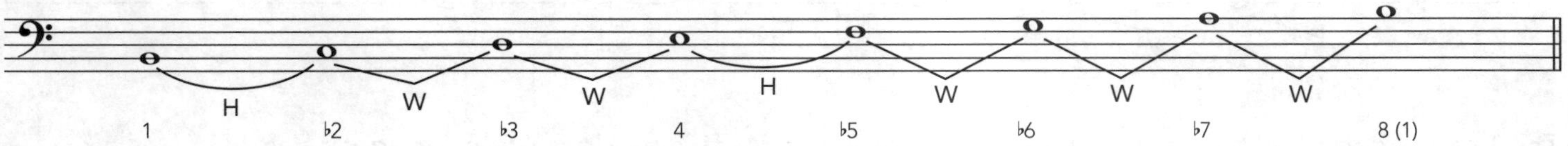

The Locrian mode can be heard as a natural minor scale with a ♭2 and a ♭5. It has a slightly strange, diminished character (due to the ♭5).

Summary of the Modes of the Major Scale

Mode	Scale Degree Derivative Approach	Scale Degrees Parallel Approach	Half-Step/Whole-Step Formula
Ionian	1	1–2–3–4–5–6–7–8	W–W–H–W–W–W–H
Dorian	2	1–2–♭3–4–5–6–♭7–8	W–H–W–W–W–H–W
Phrygian	3	1–♭2–♭3–4–5–♭6–♭7–8	H–W–W–W–H–W–W
Lydian	4	1–2–3–♯4–5–6–7–8	W–W–W–H–W–W–H
Mixolydian	5	1–2–3–4–5–6–♭7–8	W–W–H–W–W–H–W
Aeolian	6	1–2–♭3–4–5–♭6–♭7–8	W–H–W–W–H–W–W
Locrian	7	1–♭2–♭3–4–♭5–♭6–♭7–8	H–W–W–H–W–W–W

WORKSHEET 16: MODES OF THE MAJOR SCALE

1. Name the scale degrees (parallel approach) of the following modes.

   a. Aeolian ______________________

   b. Dorian ______________________

   c. Mixolydian ______________________

   d. Lydian ______________________

   e. Locrian ______________________

   f. Phrygian ______________________

2. Write the following modes using accidentals.

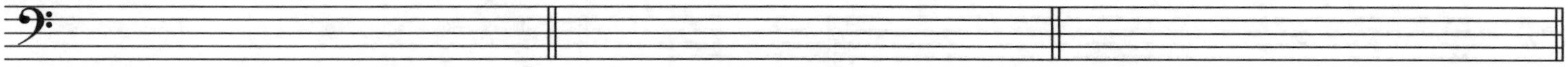

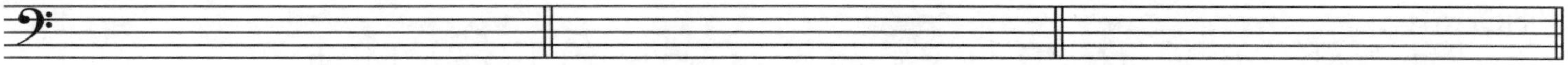

Answers

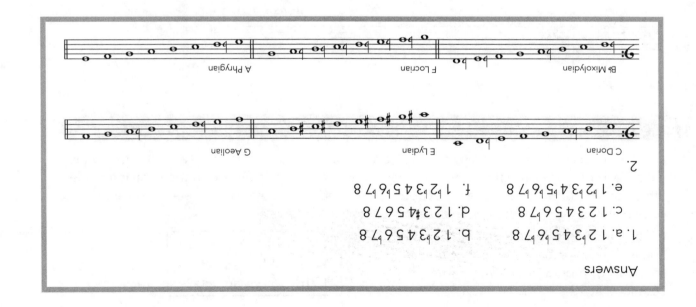

1. a. 1 2 ♭3 4 5 ♭6 ♭7 8 b. 1 2 ♭3 4 5 6 ♭7 8
c. 1 2 3 4 5 6 ♭7 8 d. 1 2 3 ♯4 5 6 7 8
e. 1 ♭2 ♭3 4 ♭5 ♭6 ♭7 8 f. 1 ♭2 ♭3 4 5 ♭6 ♭7 8

2.

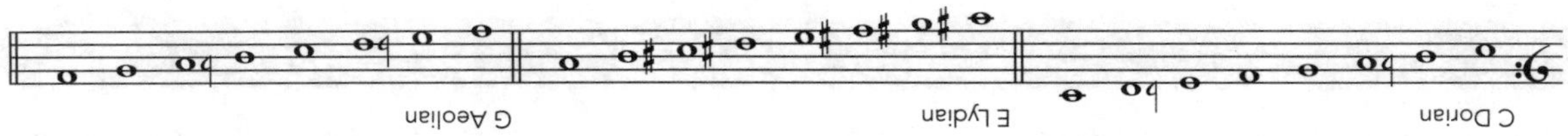

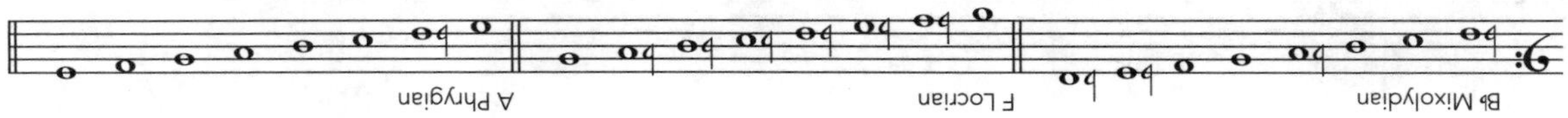

Expanding Your Chord Vocabulary

The goal of this chapter is to further your knowledge of how chords are constructed. Keep in mind, as with triads and 7th chords, a bass player is not responsible for playing every note in a chord voicing. In fact, it would not be wrong for a bass player to simply play the root over any chord voicing. While this approach will work it will not lead to many memorable bass lines, ("Running with the Devil," by Van Halen, excluded). Understanding all of the possibilities of chords will allow you the freedom to write solid, complimenting bass lines in any style.

6th Chords

MAJOR 6TH

A *major 6th* chord is a major triad with a major 6th added above the root (1–3–5–6). It is often used to replace a major triad with the same root. A major pentatonic scale sounds great over a major 6th chord. Common chord symbols for a C Major 6th chord are CMaj6 and C6. In this book, we will use CMaj6.

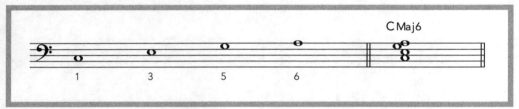

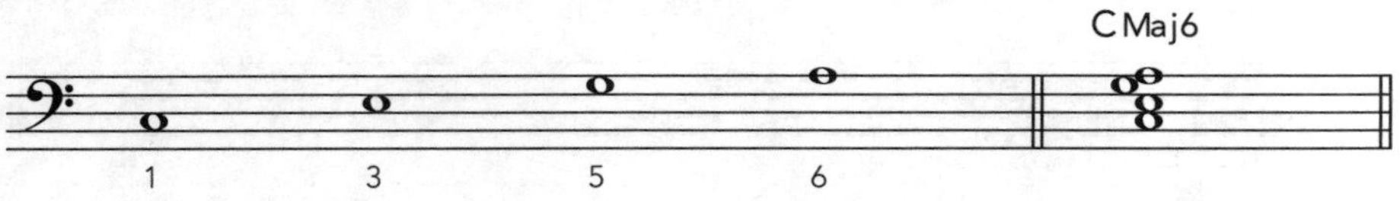

MINOR 6TH

A *minor 6th* chord is a minor triad with a major 6th added above the root (1–♭3–5–6). It is often used to replace a minor triad with the same root. Common chord symbols for a C Minor 6th chord are Cmin6 and C-6. In this book, we will use Cmin6.

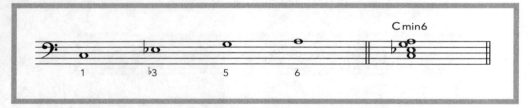

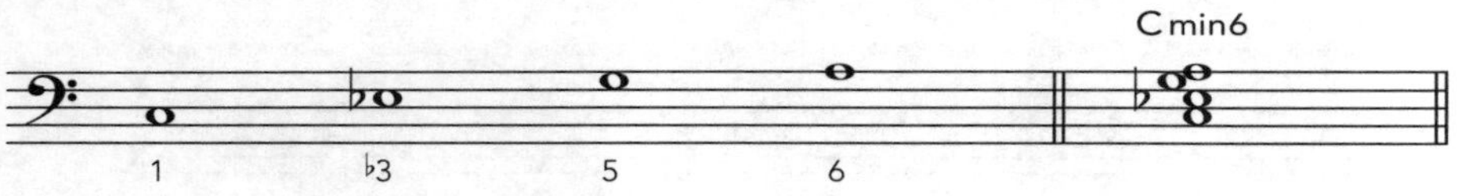

Extended Chords

An *extended* chord is made by stacking additional 3rds above the 7th. As with 7th chords, extended chords fall into three families: major, minor and dominant. Extended chords include 9th, 11th and 13th chords. The new chord tones used to create them exceed the span of an octave above the root and are analyzed as *compound intervals.*

Compound intervals are found one octave above their corresponding *simple interval* (intervals of a perfect octave or smaller). Let's look at 9ths, 11ths and 13ths.

9th	=	2nd + an octave
11th	=	4th + an octave
13th	=	6th + an octave

When trying to identify a compound interval, you can simply subtract the number 7 from the interval to find the simple interval. For example, if you need to find the 11th of C: 11 - 7 = 4. The 4th of C is F. Therefore the 11th of C is also an F.

These higher chord tones are called *extensions.* They are also sometimes called *tensions* or *colors* because of the interesting sounds they create.

9TH CHORDS: MAJOR, MINOR AND DOMINANT

9th chords are 7th chords with a 9th added above the root. Notice that the 9th is located a whole step above the octave of the root.

MAJOR 9TH
A *major 9th* (Maj9) chord is a major 7th chord with a 9th added above the root (R–3–5–7–9). Using the 9th adds a nice, melodic sound to a bass line.

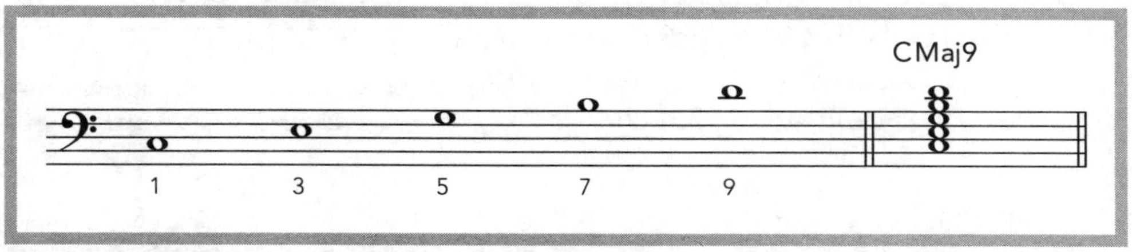

MINOR 9TH
A *minor 9th* chord (min9) is a minor 7th chord with a 9th added above the root (R–♭3–5–♭7–9).

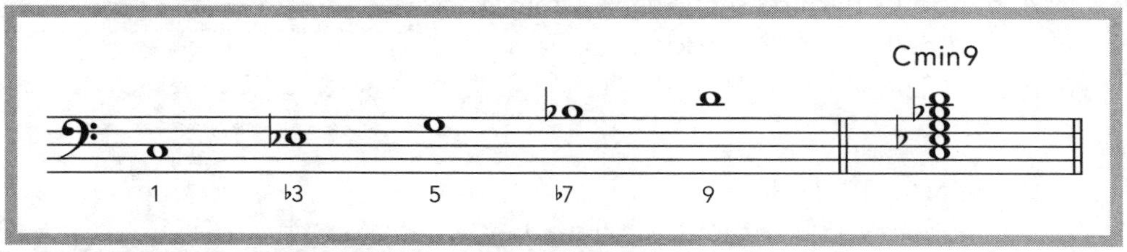

DOMINANT 9TH
A *dominant 9th* chord (9) is a dominant 7th chord with a 9th added above the root (R–3–5–♭7–9).

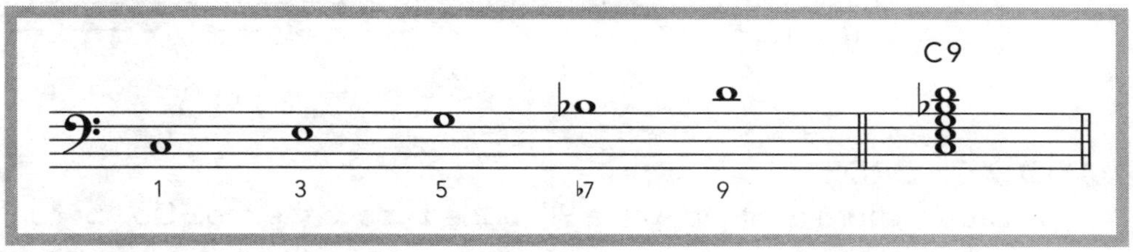

11TH CHORDS: MAJOR, MINOR AND DOMINANT

Major 11th (Maj11) and *dominant 11th* (11) chords are often avoided due to the dissonance of the harmonic minor 2nd between the 3rd and the 11th. Remember, an 11th is a 4th an octave higher. When played, the 3rd will normally be omitted to avoid this clash.

MAJOR 11TH
A *major 11th* chord is a major 9th chord with an 11th added above the root (R–3–5–7–9–11).

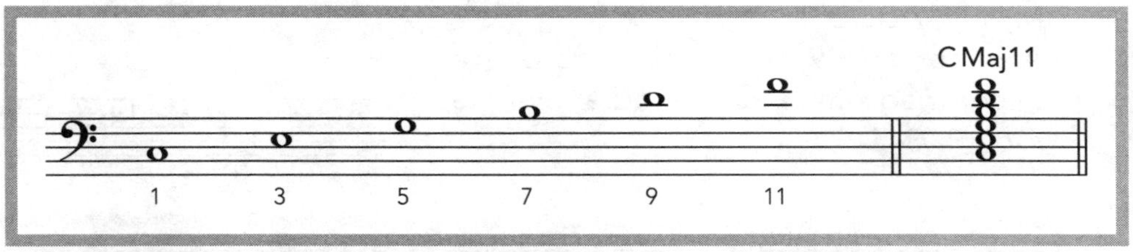

MINOR 11TH
A *minor 11th* chord (min11) is a minor 9th chord with an 11th added above the root (R–♭3–5–♭7–9–11).

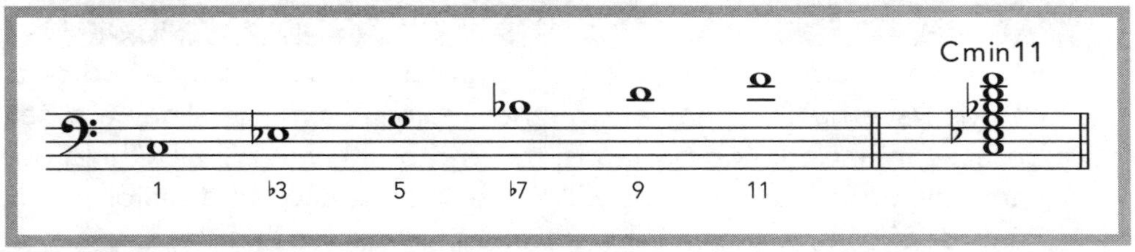

DOMINANT 11th
A *dominant 11th* chord is a dominant 9th chord with an 11th added above the root (R–3–5–♭7–9–11).

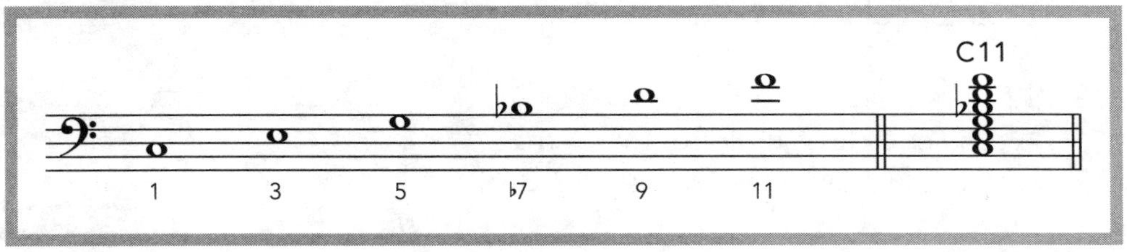

13TH CHORDS: MAJOR, MINOR AND DOMINANT

The 11th is normally omitted when playing *13th chords* to avoid clashes and make it more playable.

MAJOR 13TH

A *major 13th* (Maj13) chord is a major 11th chord with a 13th added above the root (R–3–5–7–9–[11]–13). Remember, the 11th is omitted in 13th chords.

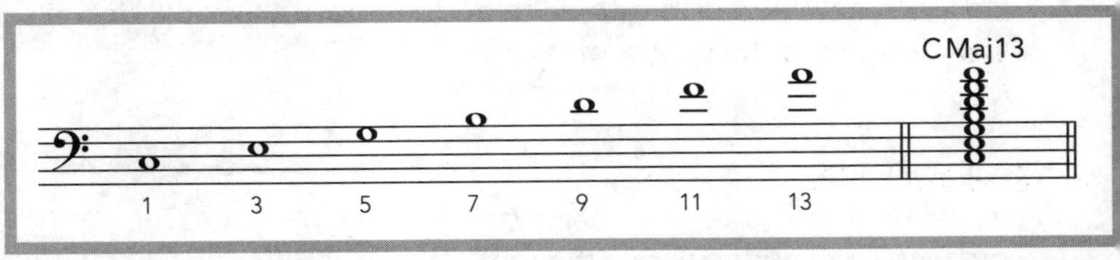

MINOR 13TH

A *minor 13th* (min13) chord is a minor 11th chord with a 13th added above the root (R–♭3–5–♭7–9–[11]–13).

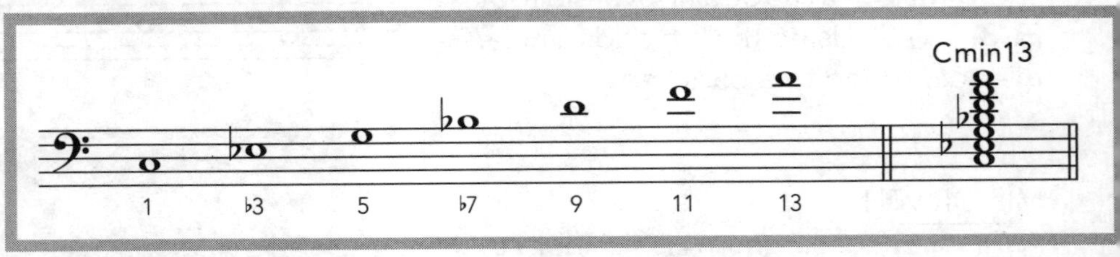

DOMINANT 13TH

A *dominant 13th* chord (13) is a dominant 11th chord with a 13th added above the root (R–3–5–♭7–9–[11]–13).

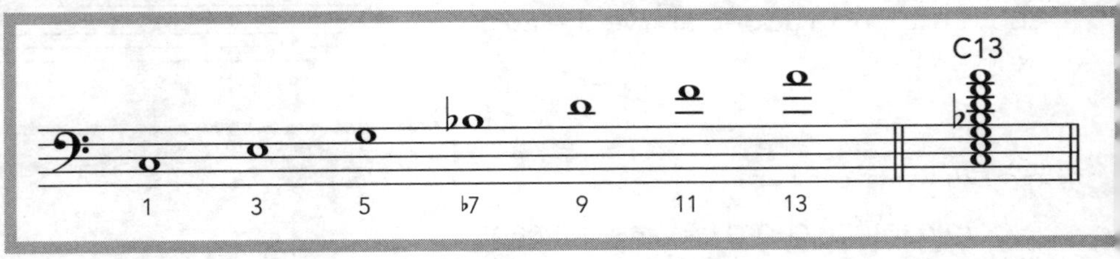

ADD 9 CHORDS

An *add 9* chord is a triad with a 9th added above the root. Do not confuse add 9 chords with 9th chords: an add 9 chord is a four-note chord with no 7th; a 9th chord always has a 7th.

MAJOR ADD 9

A *major add 9* (add9) chord is a major triad with a 9th added above the root (R–3–5–9).

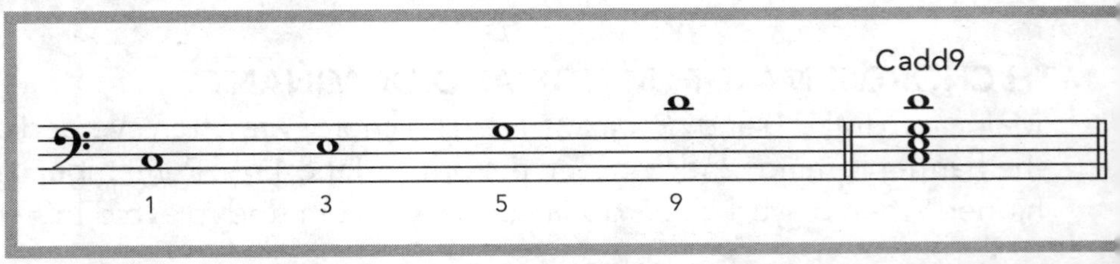

MINOR ADD 9

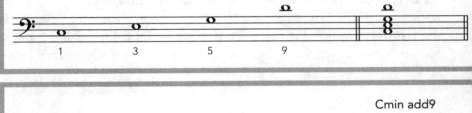

A *minor add 9* (min add9) chord is a minor triad with a 9th added above the root (R–♭3–5–9).

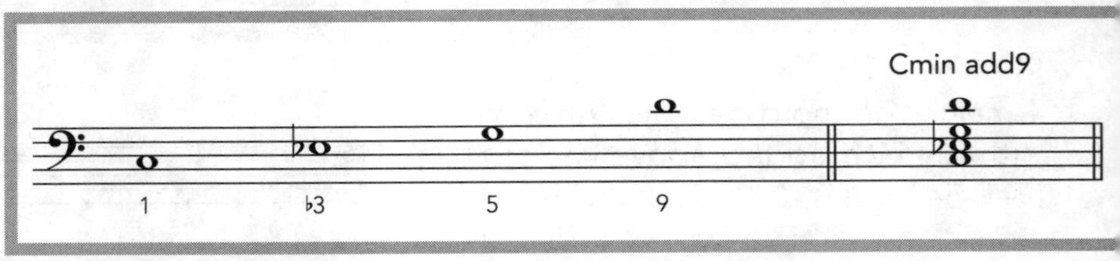

Suspended Chords

In a *suspended* chord, the 3rd of a triad is replaced with a 2nd or a 4th. Since suspended chords have no 3rd, they are neither major nor minor. They are called suspended chords because in ancient compositions, the 2nd or 4th was usually "held over" from the preceding harmony. Suspended chords will sometimes resolve to a major chord of the same root, but in modern compositions, they are often used for color and do not resolve.

SUS2

A *sus2* chord is a major or minor triad with the 3rd replaced by a 2nd (R–2–5).

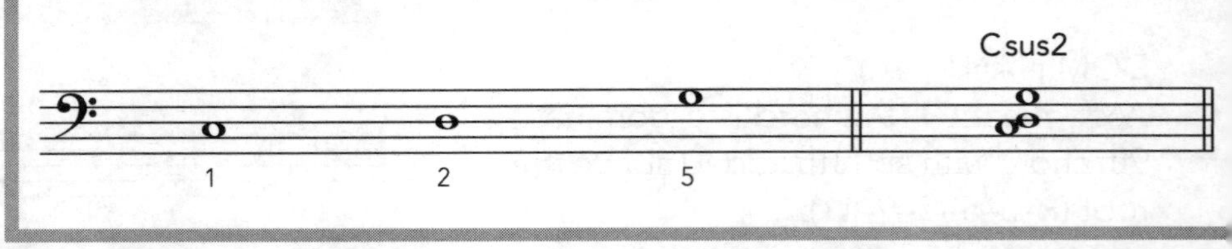

SUS4

A *sus4* is a major or minor triad with the 3rd replaced by a 4th (R–4–5).

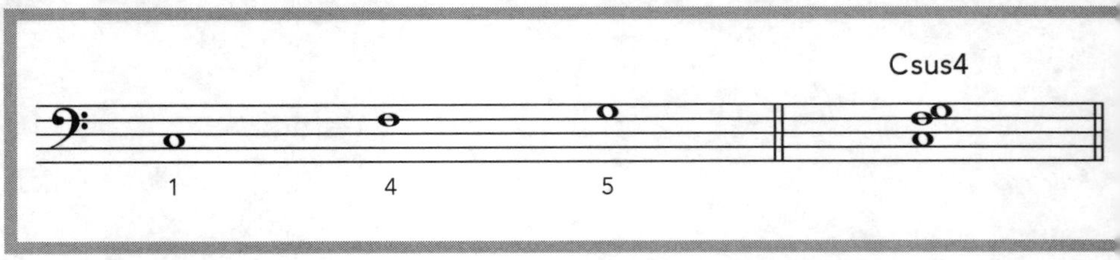

Altered Major, Minor and Dominant Chords

An *altered* chord is one in which a note of the triad or an extension is raised or lowered. Usually, the names of altered chords are self-explanatory. For example, C Major 7♯5 (CMaj7♯5) is a C Major 7th chord with a raised 5th (1–3–♯5–7). Let's look at some other altered chords.

ALTERED MAJOR CHORDS

Major7♭5

Once again, the name is self-explanatory: a *major 7♭5* chord is a major 7th chord with a lowered 5th (R–3–♭5–7).

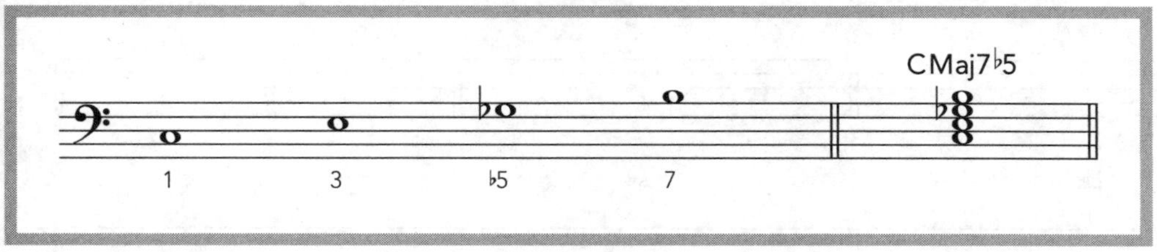

Major 7♯11

Just as 7th chords can be altered, 9th, 11th and 13th chords can be altered. The raised 11th in the *major 7♯11* chord avoids the clash between the 3rd and the 11th discussed on page 59 (R–3–5–7–9–♯11).

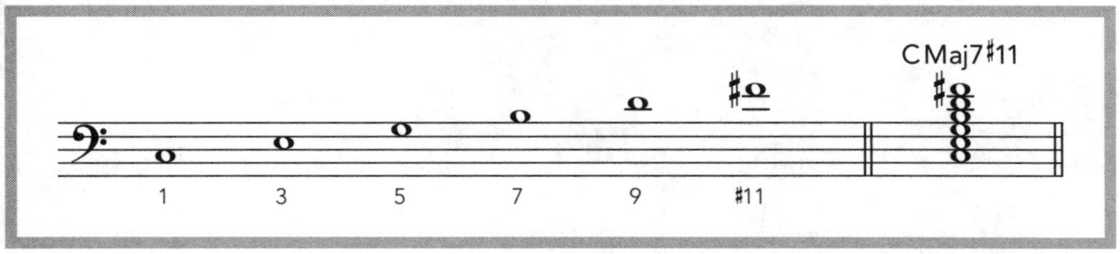

ALTERED MINOR CHORDS

Altered minor chords will also have self-explanatory names. A good example is minor 7♯5.

ALTERED DOMINANT CHORDS

Altered dominant chords are used to replace unaltered dominant chords. There are many altered chords including: *7♭5, 7♯5, 7♭9, 7♯9*. There are also altered dominant chords with more than one altered note, including: *7♯5♯9,7♭9♭13* and others. For all of these chords, simply use the notes of the dominant 7th chords and raise or lower any notes specified. Let's look at a typical altered dominant chord.

Dominant 7♯9

A 7♯9 chord is a dominant 7th chord with a raised 9th added above the root (R–3–5–♭7–♯9).

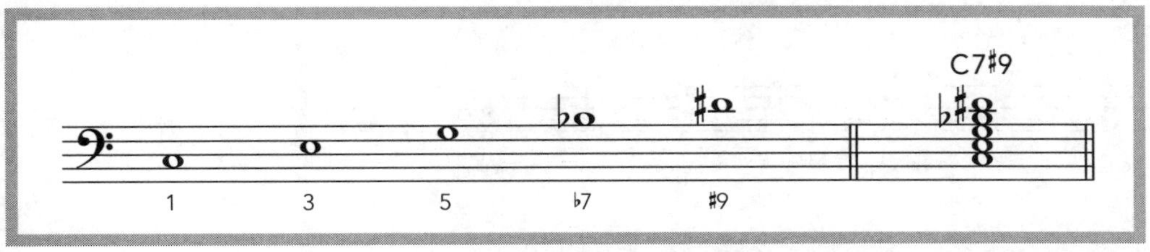

WORKSHEET 17: 6TH, EXTENDED, ADD 9, SUS AND ALTERED CHORDS

1. Write the following chords.

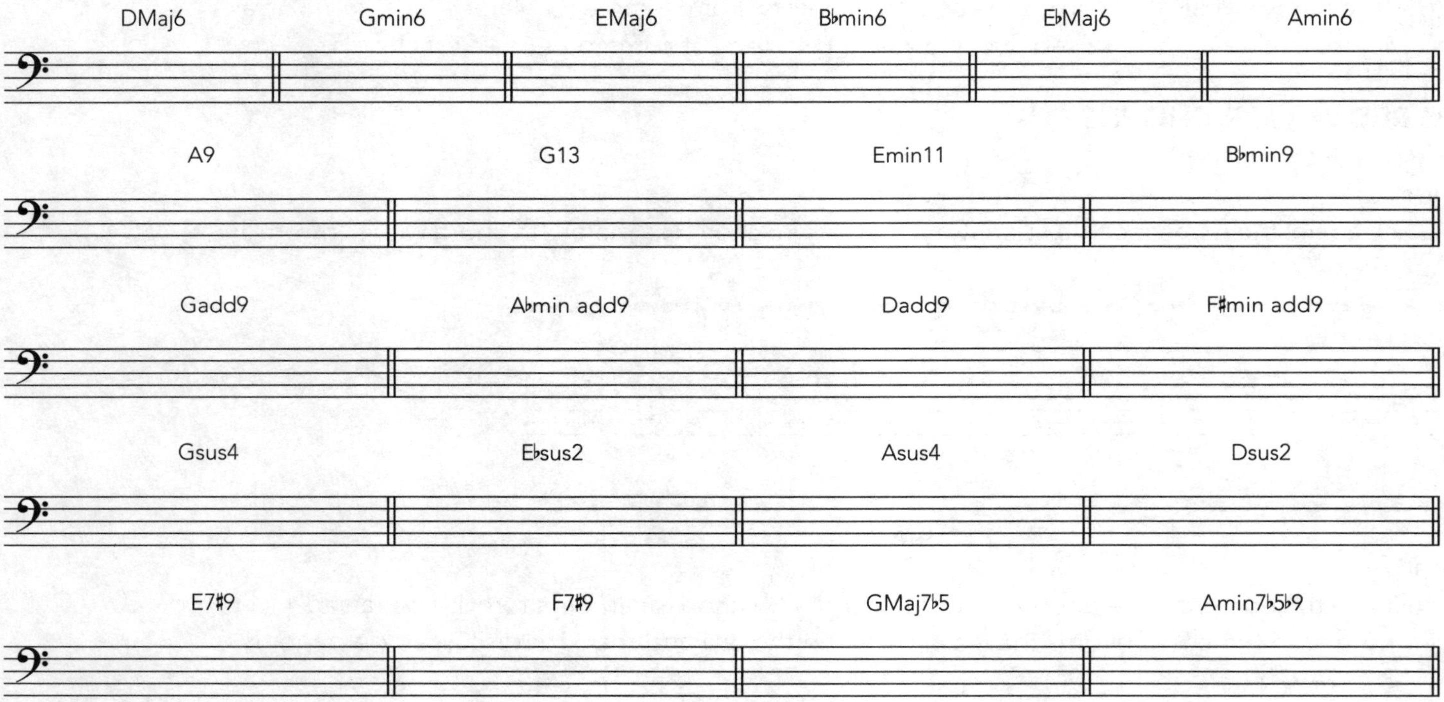

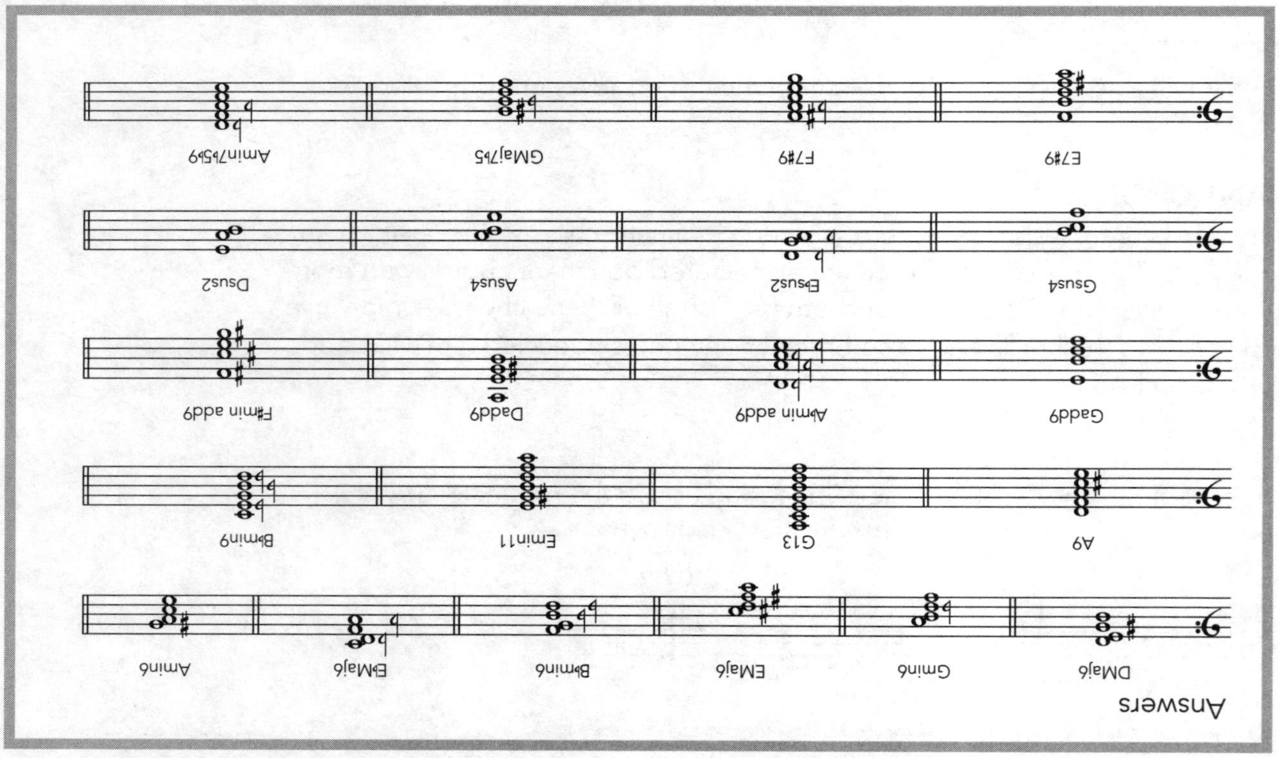

Two More Minor Scales

The Harmonic Minor Scale

The *harmonic minor* scale is a natural minor scale with a raised 7th. The harmonic minor scale formula is R–2–♭3–4–5–♭6–7–8.

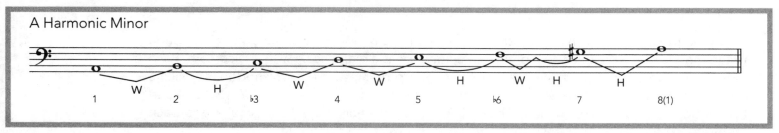

A Harmonic Minor

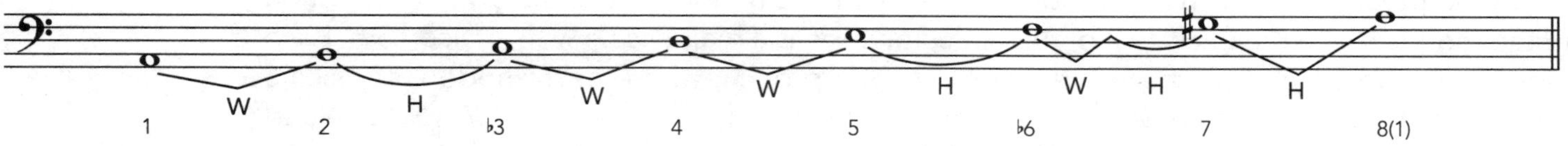

Notice the distance of three half steps (an interval of an augmented 2nd) between the 6th and 7th scale degrees. This gives the harmonic minor scale a very distinctive, exotic, Middle-Eastern sound.

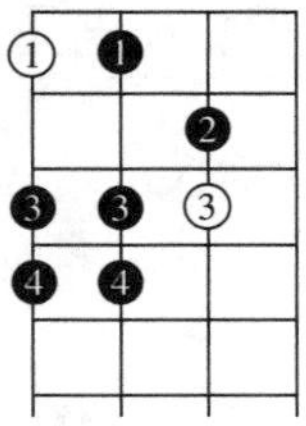

HARMONIC MINOR DIATONIC TRIADS AND 7TH CHORDS

As with the major and natural minor scales, the harmonic minor scale can be harmonized to find diatonic triads and 7th chords.

DIATONIC TRIADS OF THE HARMONIC MINOR SCALE

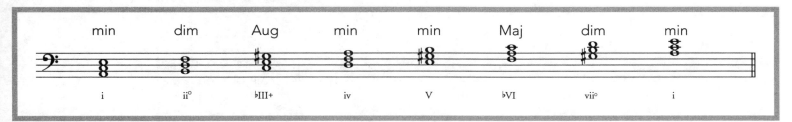

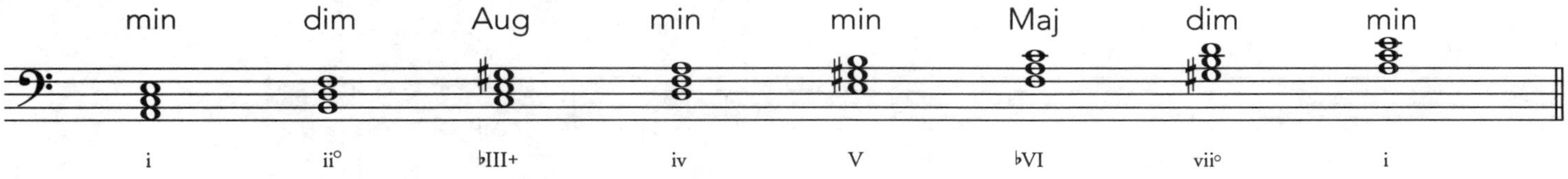

DIATONIC 7TH CHORDS OF THE HARMONIC MINOR SCALE

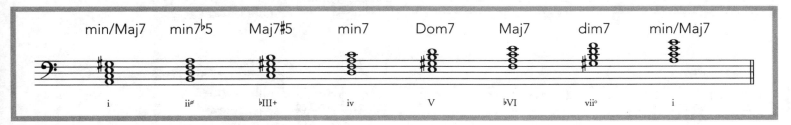

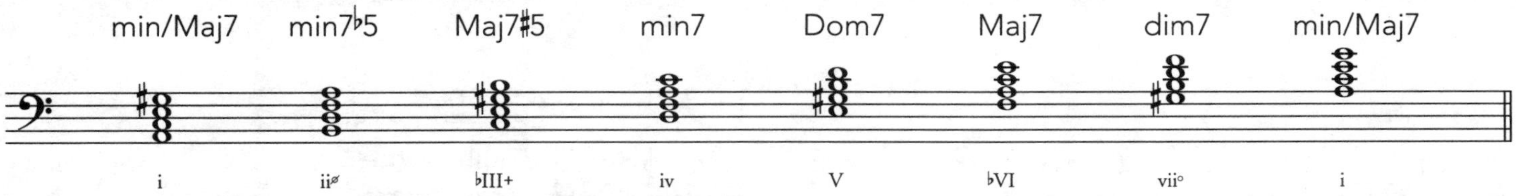

Notice the two new chord qualities that result from harmonizing the scale in 7th chords: a minor/major 7th (min/Maj7) on the first scale degree (1–♭3–5–7) and an augmented major 7th (Maj7♯5) on the 3rd scale degree (1–3–♯5–7).

Maj	=	Major triad
Dom7	=	Dominant 7th chord

It is also important to note that the 5th scale degree in harmonic minor is a major triad or a dominant 7th chord. The 5th scale degree of a natural minor scale is minor. It is common to use (*borrow*) the V or V7 chord from harmonic minor when playing in a minor key, even if the other harmonies in the piece come from the natural minor scale.

Modes of the Harmonic Minor Scale

The modes of the harmonic minor scale are found in the same way as the modes from the major scale. Simply build a seven-note scale from each scale degree of the harmonic minor scale.

There are six modes of the harmonic minor scale. The harmonic minor scale itself has no modal name.

Using the parallel approach, the modes of the harmonic minor scale are analyzed in relation to the modes of the major scale. For example, Ionian ♯5 is a major scale with a raised 5th. Each mode can also be analyzed using the derivative approach, where each mode is the scale starting from a specific scale degree. Here are the modes of the C Harmonic Minor scale and the harmonies associated with them. The scale degrees are analyzed with the parallel approach underneath each, and the derivative approach is shown at the right.

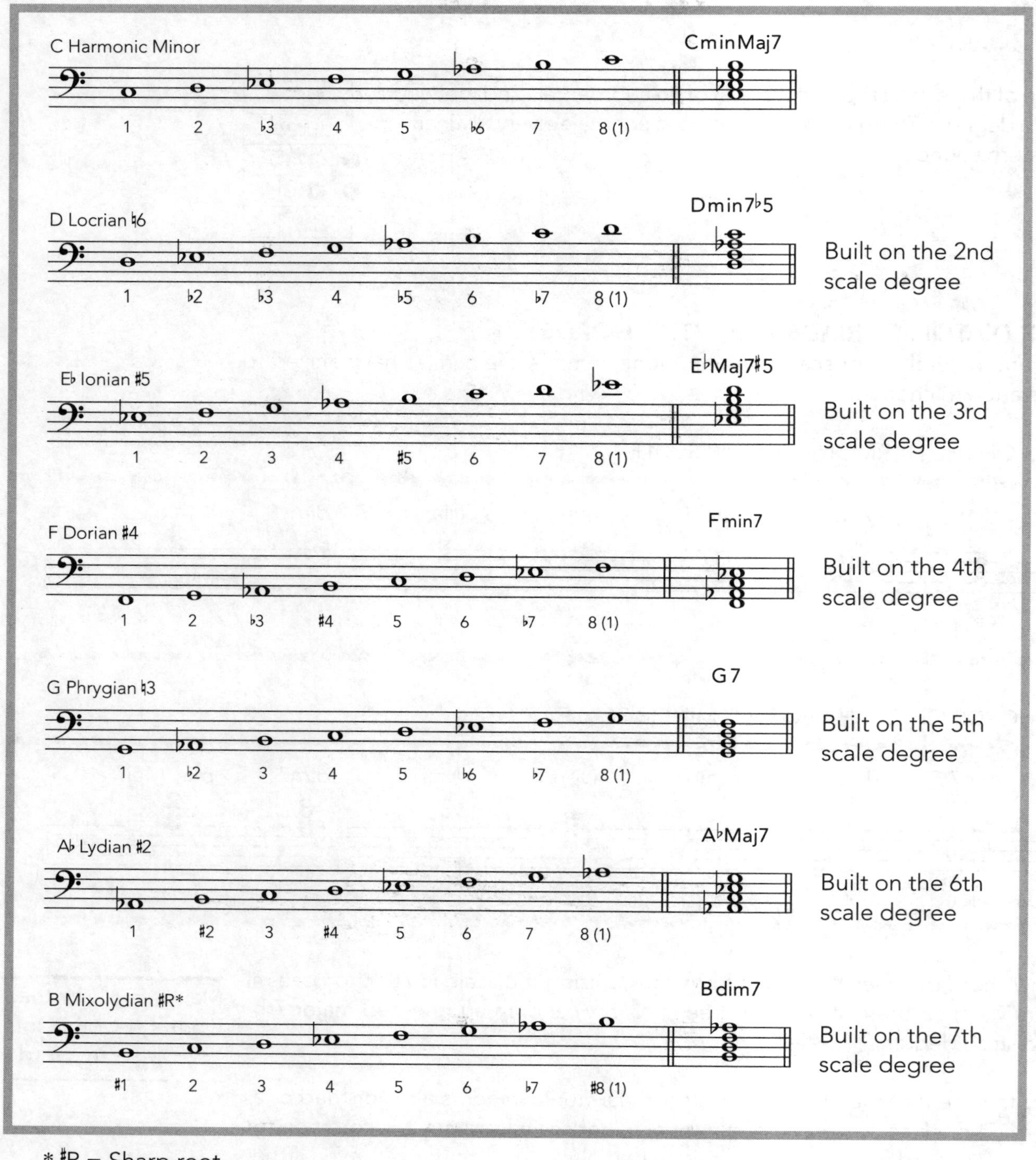

* ♯R = Sharp root.

WORKSHEET 18: THE HARMONIC MINOR SCALE

1. List the scale degrees (parallel to the major scale) of the harmonic minor scale.

______ ______ ______ ______ ______ ______ ______ ______

2. Name the diatonic triads of the C Harmonic Minor scale using Roman numerals and the chord symbols.

Roman Numerals: ______ ______ ______ ______ ______ ______ ______

Chord Symbols: ______ ______ ______ ______ ______ ______ ______

3. Name the diatonic 7th chords of the harmonic minor scale using Roman numerals and the chord symbols.

Roman Numerals: ______ ______ ______ ______ ______ ______ ______

Chord Symbols: ______ ______ ______ ______ ______ ______ ______

4. Write the following scales:

E Harmonic Minor B♭ Harmonic Minor G Harmonic Minor

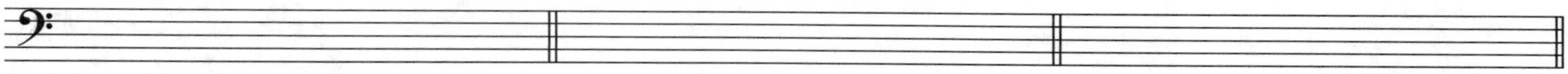

Answers

1. 1 2 ♭3 4 5 ♭6 7 8

2. Roman numerals: i ii° ♭III+ iv V ♭VI vii°

Chord symbols: Cmin Ddim E♭Aug Fmin G A♭ Bdim

3. Roman numerals: i iiø ♭III+ iv V ♭VI vii°

Chord symbols: Cmin/Maj7 Dmin7♭5 E♭Maj7♯5 Fmin7 G7 A♭Maj7 Bdim7

4.

E Harmonic Minor B♭ Harmonic Minor G Harmonic Minor

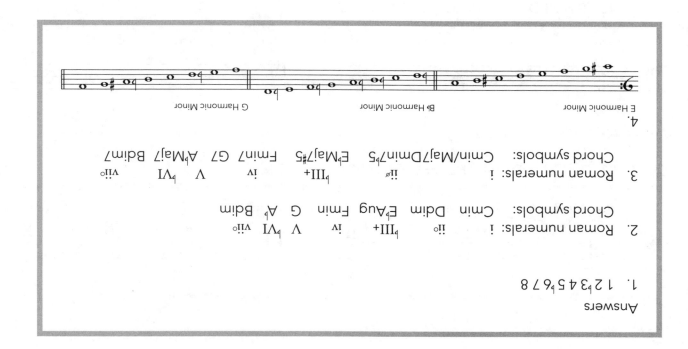

The Melodic Minor Scale

The *melodic minor* scale is a natural minor scale with raised 6th and 7th scale degrees. It can also be thought of as a major scale with a ♭3. The melodic minor scale formula is R–2–♭3–4–5–6–7–8.

In classical music theory, the melodic minor scale descends as a natural minor scale. In rock or jazz, it ascends and descends using the raised 6th and 7th. This is sometimes called *jazz minor*.

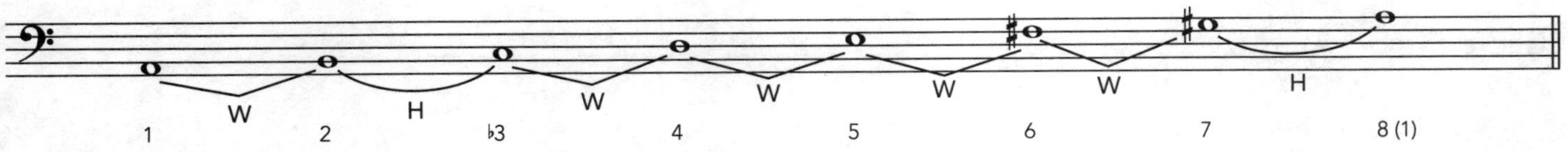

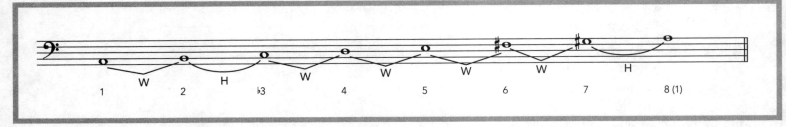

Ascending, the melodic minor scale sounds minor at first, but ends sounding major.

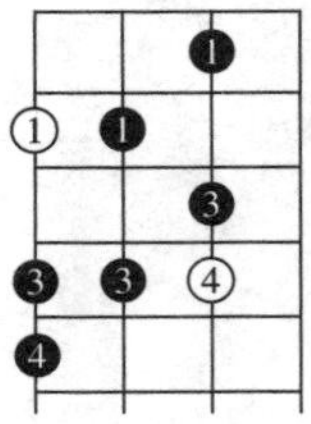

MELODIC MINOR DIATONIC TRIADS AND 7TH CHORDS

Here is the harmonization of a C Melodic Minor scale in triads and 7th chords. Notice the major V and the dominant V7 chord, as was the case with harmonic minor scale.

DIATONIC TRIADS OF THE MELODIC MINOR SCALE

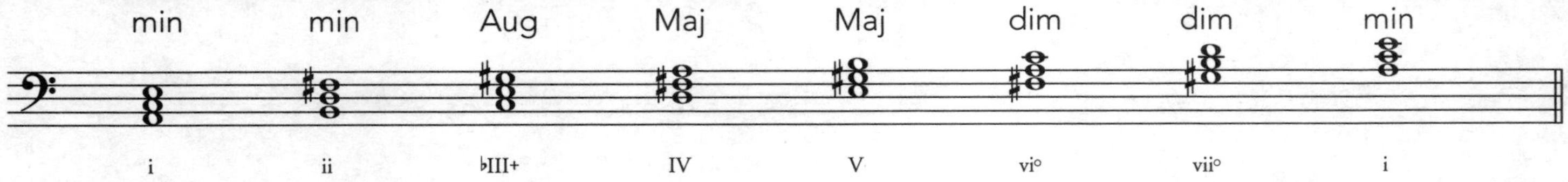

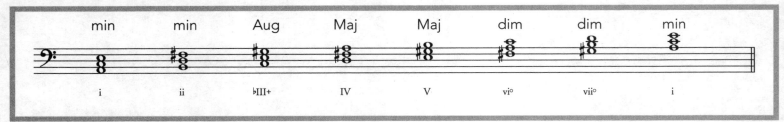

DIATONIC 7TH CHORDS OF THE MELODIC MINOR SCALE

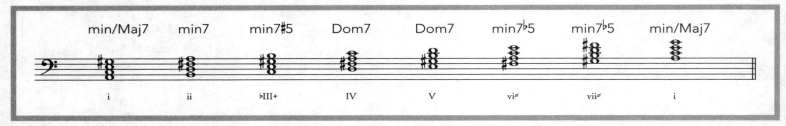

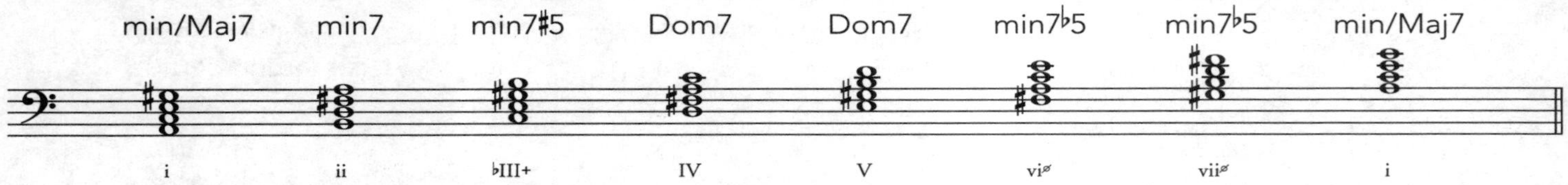

Modes of the Melodic Minor Scale

The modes of the melodic minor scale are more commonly used than those of the harmonic minor scale. With the exception of the last mode, which is commonly called *altered dominant*, the modes of melodic minor scale are named as alterations of the modes of the major scale. These modes are commonly used in jazz.

Once again, each mode can be thought of using the derivative approach, where each mode is the melodic minor scale starting on a different scale degree. Here are the modes of the C Melodic Minor scale and the harmonies associated with them. The scale degrees are analyzed with the parallel approach underneath each, and the derivative approach is shown at the right.

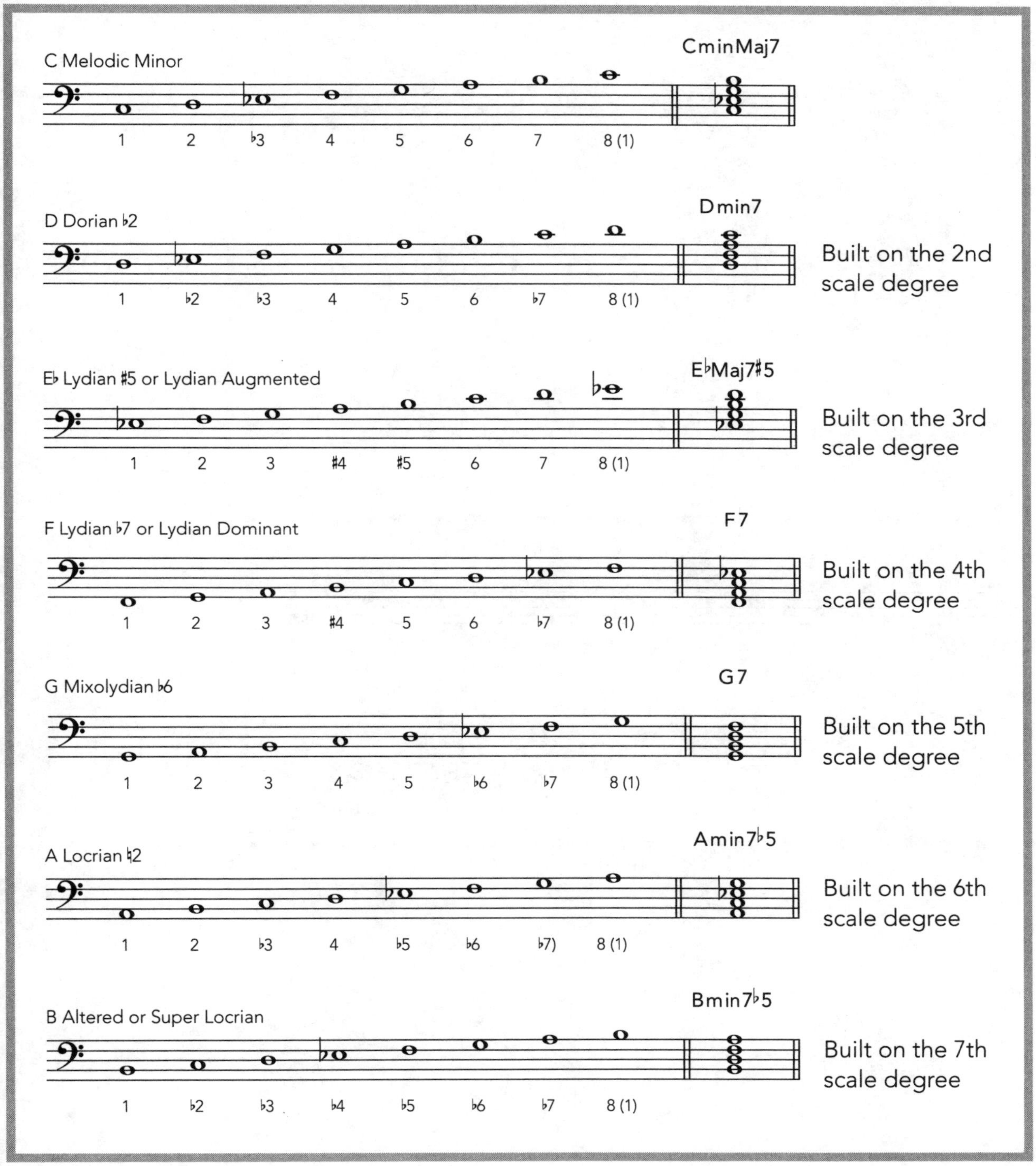

WORKSHEET 19: THE MELODIC MINOR SCALE

1. List the scale degrees (parallel to the major scale) of the melodic minor scale.

_____ _____ _____ _____ _____ _____ _____ _____

2. Write the following scales:

A Melodic Minor G Jazz Minor E♭ Jazz Minor

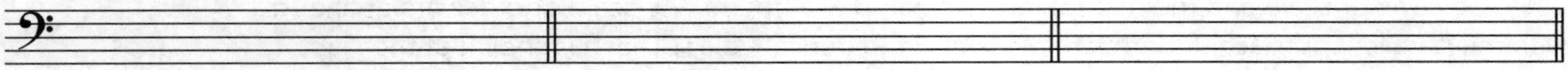

Answers:

1. 1 2 ♭3 4 5 6 7 8

2.

A Melodic Minor G Jazz Minor E♭ Jazz Minor

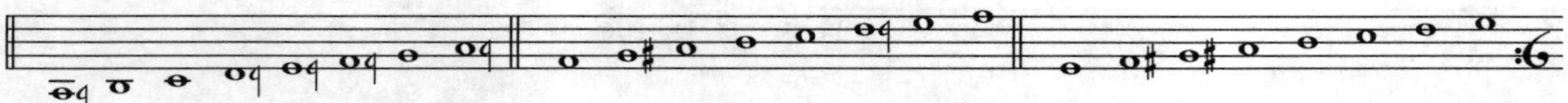

Symmetrical Scales

A *symmetrical scale* is one that is built with a repeating interval or a repeating pattern of intervals.

THE CHROMATIC SCALE

A *chromatic scale* features the repeating minor 2nd interval (half steps) and always contains all 12 notes of the musical alphabet. Since all 12 notes are always used, there is only one chromatic scale.

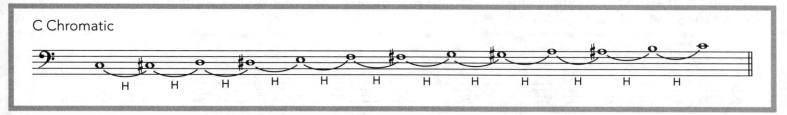

C Chromatic

The chromatic scale is easy to identify. Listen for a series of half steps!

THE WHOLE-TONE SCALE

A *whole-tone* scale is a six-note scale featuring a major 2nd (whole step) between every scale degree. As with the other scales you have learned, the tonic is usually repeated at the end. The formula for a whole-tone scale is R–2–3–♯4–♯5–♭7–8. Let's look at the C and C♯ Whole-Tone scales.

C Whole Tone — C♯ Whole Tone

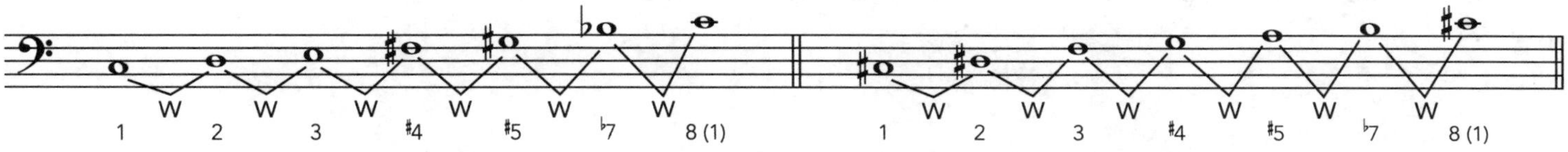

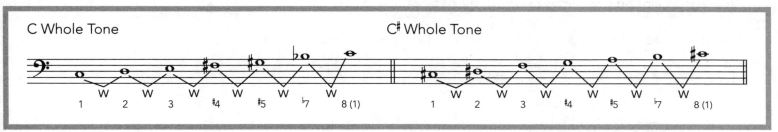

There are only two different whole-tone scales. The scale repeats itself every major 2nd. The C, D, E, F♯/G♭, G♯/A♭ and A♯/B♭ Whole-tone scales are identical.

The C♯/D♭, D♯/E♭, F, G, A and B Whole-tone scales are also identical.

The whole-tone scale is commonly used over augmented triads and dominant chords with a ♭5 or ♯5.

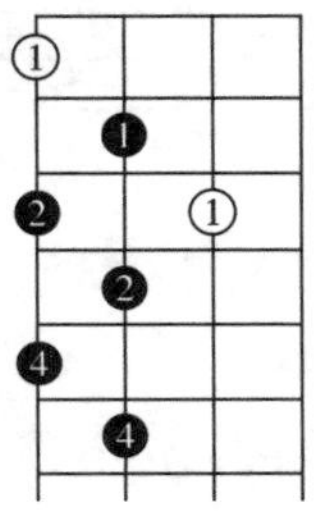

The whole-tone scale is easy to identify. Listen for the series of repeating whole steps.

Diminished Scales

A *diminished* scale is an eight-note symmetrical scale that features a series of alternating half steps and whole steps. The tonic is repeated at the end. There are two types of diminished scales: one beginning with a half step, and one beginning with a whole step.

HALF/WHOLE DIMINISHED

The *half/whole diminished* scale starts with a half step which is followed by a whole step and continues to ascend in alternating half steps and whole steps. The formula for a half/whole diminished scale is R–♭2–♯2–3–♯4–5–6–♭7–8(1).

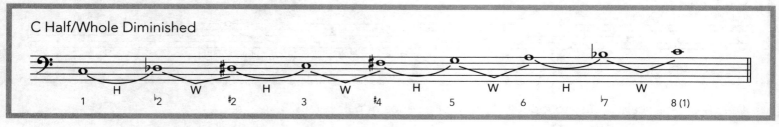

C Half/Whole Diminished

The half/whole diminished scale repeats itself every minor 3rd. For example, a half/whole diminished scale starting on E♭ has the same pitches as one starting on C. Because of this fact, there are only three half/whole diminished scales: C, C♯/D♭ and D. All of the other half/whole diminished scales are simply different enharmonic spellings of one of these three scales.

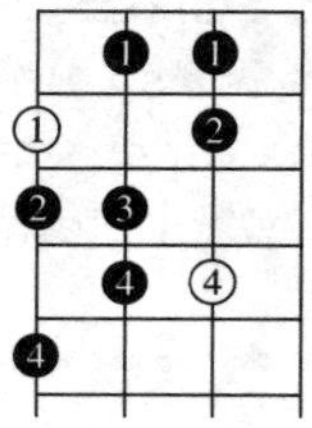

The half/whole diminished scale is commonly used over dominant chords with a ♯9 or ♭9.

WHOLE/HALF DIMINISHED

The *whole/half diminished* scale starts with a whole step which is followed by a half step and continues to ascend, alternating half steps and whole steps. The formula for a whole/half diminished scale is R–2–♭3–4–♭5–♭6–𝄫7–7–8.

C Whole/Half Diminished

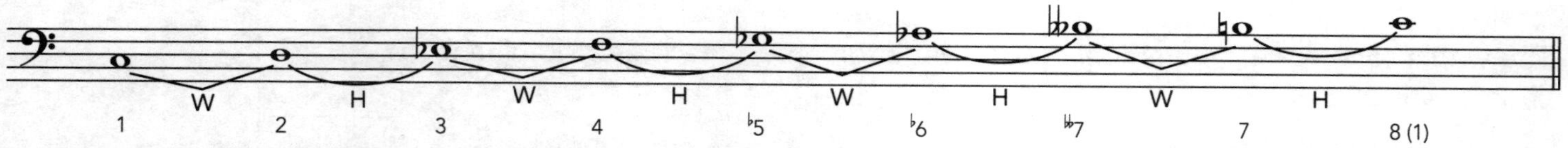

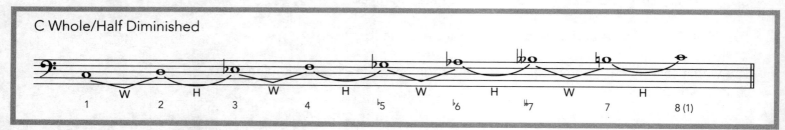

Just as with the half/whole diminished scale, there are only three whole/half diminished scales and they repeat themselves every minor 3rd.

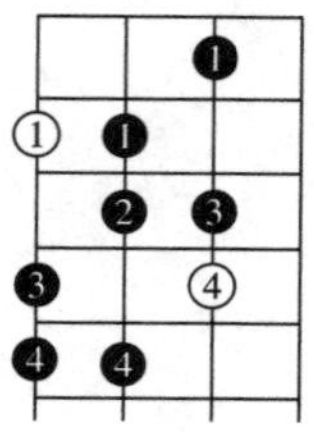

The whole/half diminished scale is commonly used over diminished triads and diminished 7th chords.

Chord Progressions

A *chord progression* is a series of chords. When we speak of a chord progression, we are speaking of the movement of one chord to another. Typically, we use Roman numerals for such discussions. This is very handy, because once a progression is understood in these terms, it can be played in any key.

The Primary Chords—I, IV and V

The most important chords in any key are I, IV and V. These are called the *primary chords*. Many rock and blues tunes are composed entirely of these three chords alone. In the key of C Major, these chords are C Major (I), F Major (IV) and G Major (V); in the key of G Major they are G Major (I), C Major (IV) and D Major (V).

Over thousands of years of musical and cultural development, the interval of a perfect 5th became deeply important to our musical structures. It is probably the relationship of a descending perfect 5th from I to IV, and an upward perfect 5th from I to V, that accounts for the predominance of the primary chords in our music. They most often appear in this order: IV–V–I. The sound of IV–V–I is so definitive for us that it, or one of its variants, is needed to firmly establish the sound of any key in our ears.

Diatonic Chord Progressions in Major Keys

There are common chord progressions that surface time and again in popular music. This chapter will explore some of these progressions. Whether you are writing songs or working as a *sub* (substitute) on a gig, you will need to be able to recognize these chord patterns and supply complimenting bass lines to support them in a song.

Diatonic chord progressions are those in which all of the chords revolve around a tonal center or key. All of the chords in the song will eventually want to resolve back to the tonic. Saying "a diatonic progression in the key of C" is the same as saying "a song is in the key of C." The following are some of the most common diatonic major chord progressions.

I–IV–V–I

The three primary chords, I, IV and V, are used constantly in popular music. In a typical I–IV–V–I, they are played as all major chords. The song "Lay Down Sally" by Eric Clapton uses a I–IV–V–I progression. Let's look at a I–IV–V–I progression in the key of G Major.

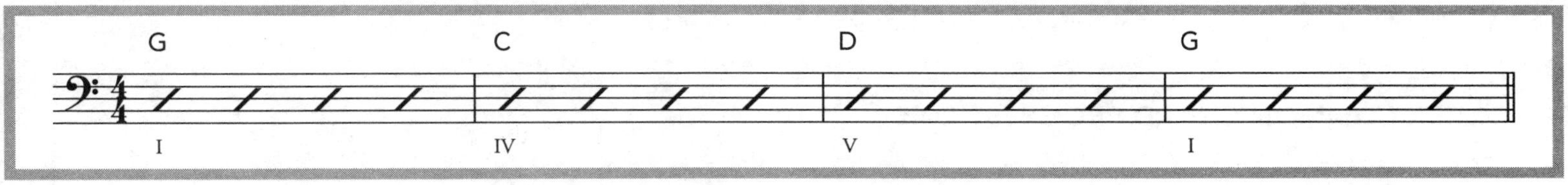

You will notice that the progression begins and ends on the I chord. When analyzing chord progressions, start with the first and last chord. If they are the same chord, check if all of the other chords fit in the key of that chord. If they all fit, you can be reasonably sure you have found the key.

Here is a I–IV–V progression that starts on the IV chord.

Although this progression starts on F Major, it is still considered in the key of C. C is the only major key that contains all three of these chords, and C Major is also the only chord in this progression that sounds fully resolved. Since A Minor is the relative minor of C Major, all of these chords could be found in A Minor as well. The reason it is considered C Major and not A Minor is that the progression ends on C.

I–vi–IV–V–I

The I–vi–IV–V–I is another extremely common progression. This progression has a very distinct sound and can be heard on the classic "Stand By Me," made famous by Ben E. King. The following I–vi–IV–V–I progression is in the key of C Major. Again, since A Minor is the relative minor of C Major, all of these chords could be found in A Minor as well. The reason it is considered C Major and not A Minor is the fact that the progression starts, and usually ends, on C.

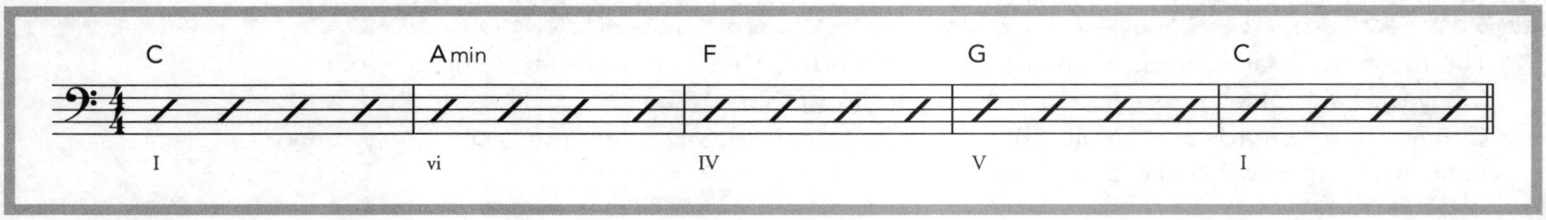

I–IV–ii–V–I

The I–IV–ii–V–I progression can be heard in the song "Run Around" by Blues Traveler. This progression is easy to hear in that it is comprised of two sets of chords, a whole step apart, that move down a 5th (or up a 4th). Here is the progression in the key of D Major.

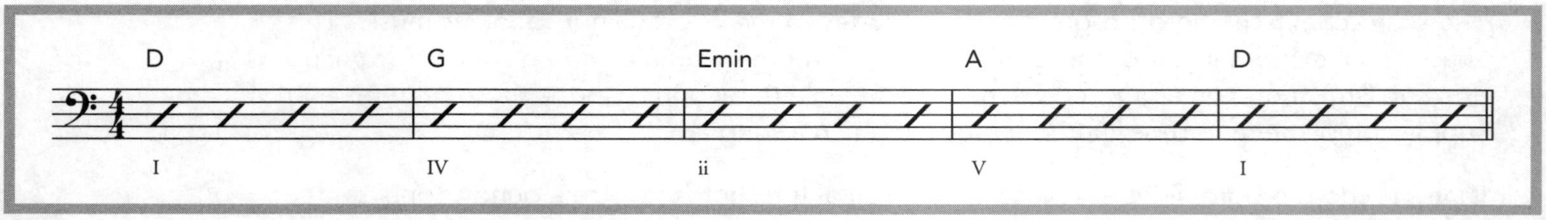

As with the last two progressions, all of these chords could fit in the relative minor key (E Minor), but arranged in this manner, followed by the typical resolution back to I, creates the sense of the major key.

There are many other major chord progressions that are used in all styles of music. Starting to hear how chords move and work together will help your playing tremendously. The following is a list of a few major key progressions and songs that use them.

OTHER COMMON CHORD PROGRESSIONS

Progression	**Song**	**Artist**
I–IV–I–V	"Brown Eyed Girl"	Van Morrison
I–V–IV	"Blue Sky"	The Allman Brothers Band
I–iii–IV–I	"The Weight"	The Band
I–ii–iii–IV–V	"Like a Rolling Stone"	Bob Dylan
I–V–vi–IV–ii–V–ii–V–I–IV–I–V	"Oh Darlin' "	The Beatles

Diatonic Chord Progressions in Minor Keys

In a minor key chord progression, all of the chords will revolve around and want to eventually resolve to the minor i chord. Songs in minor keys normally have a somber, sad sound.

i–V–i–iv–i

The i–V–i–iv–i is a very common progression and is the basis of the Santana classic, "Black Magic Woman." Notice that the V chord is a dominant 7th rather than minor. The V7 chord of harmonic minor is often used in place of the minor v chord found in natural minor.

Amin E7 Amin Dmin Amin

i V i iv i

i–♭VI–iv–♭VII–i

An example of the i–♭VI–iv–♭VII–i progression can be found in the verse to "Mr. Jones" by Counting Crows. The following progression is in the key of A Minor. Try arpeggiating each chord. This will help you hear the harmony.

Amin F Dmin G Amin

i ♭VI iv ♭VII i

WORKSHEET 20: CHORD PROGRESSIONS

Write out the following chord progressions in the given keys.

1. I–vi–IV–V–I

   a. D Major ____________ b. B♭ Major ____________

   c. E Major ____________ d. F♯ Major ____________

2. i–♭VI–iv–♭VII–i

   a. A Minor ____________ b. C Minor ____________

   c. E Minor ____________ d. B♭ Minor ____________

3. Analyze the following progressions using Roman numerals.

   a. D F♯min Emin A7
   Analysis ___ ___ ___ ___

   b. Emin Amin G C B7
   Analysis ___ ___ ___ ___ ___

   c. G C D G
   Analysis ___ ___ ___ ___

   d. Dmin C B A7
   Analysis ___ ___ ___ ___

Answers

1.a. D–Bmin–G–A–D b. B♭–Gmin–E♭–F–B♭ c. E–C♯min–A–B–E d. F♯–D♯min–B–C♯–F♯

2. a. Amin–F–Dmin–G–Amin b. Cmin–A♭–Fmin–B♭–Cmin c. Emin–C–Amin–D–Emin d. B♭min–G♭–E♭min–A♭–B♭min

3.a. I–iii–ii–V b. i–iv–♭III–♭VI–V c. I–IV–V–I d. i–♭VII–♭VI–V

More Chord Progressions

The ii–V–I Progression

One of the most common variants on the IV–V–I progression is the ii–V–I, in which ii takes the place of IV. This can be played in major or minor keys, and it works because the 3rd and 5th of the ii chord are the same pitches as the root and 3rd of the IV.

THE MAJOR ii–V–I

As the name implies, a major ii–V–I is a three-chord progression that starts on a ii or ii7 (min7) chord, moves down a 5th (or up a 4th) to a V or V7 chord and finally down a 5th (or up a 4th) to a I or I7 (Maj7) chord. This movement creates what is called *tension and release.* The V chord, which creates this tension, has a natural tendency to resolve to the I chord, which, as the tonic, gives us a feeling of release.

To recognize a ii–V–I, you must find a group of three chords that descend in 5ths (or ascend in 4ths). All of the chords should be in the key of the I chord. The qualities will follow the diatonic harmony of a major scale in triads or 7th chords. Let's look at an example in C Major, first in triads and then in 7th chords.

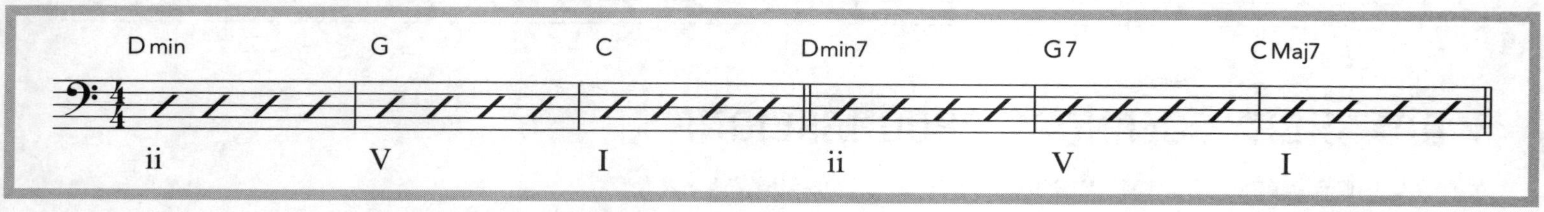

THE MINOR ii–V–i

The minor ii–V–i has a diminished ii° (or min7♭5) and a minor (or min7) tonic. The V7 chord comes from the harmony of a harmonic minor scale (see page 63). Let's look at a minor ii–V–i first in triads, then in 7th chords.

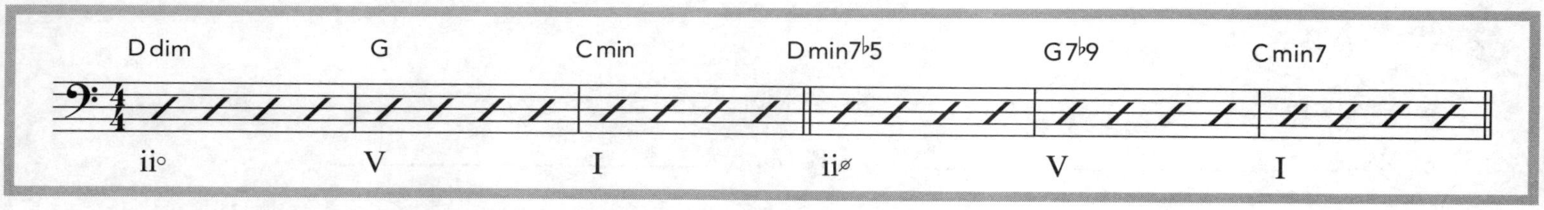

When using triads, it is a common practice to substitute a minor ii for the diminished ii°.

Notice that the V chord in the last progression is played as a G7♭9. This chord fits with the 5th mode of harmonic minor, which has a ♭2. Practice playing bass lines over ii–V–I progressions in C Major and C Minor. Once you feel comfortable in these keys, try to master all 12 major and minor ii–V–i progressions. Use the major scales on pages 21 and 22 and your knowledge of relative minor scales to do this.

Secondary Dominants

Secondary dominants are dominant 7th chords that are used to replace other quality chords of the same root in a chord progression. A dominant 7th chord has a tendency to pull to a chord whose root is a 5th below (or a 4th above), as in V7 to I. For this reason, a dominant chord can replace any chord in a progression when the following chord is a 5th below (or a 4th above). Let's look at a ii–V–I in the key of C Major.

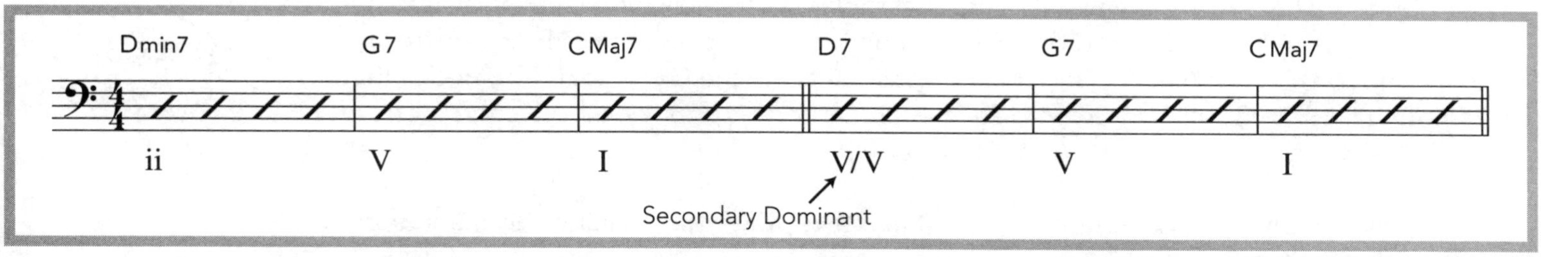

V/V = The secondary dominant of V

Notice that the Dmin7 has been replaced with a D7. The D7 is a secondary dominant.

BACKCYCLE

Let's look at a five-bar progression in the key of C Major. There are two versions.

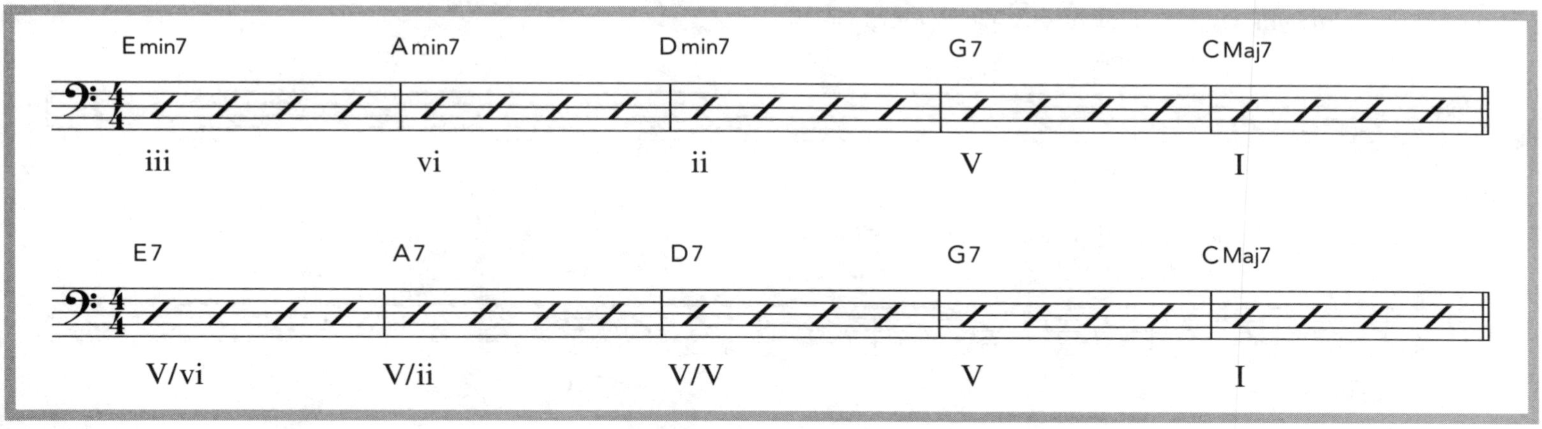

Changing all of the minor chords to dominant 7th chords creates tension throughout the progression until the final resolution to the I chord in the final measure. Although not all of these dominant chords are normally in the key of C Major, this progression would still be considered to be in the key of C Major because of how it ends (G7–CMaj7). Going backwards from the final CMaj7, each chord is a perfect 5th above the last. This cycle-of-5ths motion is often called a *backcycle*. The E7, A7 and D7 can all be analyzed as secondary dominants of the chords they precede, and it all comes to a conclusion with a movement from V7 to I, which is called a *perfect cadence*.

Try arpeggiating each of the two progressions above, listening to the difference created by the backcycle of secondary dominants.

Tritone Substitutions

As you know, the interval of a diminished 5th (or augmented 4th) is also known as a tritone (see page 31). Every dominant 7th chord has the interval of a tritone between the 3rd and the ♭7th. For example, in a C7 chord, the 3rd is E and the ♭7 is B♭. These two notes are a tritone apart. This tritone interval creates additional tension in a dominant 7th chord.

A *tritone substitution* is a dominant chord that replaces another dominant chord a tritone away. For example, G♭7 is the tritone substitution for C7. Notice that the E-note is the 3rd in C7 and the ♭7 in G♭7 (E is enharmonically spelled as F♭ in the G♭7 chord). Also notice that B♭-note is the ♭7 in C7 and the 3rd in G♭7. *The same tritone is present in both chords.* These common chord tones are what allow a tritone substitution to take place.

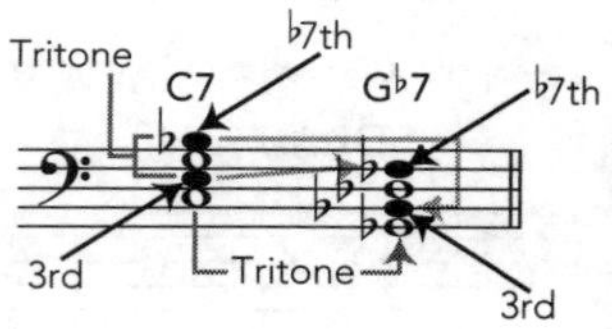

Let's look at a tritone substitution in a ii–V–I in the key of C Major, first without and then with a tritone substitution for the V7.

Notice that the G7 was replaced with a D♭7. This tritone substitution creates a chromatic movement of the chords in the harmony from Dm7 to D♭7 to Cmaj7. Tritone substitutions are commonly used to create chromatic progressions along with chromatic bass lines.

Let's review the iii–vi–ii–V–I progression from page 75.

Here is the progression with the secondary dominants.

Finally, here is the same progression with tritone substitutions. Notice how the progression is a series of dominant 7th chords, descending in half steps until the final resolution to the I chord.

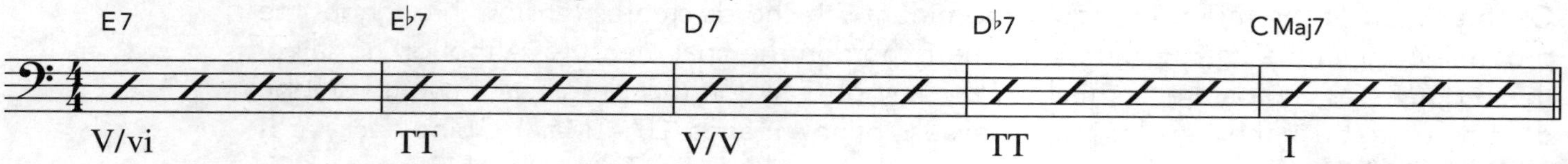

TT = Tritone substitution

Borrowed Harmony

In theory, any chord from a parallel key (a different key with the same tonic, for example, C Major and C Minor are parallel keys) can be *borrowed*. In practical use, there are only a few commonly borrowed chords. For example, in a major key, the ♭VII and the ♭VI are often borrowed from the parallel minor key.

In this A Major progression, the G7 and F Major are borrowed from the key of A Minor. Notice how this substitution creates an interesting chromatic movement from the ♭VII down to the V.

Modulation

A *modulation* is a change of key. Depending on the songwriter's intention, modulations can be quite drastic or very subtle. Secondary dominant chords often smooth out the transition from key to key. Here is a progression that modulates.

	G	C	D	G	C	D	G
G:	I	IV	V	I	IV	V	I
	C	Bmin	B7	E	A	E	B	E
	IV	iii	V/vi					
			E: V	I	IV	I	V	I

WORKSHEET 21: PRIMARY CHORDS, ii–V–I PROGRESSIONS, SECONDARY DOMINANTS AND TRITONE SUBSTITUTIONS

1. Name the primary chords (I–IV–V) in the given keys.
   a. D Major ________ b. F Major________ c. A Major ________
   d. B♭Major________
2. Give the chords and qualities of a major ii–V–I progression in the following keys.
   a. G Major ________ b. D Major ________ c. E Major ________
   d. F Major ________ e. A Major ________ f. B♭ Major
3. Give the chords and qualities of a minor ii–V–i progression in the following keys using 7th chords.
   a. C Minor ________ b. E♭ Minor ________ c. G Minor ________
   d. F# Minor ________ e. G# Minor ________
4. Change all of the minor chords in the following progression to secondary dominants.

____ ____ ____

Dmin7 Gmin7 Cmin7 F7 B♭Maj7

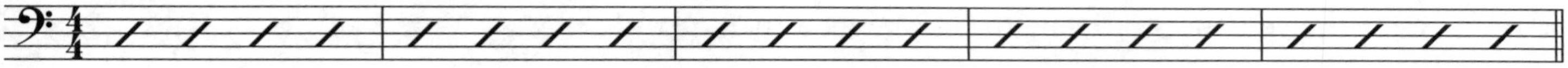

5. Name the tritone substitutions of the following chords.
   a. B♭7 ___ b. A7 ___ c. G7 ___ d. E♭7 ___ e. F#7 ___ f. E7 ___ g. D7 ___

Answers

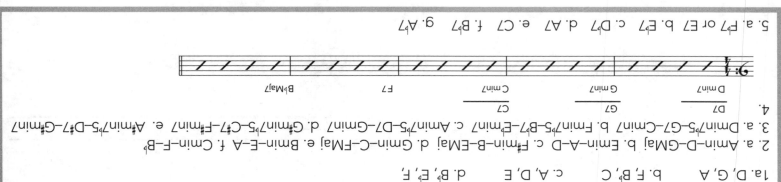

1a. D, G, A b. F, B♭, C c. A, D, E d. B♭, E♭, F

2. a. Amin–D–GMaj b. Emin–A–D c. F#min–B–EMaj d. Gmin–C–FMaj e. Bmin–E–A f. Cmin–F–B♭

3. a. Dmin7♭5–G7–Cmin7 b. Fmin7♭5–B♭7–E♭min7 c. Amin7♭5–D7–Gmin7 d. G#min7♭5–C#7–F#min7 e. A#min7♭5–D#7–G#min7

4. D7 G7 C7

Dmin7 Gmin7 Cmin7 F7 B♭Maj7

5. a. F♭7 or E7 b. E♭7 c. D♭7 d. A7 e. C7 f. B♭7 g. A♭7

Passing Tones and Approach Notes

One of the main responsibilities of a bass player is to create forward motion within chords and from one chord change to the next. Much of this motion is accomplished by using *passing tones* and *approach notes.* These devices are used constantly in *walking* (mostly stepwise) bass lines. All of the concepts covered in this chapter will be analyzed in the context of a walking bass line.

Passing Tones

A *passing tone* is a non-chord tone melodically placed between two chord tones that is approached by step. For example, in a C Major chord, E and G are chord tones (3rd and 5th). In a bass line, an F placed between E and G is a passing tone.

Chromatic passing tones can be used to connect two scale tones. C and D are the first two scale tones in a C Major scale. C♯ or D♭ can be used in a bass line as a chromatic passing tone to connect these two notes. The following is an example of a line that uses passing tones. A chromatic passing tone can also connect a passing tone to a chord tone.

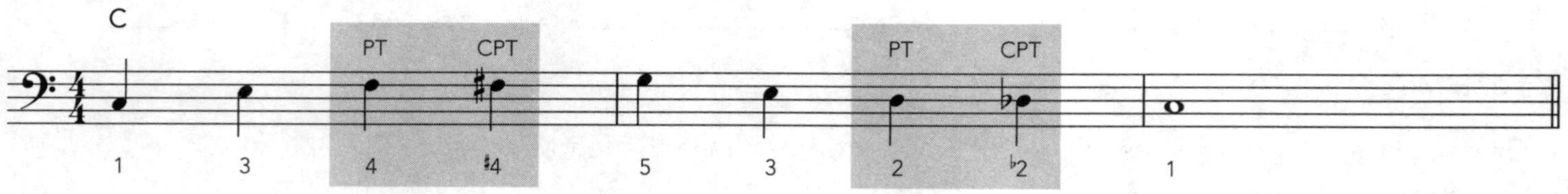

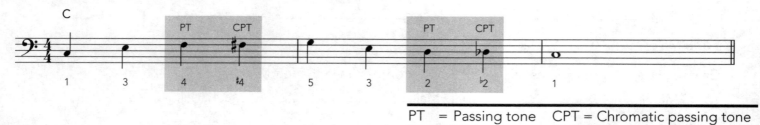

PT = Passing tone CPT = Chromatic passing tone

The F♯ pulls the listener's ear to the chord tone, G, and the D♭ pulls the listener's ear to the resolution on the root of the C chord, C. Used sparingly, passing tones are a great way to spice up a bass line. When overused, passing tones can confuse the harmony.

Approach Notes

Approach notes are melodically placed directly before a chord tone that are not approached by step. Often but not always non-chord tones, they are used to create forward motion to a *target note.* Approach notes normally prepare a listener to hear the next chord change. They can also be used to move from chord tone to chord tone within a chord.

CHROMATIC APPROACHES

A *chromatic approach* is played one half step above or below a target note. These target notes are usually chord tones. Chromatic approaches can be used when moving from chord tone to chord tone within a single chord or when changing from chord to chord. Let's look at an example of each.

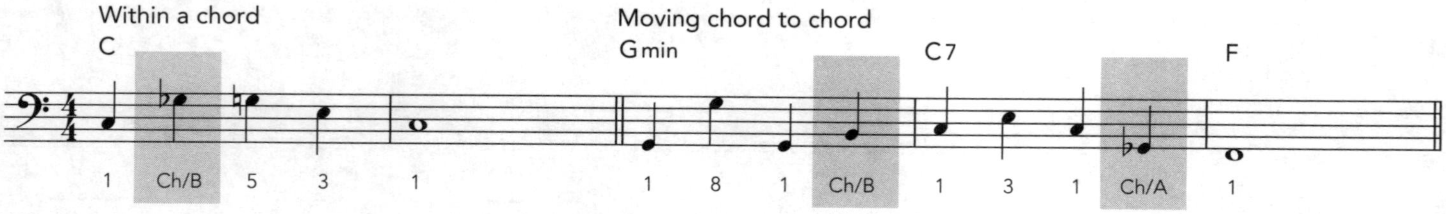

Ch/A = Chromatic above Ch/B = Chromatic below

Double-Chromatic Approaches

Double-chromatic approaches are played two half steps above or below a target note. For example, $B^\flat$ to $B^\natural$ is a double-chromatic approach below the target note, C. Double-chromatic approaches are used in the same way as chromatic approaches.

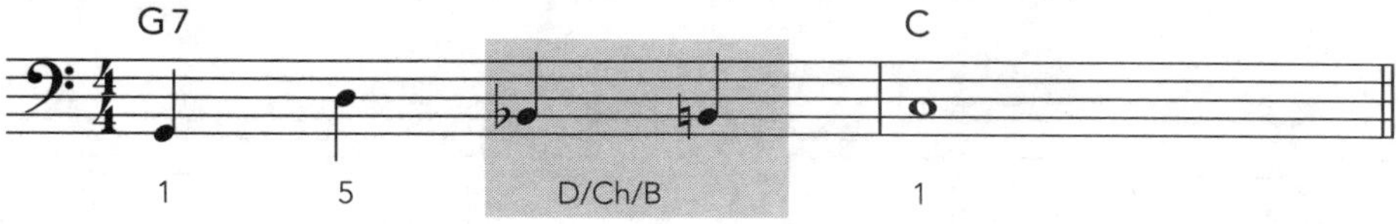

Scale-Step Approaches

A *scale-step approach* is played one scale-step above or below a target note. The following is an example of a scale-step approach.

SS/A= Scale step above

MULTIPLE SCALE-STEP APPROACHES

Target notes can also be approached by more than one scale-step above or below. The trick is to land on the target note on the desired beat. You can also use combinations of a scale step above and a scale-step below, or vice-versa, to approach a target note. The following example shows a few of the possible multiple scale-step approaches.

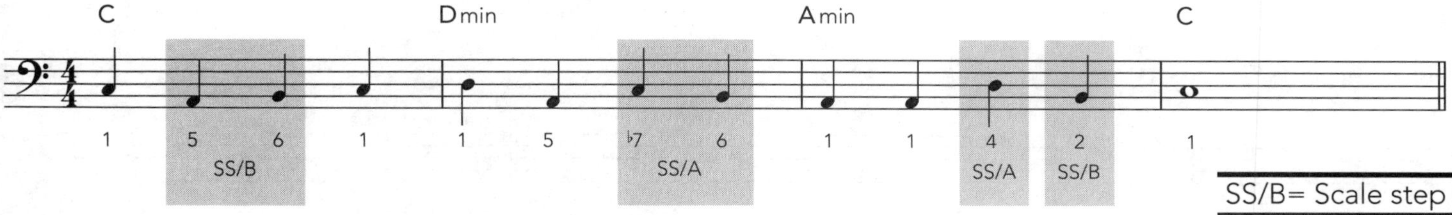

SS/B= Scale step below

Combining Scale and Chromatic Approaches

Chromatic and scale-step approaches can be used in combination with one another. Among these possibilities are combining scale-step approach above and a chromatic approach below a target note, and combining a scale-step below and a chromatic approach above a target note. Some combinations may sound better to you than others. Experiment and trust your ear when playing any kind of approach. The following example shows some of the possible combinations.

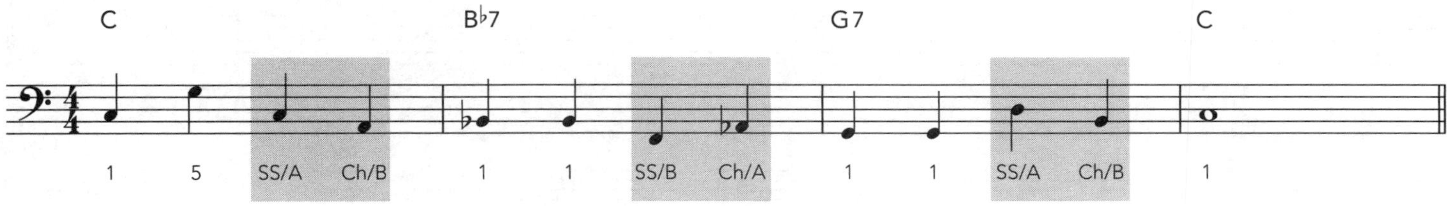

Surround Approaches

Target notes can be approached by surrounding the note with a half step on either side. This is called a *surround approach*. For example, C can be approached using a surround by playing C♯–B–C, or B–C♯–C. The following is an example of a surround approach.

Dominant Approaches

A *dominant approach* is one that resolves to a target note from a 5th above or below. A G-note played above or below C would be considered a dominant approach to the C. Let's look at some examples of dominant approaches.

Dom = *Dominant approach*

WORKSHEET 22: APPROACH NOTES

In all of the following questions, you'll be asked to write in the requested approach to the given target note.

1. Chromatic above

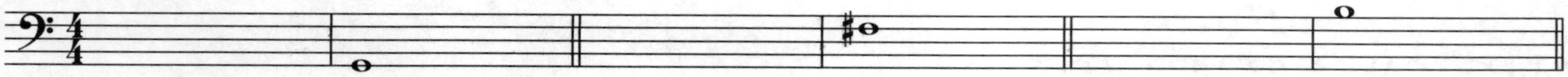

2. Double chromatic below

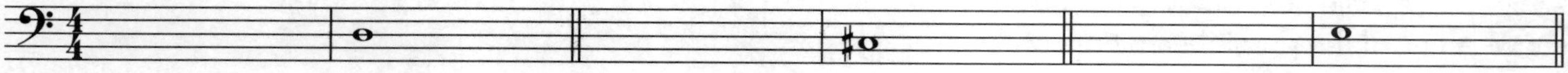

3. Scale-step above

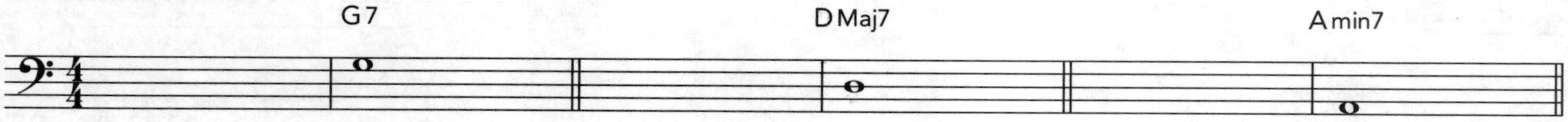

4. Scale-step above chromatic below

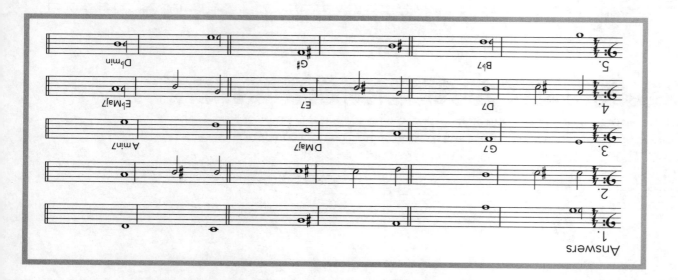

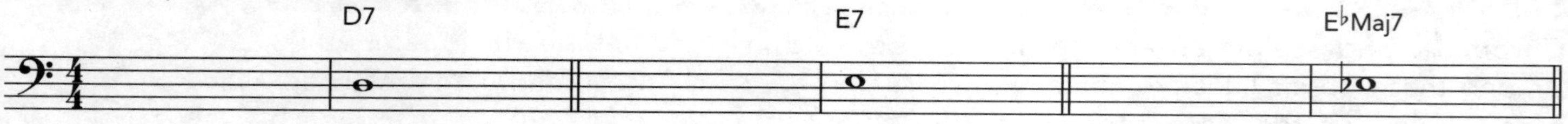

5. Dominant approach

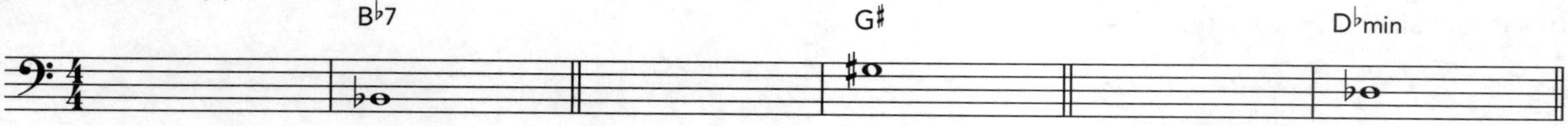

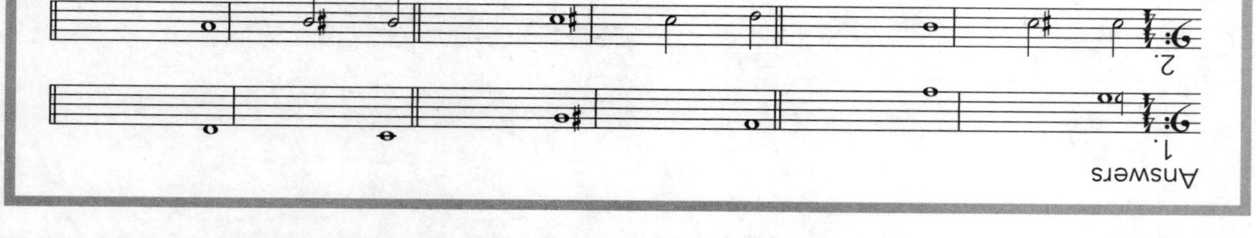

The 12-Bar Blues

The *12-bar blues* appears in many styles of music including rock, jazz, country and, of course, blues. The basic 12-bar blues is a 12-measure progression that uses the I, IV and V chords of a key. This form is sometimes referred to as "a I–IV–V blues" or just "a blues."

The Major 12-Bar Blues

In a basic, major 12-bar blues, all of the chords are played as dominant 7th chords. Although the first chord is an E7 chord, which is not diatonic to the key of E, this blues is still considered in the key of E. In other words, the dominant 7th chords do not all *function* as dominant (V). In the blues, the dominant 7th sound is a desireable "color;"we want the sound of the chord, and there is not the usual imperative to resolve to I every time we hear this sound.

The form below is a basic blues in its most stripped-down form. It is used in rock, basic blues and country music. Notice that all of the Roman numerals are accompanied by the number 7, indicating dominant 7th chords.

Notice the Roman numerals below each chord change. Following this harmony will allow you to play blues in any key. Simply start on the I chord of the given key and use the IV and V chords of that key where needed. Assume they are all dominant 7th chords.

The Quick IV

To add interest to a blues progression, a IV chord is often played in the second bar. This change is called a *quick four*. Always listen closely in the first chorus of a blues to hear if a quick four is being played.

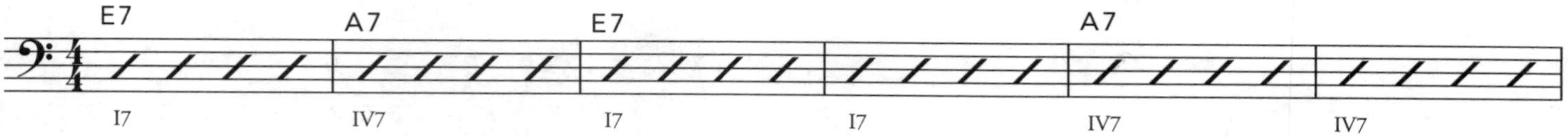

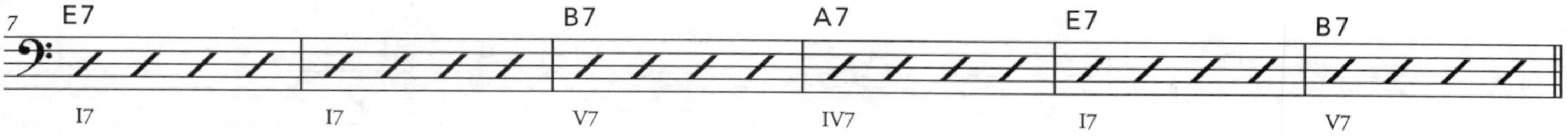

Notice that a V (B7) appears in bar 12. The V chord on the final measure is another common variation, because it leads back to the I chord in bar 1. Once again, you will need to listen for this change.

More Variations

Another way to spice up a blues is to play different chord extensions. The I, IV and V are all usually played as dominant 7th chords and can therefore be replaced with any dominant-type chord. The most typical chord extensions used are dominant 9th and 13th chords, played with or without altered tones. Let's look at an example of a blues with some common chord variations. Notice that in the Roman Numerals, we are still thinking of these as dominant chords.

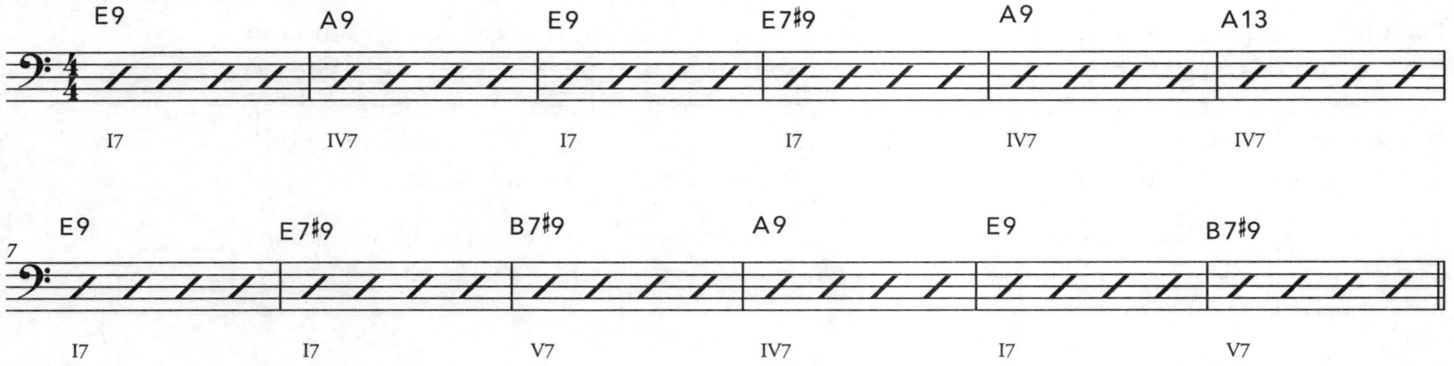

Your guitarist and/or keyboard player will supply the harmony of these chords. You can still play basic lines over extended chords, or you can choose to emphasize these extensions in your lines.

SECONDARY CHORDS AND PASSING CHORDS IN THE BLUES

Secondary dominants can also be used to set-up changes in a blues. For example, in a C blues, a D7 chord can be played in bar 8, which will act as a secondary dominant of the G7 in bar 9.

Quick ii–V changes can also be used to set-up chord changes in the blues. Using the same example of a C blues, Amin7–D7 (ii–V) can be played in bar 8, which also leads to the G7 in bar 9. Together, these chords act as a *secondary ii–V* of the G7.

Chromatic passing chords are often placed on beat 4 of a measure, leading to a new chord in the next measure. A passing chord is a non-diatonic chord placed between diatonic chords, approached and resolved by step. Approaching and resolving the passing chord by half step makes it a chromatic passing chord. For example, in a C blues, F♯7 (or any other F♯ dominant chord) can be played on beat 4 of bar 4, which leads chromatically to the F7 in bar 5. The following are examples of secondary chords in a major blues.

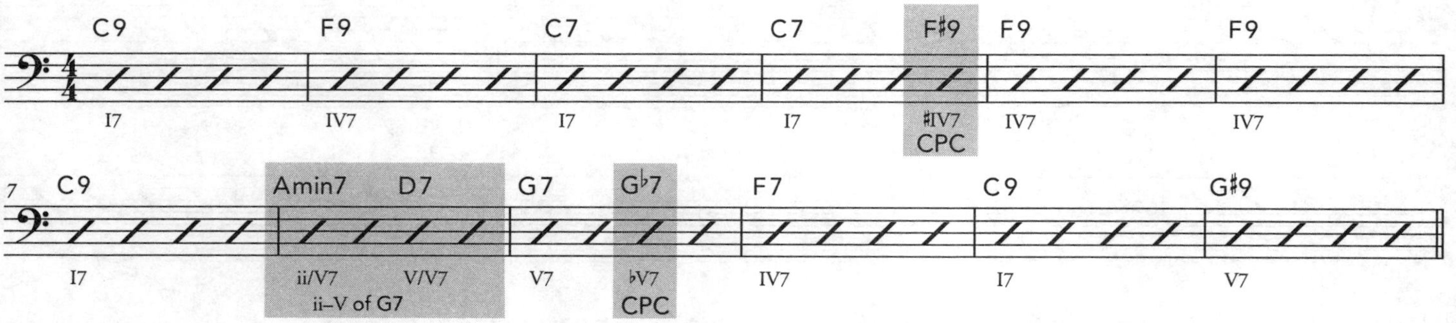

CPC = Chromatic passing chord
ii/V = The ii in a secondary ii–V, in this case, a ii–V of the V.

Turnarounds

A *turnaround* is a group of chords at the end of a piece of music that leads back to the beginning of the form. In a blues, the last four bars are the turnaround.

In a rock or blues situation, bars 9 and 10 are usually V–IV. Bars 11 and 12 are much more open to interpretation. The following are two of the more common turnarounds in the key of C. One descends while the other ascends.

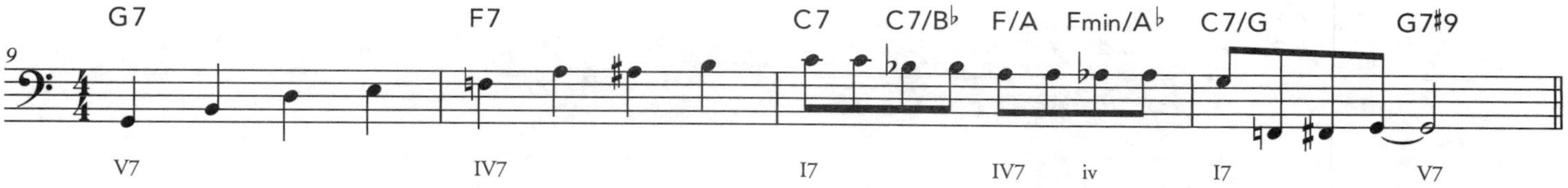

The written bass lines in the last two measures of both examples are cliché lines commonly used by bass players. In a faster blues, guitar players will often forgo the harmony and play just the roots of these chords as well.

Endings

A blues will always resolve back to the I chord at the very end. A turnaround easily becomes an ending when reworked to finish on I. The following are common endings you will likely encounter.

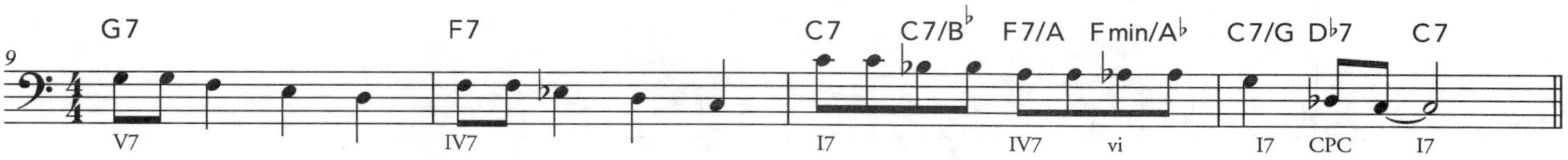

There are many variations that can be played on turnarounds and endings. Always keep your ears open and be ready to react to what is being played. If you find yourself stumped by a variation, turnaround or ending, don't be afraid to ask your fellow musicians what they played.

Minor 12-Bar Blues

A *minor blues* is a 12-measure progression that uses the harmony of a minor scale. The basic chords of a minor blues are i, iv and v. Unlike a major blues, which is often referred to as simply a blues, a minor blues is always referred to as a "minor blues." The following is a basic minor blues in G Minor.

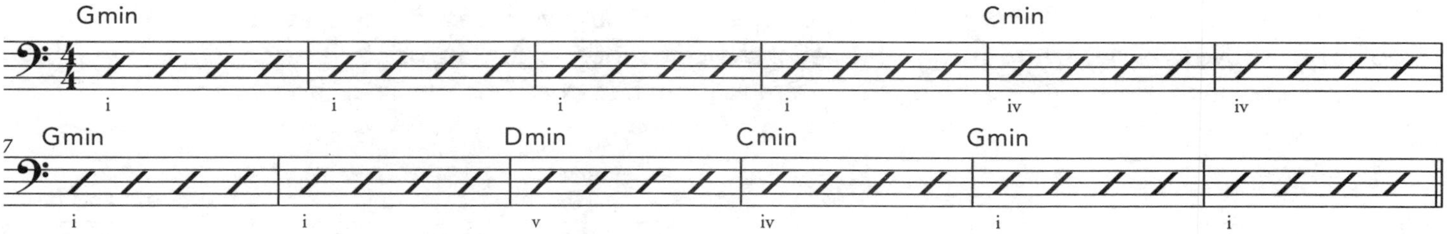

As with a major blues, memorizing the Roman numerals will allow you to play a minor blues in any key.

Minor Blues Variations, Turnarounds and Endings

As with a major blues, the iv chord is often used in bar 2 of a minor blues. The turnaround of a minor blues can be played differently as well. The usual v–iv–i–v is often replaced with ♭VI–V7–i–V7 (the dominant 7th V chord is borrowed from harmonic minor). Let's look at these changes in a C Minor blues.

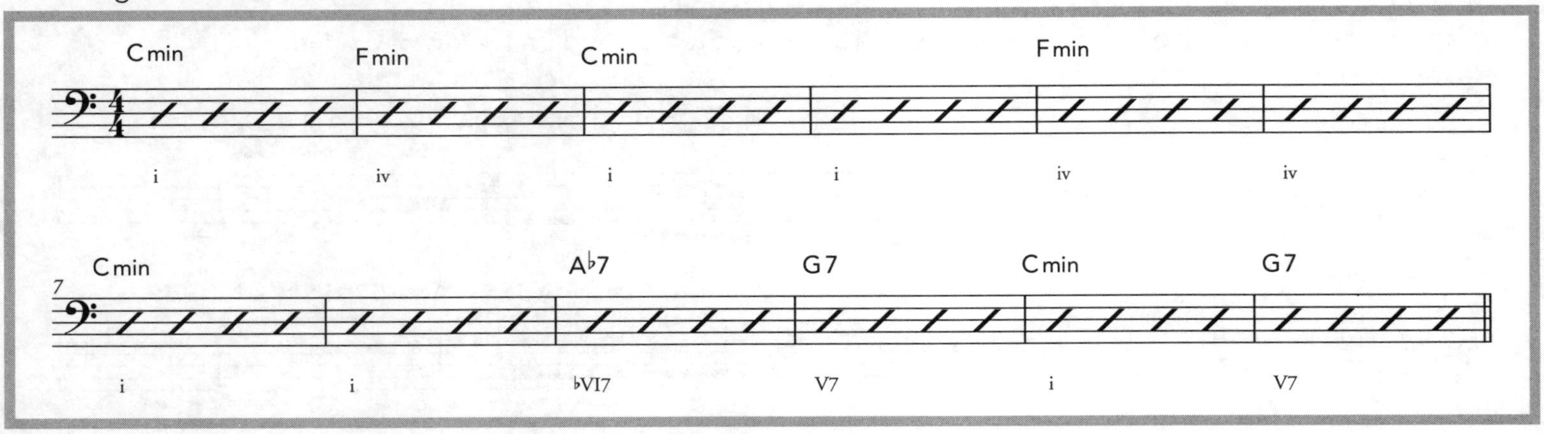

Endings

It is common to *tag* (repeat) the turnaround of a minor blues three times before ending on the i chord. Let's look at an example of this starting from the *top* (beginning) of the final chorus.

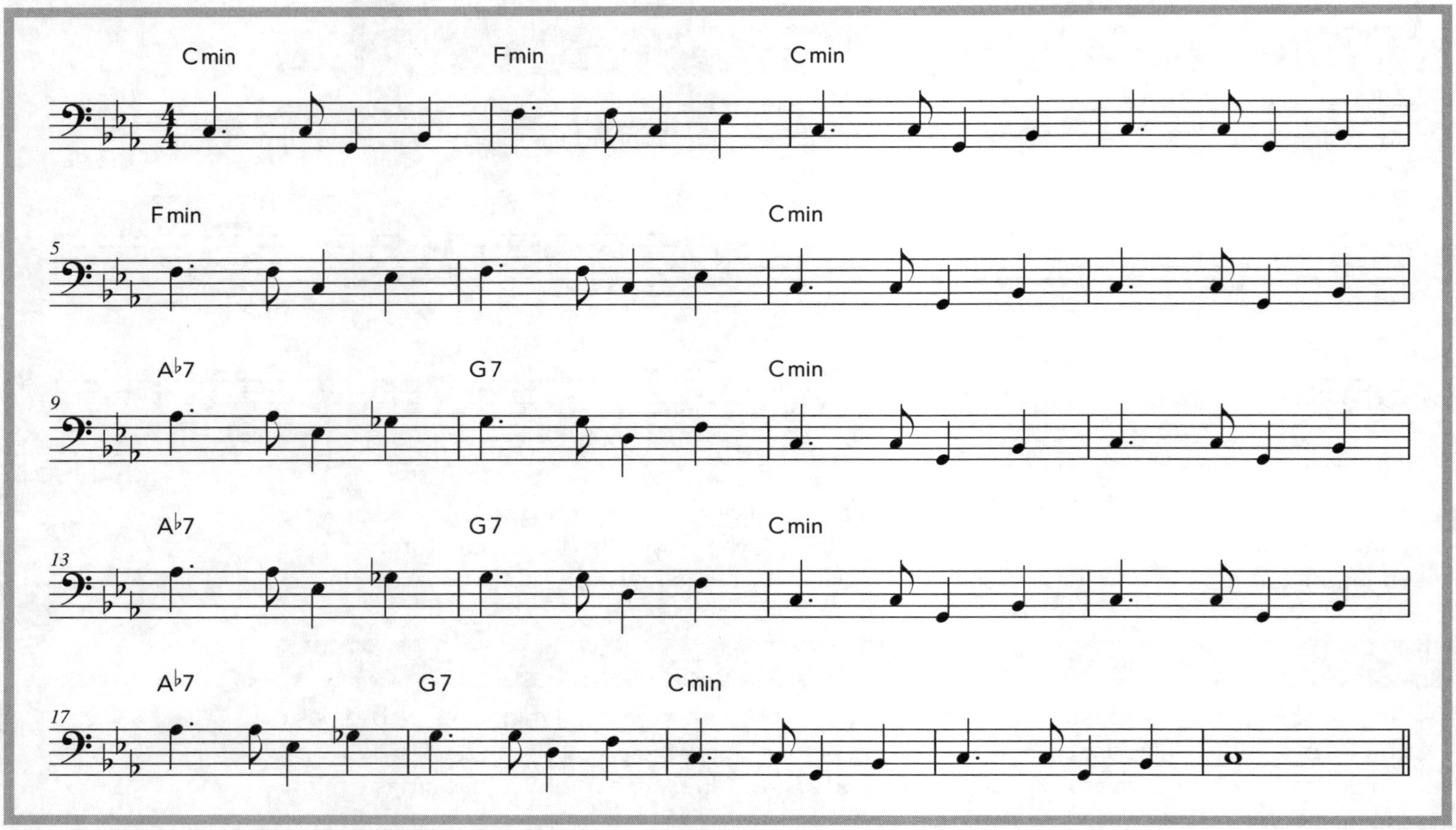

Another common ending for a minor blues is to repeat the final two measures as a *vamp* (a repetitive groove over one chord change or a set of chord changes). This vamp is often faded until a final resolution. Here is an example of this starting from the turnaround of a final chorus.

WORKSHEET 23: MAJOR AND MINOR BLUES

1. Give the Roman numerals of a basic major 12-bar blues.

_____ _____ _____ _____ _____ _____ _____ _____ _____ _____ _____ _____

2. Give the Roman numerals of a basic minor 12- bar blues.

_____ _____ _____ _____ _____ _____ _____ _____ _____ _____ _____ _____

3. Using the following changes, write the chord symbols for the given major blues keys. Use dominant chords.

I7–IV7–I7–I7♯9–IV7–IV7–I7–I7–V7–IV7–I7–V7♯9

a. E Major

_____ _____ _____ _____ _____ _____ _____ _____ _____ _____ _____ _____

b. A Major

_____ _____ _____ _____ _____ _____ _____ _____ _____ _____ _____ _____

c. G Major

_____ _____ _____ _____ _____ _____ _____ _____ _____ _____ _____ _____

4. Using the following changes, write the chords for the given minor blues keys. Use minor 7th on i and iv and dominant 7th chords on all other chords.

i–iv–i–i–iv–iv–i–i–♭VI7–V7–i–V7

a. G Minor

_____ _____ _____ _____ _____ _____ _____ _____ _____ _____ _____ _____

b. A Minor

_____ _____ _____ _____ _____ _____ _____ _____ _____ _____ _____ _____

c. F Minor

_____ _____ _____ _____ _____ _____ _____ _____ _____ _____ _____ _____

Answers

1. I–I–I–I–IV–IV–I–I–V–IV–I–I

2. i–i–i–i–iv–iv–i–i–v–iv–i–i

3.
   a. E7–A7–E7–E7♯9–A7–A7–E7–E7–B7–A7–E7–B7♯9
   b. A7–D7–A7–A7♯9–D7–D7–A7–A7–E7–D7–A7–E7♯9
   c. G7–C7–G7–G7♯9–C7–C7–G7–G7–D7–C7–G7–D7♯9

4.
   a. Gmin7–Cmin7–Gmin7–Gmin7–Cmin7–Cmin7–Gmin7–Gmin7–E♭7–D7–Gmin7–D7
   b. Amin7–Dmin7–Amin7–Amin7–Dmin7–Dmin7–Amin7–Amin7–F7–E7–Amin7–E7
   c. Fmin7–B♭min7– Fmin7–Fmin7–B♭min7–B♭min7–Fmin7–Fmin7–D♭7–C7–Fmin7–C7

Jazz-Blues

The basic *jazz-blues* is very similar to a basic blues with a few exceptions: the quick IV is *always* played in a jazz situation, and the turnaround is usually played differently. A ii–V is used over bars 9 and 10 instead of the V–IV of a basic blues. Below is an example of a basic jazz-blues. This would be the basic form you would play on a jazz gig when someone says, "Let's play an F Blues."

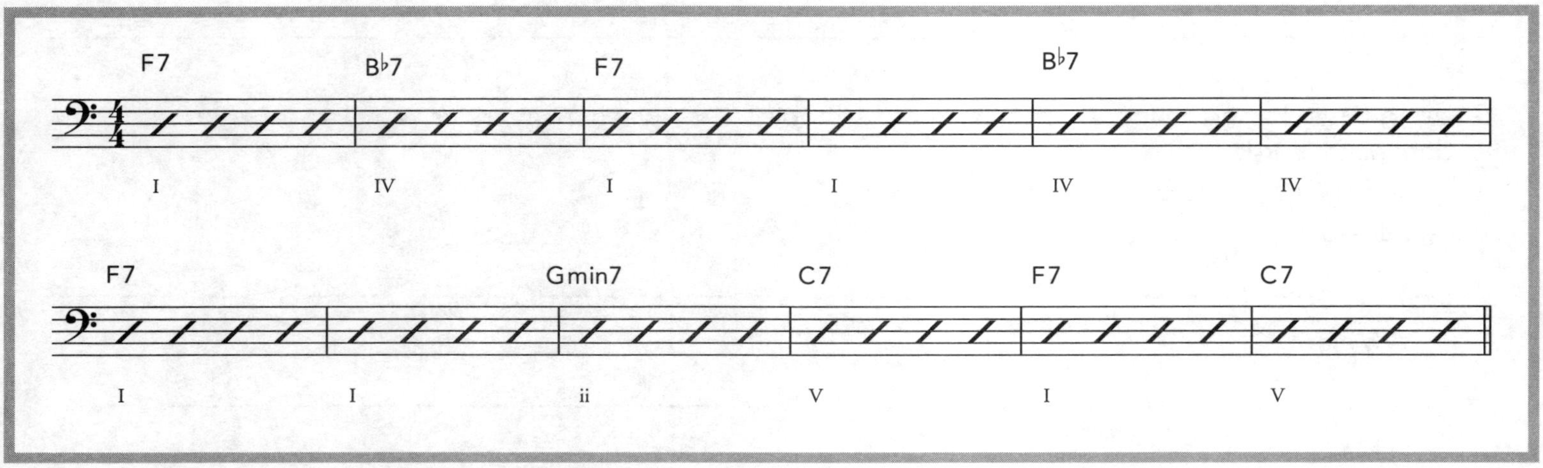

Jazz-Blues Variations

While a basic blues is sometimes played, it is rare that a jazz musician will stick to this simple form. Chord substitutions take place all the time in jazz situations. A ♯iv° in bar 6 and secondary ii–V changes are often used to spice up a jazz-blues. Let's look at these devices being used in an F blues.

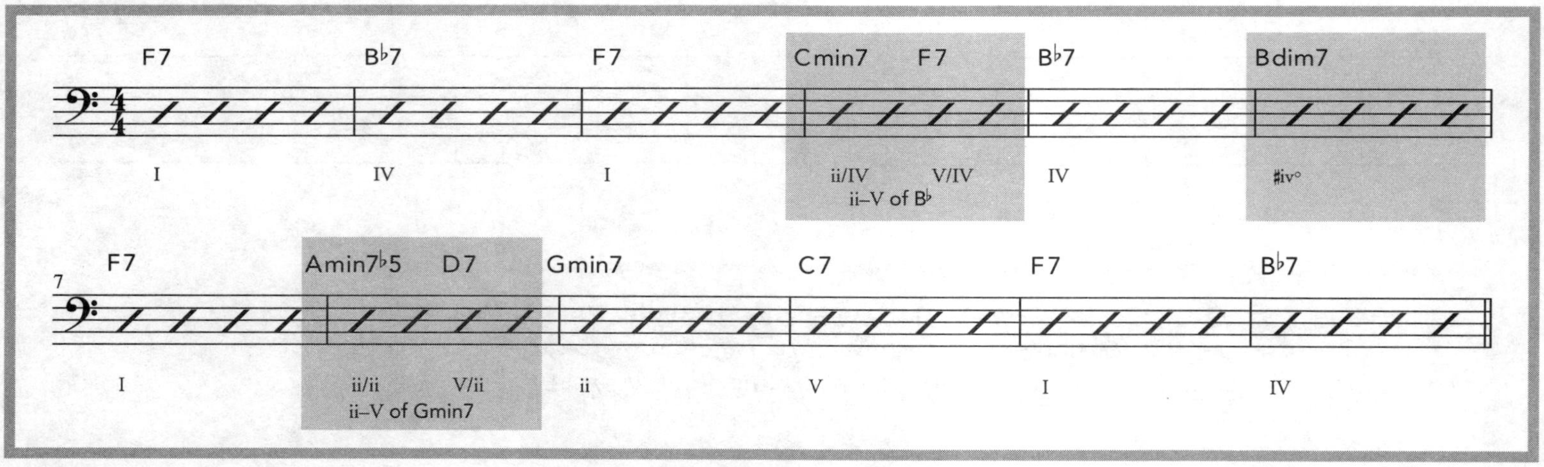

ii/V = The ii in a secondary ii–V, in this case, a ii–V of the V.

The last two measures of the turnaround are also often played differently in a jazz-blues. The following are some common turnarounds over an F blues. Notice how each turnaround is progressively altered further using secondary dominants and tritone substitutions. As with many other situations, you will need to use your ear to determine which turnaround is being used at a gig or jam session.

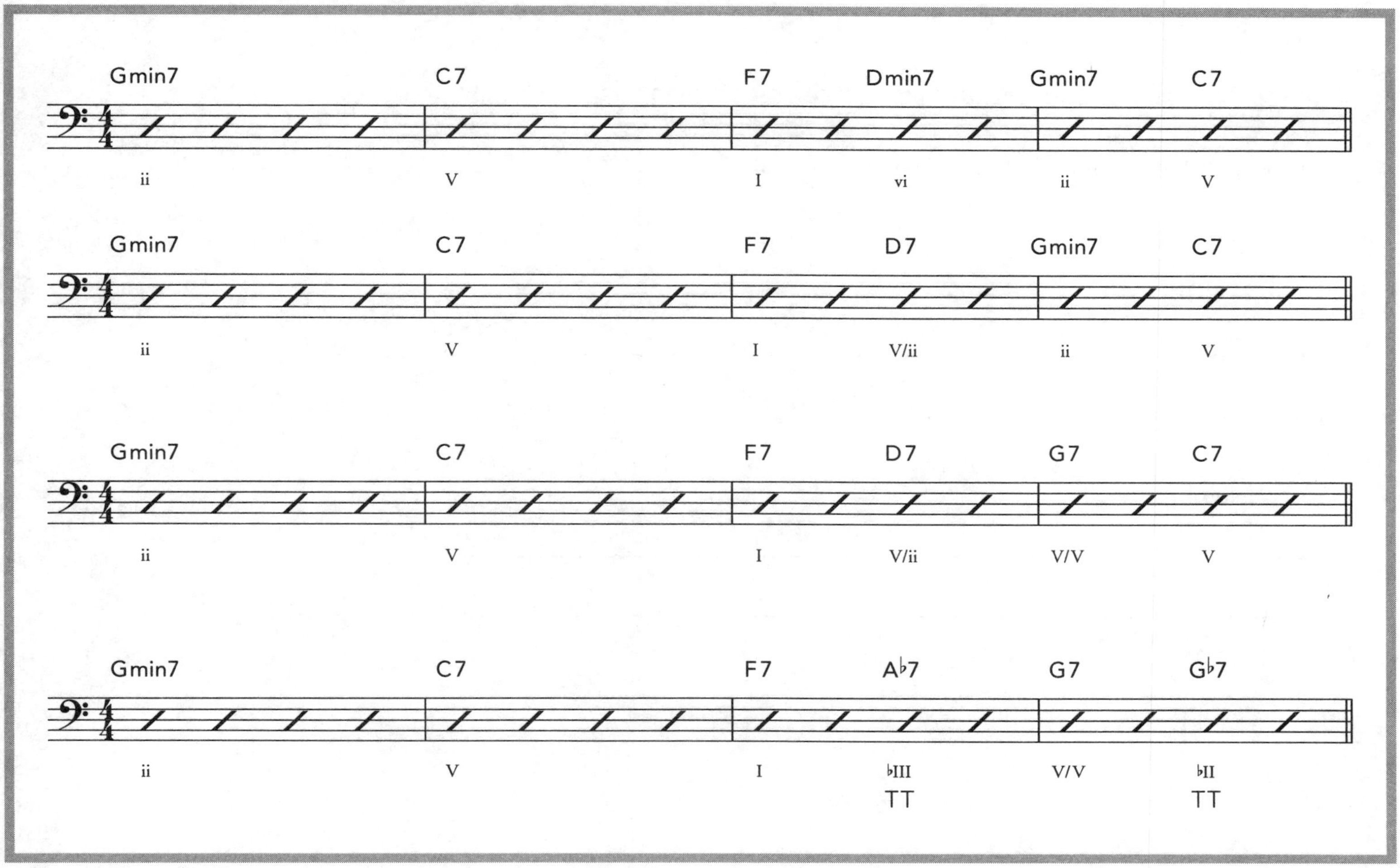

Finally, after all of these substitutions, a jazz-blues might look something like this.

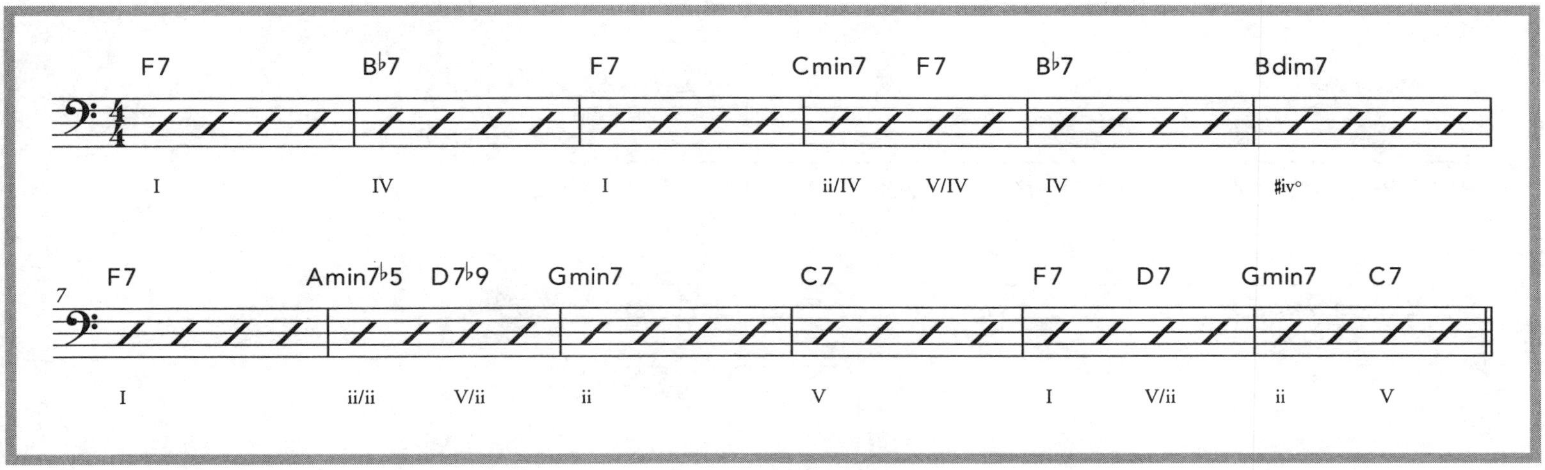

WORKSHEET 24: JAZZ-BLUES

1. Give the Roman numerals of a basic jazz blues.

1. ______ 2. ______ 3. ______ 4. ______ 5. ______ 6. ______

7. ______ 8. ______ 9. ______ 10. ______ 11. ______ 12. ______

2. Using the following changes, give the chord symbols for a jazz blues in the given keys.

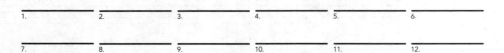

I–IV–I–I–IV–♯iv°7–I–iimin7♭5/ii–V/ii–ii–V–I–V/ii–ii–V

a. C Major

1. ______ 2. ______ 3. ______ 4. ______ 5. ______ 6. ______

7. ______ 8. ______ 9. ______ 10. ______ 11. ______ 12. ______

b. E♭ Major

1. ______ 2. ______ 3. ______ 4. ______ 5. ______ 6. ______

7. ______ 8. ______ 9. ______ 10. ______ 11. ______ 12. ______

Answers

1. I–IV–I–I–IV–IV–I–I–ii–V–I–V

2. a. C7–F7–C7–C7–F7–F♯dim7–C7–Emin7♭5–A7–Dmin7–G7–C7–A7–Dmin7–G

   b. E♭7–A♭7–E♭7–E♭7–A♭7–Adim7–E♭7–Gmin7♭5–C7–Fmin7–B♭7–E♭7–C7–Fmin7–B♭7

Rhythm Changes

Rhythm Changes is a jazz form that is derived from the song "I've Got Rhythm," by George Gershwin. Many different melodies have been written over these changes to create many different songs. Rhythm Changes has an A–A–B–A form, meaning that there are two sections to the song, an A section and a B section. The A section is played twice followed by the B section and finally the A returns. This form is then repeated until the end of the song. Rhythm Changes is commonly played in the key of $B^{\flat}$. Let's look at the A section first.

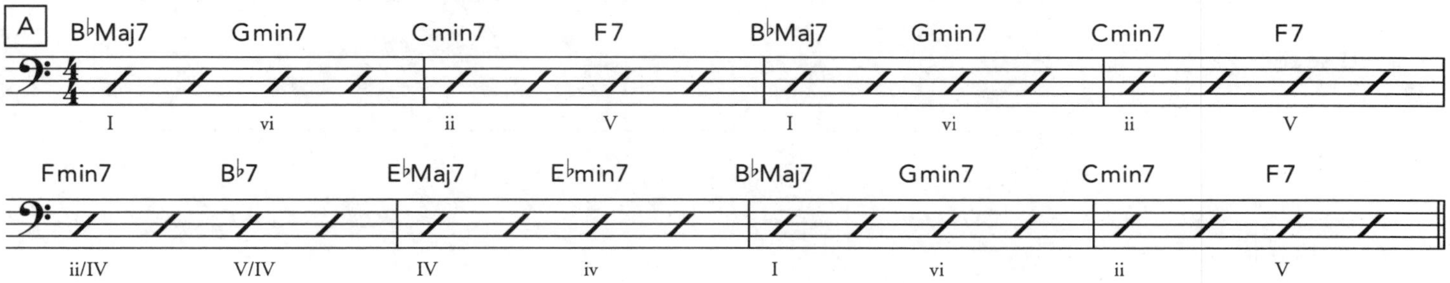

Notice that a I–vi–ii–V cycle takes place on bars 1–2, 3–4, and 7–8. This repetition makes it easy to memorize the A section. Bar 5 is a secondary ii–V progression to the IV chord in bar 6, which starts on the major IV and *mutates* (changes from major to minor or vice versa) to a minor iv.

The B section, often called the *bridge* (a section that connects two other sections, usually composed of materials that contrast the rest of the piece) is quite easy to remember. It is a backcycle (see page 75) of dominant 7th chords, beginning with a V/vi. Each chord is played for two measures. Here is the B section in the key of $B^{\flat}$.

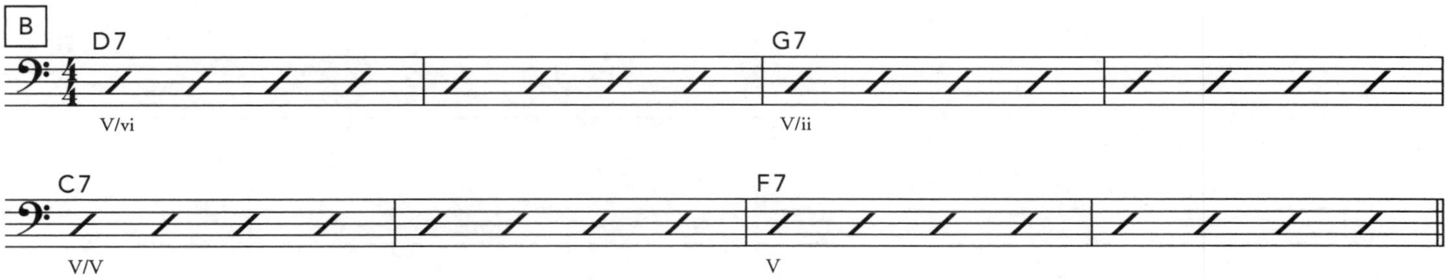

This cycle of dominant chords creates constant tension until the resolution to the I upon the return of the A section.

Alternate Bridge

A common variation for the bridge of Rhythm Changes is accomplished using tritone substitutions. Playing the tritone substitution of the second and fourth chord change creates a chromatic line that descends back to the I chord of the A section.

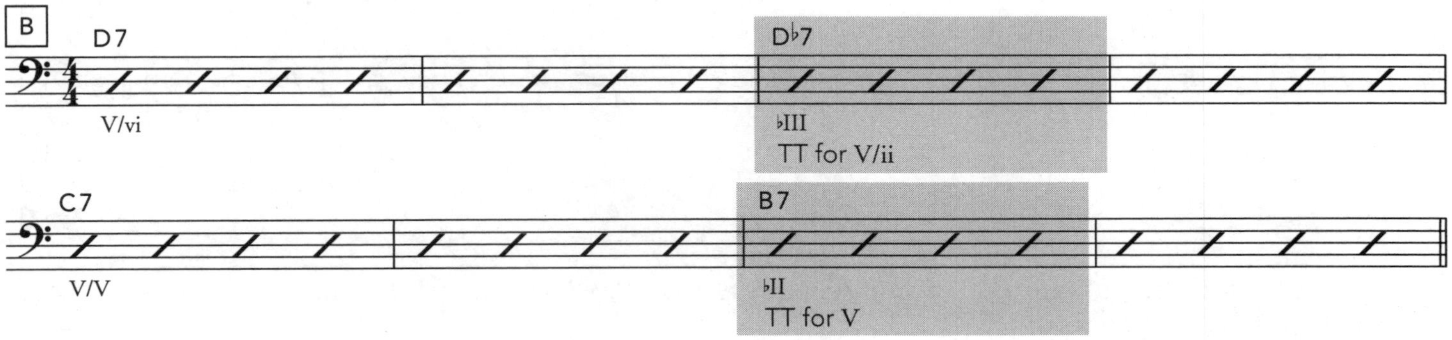

This bridge can be used for every chorus, or as a substitution for the original bridge at any point in the song. You will have to keep your ears open and respond when this variation of the bridge is used. At the same time, don't be afraid to use this bridge yourself. Good players will in turn be listening to you and will respond.

WORKSHEET 25: RHYTHM CHANGES

1. What is the form (using A and B) of Rhythm Changes? ________________________

2. Write the chord changes of the A and B section for Rhythm Changes in the given keys.

a. E♭ Major

A section:

1. ______ 2. ______ 3. ______ 4. ______ 5. ______ 6. ______ 7. ______ 8. ______

B section:

9. ______ 10. ______ 11. ______ 12. ______ 13. ______ 14. ______ 15. ______ 16. ______

b. B♭ Major

A section:

1. ______ 2. ______ 3. ______ 4. ______ 5. ______ 6. ______ 7. ______ 8. ______

B section:

9. ______ 10. ______ 11. ______ 12. ______ 13. ______ 14. ______ 15. ______ 16. ______

c. C Major

A section:

1. ______ 2. ______ 3. ______ 4. ______ 5. ______ 6. ______ 7. ______ 8. ______

B section:

9. ______ 10. ______ 11. ______ 12. ______ 13. ______ 14. ______ 15. ______ 16. ______

Answers

1. A–A–B–A

2a. A section

E♭Maj7–Cmin7–Fmin7–B♭7–E♭Maj7–Cmin7–Fmin7–B♭7–B♭min7–E♭7–A♭7–A♭min7–E♭Maj7–Cmin7–Fmin7–B♭7

B section

G7–G7–C7–C7–F7–F7–B♭7–B♭7

2b. A section

B♭Maj7–Gmin7–Cmin7–F7–B♭Maj7–Gmin7–Cmin7–F7–Fmin7–B♭7–E♭Maj7–E♭min7–B♭Maj7–Gmin7–Cmin7–F7

B section

D7–D7–G7–G7–C7–C7–F7–F7

2c. A section

CMaj7–Amin7–Dmin7–G7–CMaj7–Amin7–Dmin7–G7–Gmin7–CMaj7–FMaj7–Fmin7–CMaj7–Amin7–Dmin7–G7

B section

E7–E7–A7–A7–D7–D7–G7–G7

Bebop Scales

Bebop scales are scales with added chromatic passing tones which are used in a jazz setting. The two most common bebop scales are the *major bebop scale* and the *dominant bebop scale*.

Major Bebop Scale

A major bebop scale is built by adding a chromatic passing tone between the 5th and 6th scale degrees of a major scale. For example, a G♯ would be added between the G and A of a C Major scale to create a C Major Bebop scale.

C Major Bebop Scale

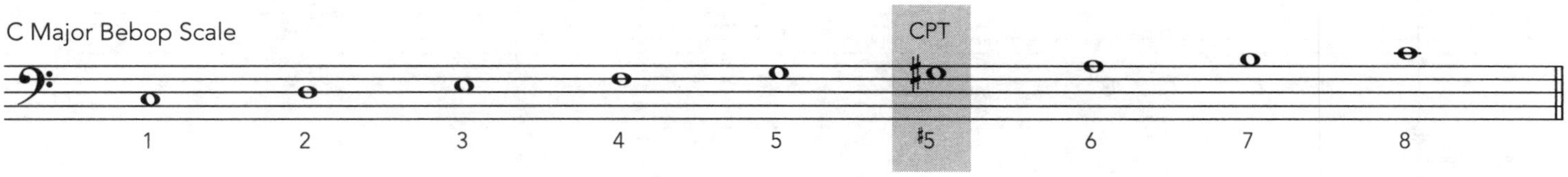

Playing a major bebop scale starting on the root of a chord, ascending or descending in eighth notes, will give you a line that spells out all of the consonant tones of the chord on the beats. This technique makes major bebop scale–lines sound very strong in relation to a major chord.

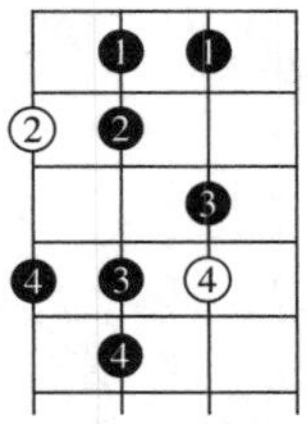

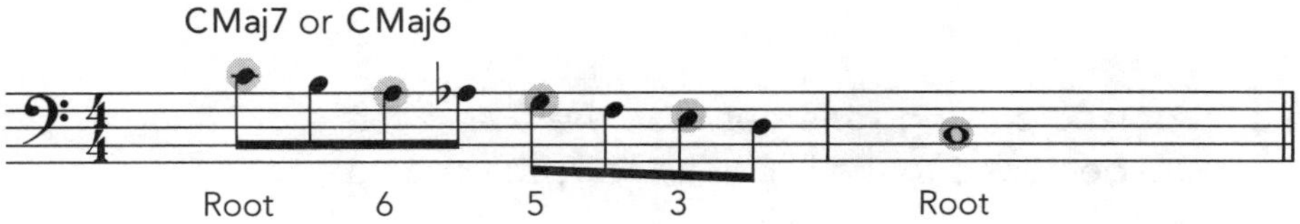

DOMINANT BEBOP SCALE

The dominant bebop scale is the Mixolydian mode with a chromatic passing tone added between the ♭7 and the octave. For example, to create a C Dominant Bebop scale from the C Mixolydian mode, a B would be added between the B♭ and C.

C Dominant Bebop Scale

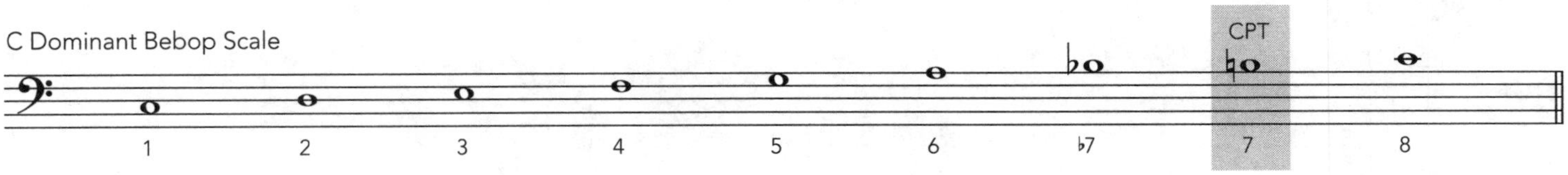

Here is the dominant bebop scale descending in eighth notes. Notice once again how all of the chord tones fall on downbeats.

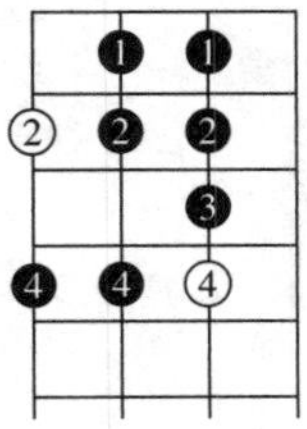

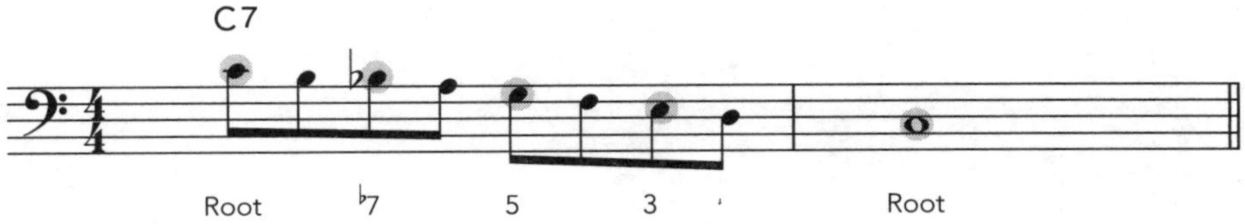

Minor Bebop Scale

Since there are several minor scales, there are also several *minor bebop* scales. The following are two of the more common minor bebop scales.

NATURAL MINOR BEBOP SCALE

A *natural minor bebop* scale is built by adding a chromatic passing tone between the $^{\flat}7$ and the octave of a natural minor scale. For example, a G♯ would be added to the A Natural Minor scale to create the A Natural Minor Bebop scale.

A Natural Minor Bebop Scale

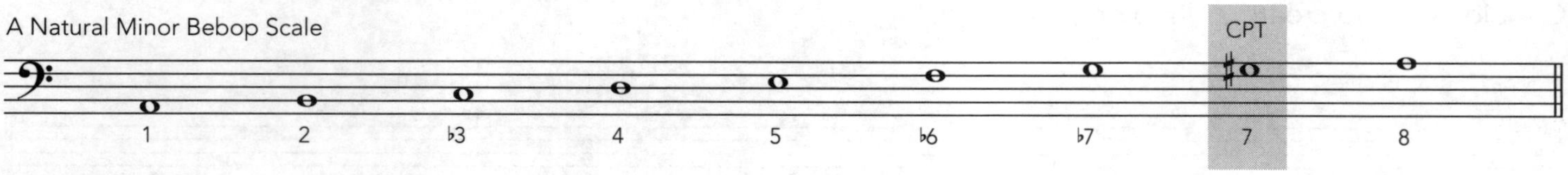

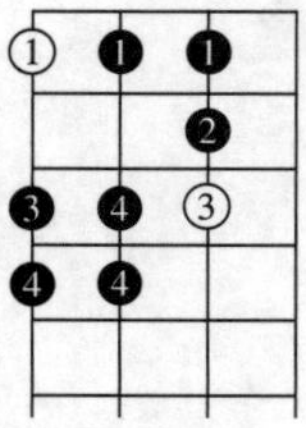

DORIAN BEBOP SCALE

A *Dorian bebop* scale is built by adding a chromatic passing tone between the $^{\flat}7$ and the octave of a Dorian scale. For example, a C♯ would be added to the D Dorian scale to create a D Dorian Bebop scale.

A Dorian Bebop Scale

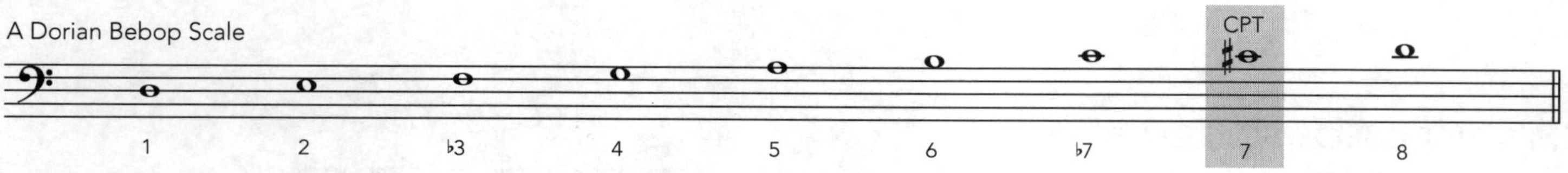

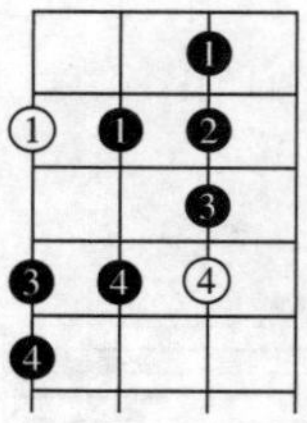

Revisiting Slash Chords

We first covered slash chords on page 36. Slash chords are sometimes written right into the harmony of a song. In these cases, it is most common for a bass player to simply follow the bass movement as indicated in the slash chords. There are also many cases where the guitar or keyboard will play a chord in root position for multiple measures. When this happens, the bass line has a natural tendency to descend. When combined with the original chord, this type of bass line creates slash chords.

Descending Bass Lines for One Chord

DESCENDING BASS LINE FOR A MAJOR CHORD

When major chords are played for more than one measure, it is common to play a bass line starting on the root and descending through a major scale. This technique creates interest and gives the harmony a moving sound. Let's look at a bass line for a C Major chord.

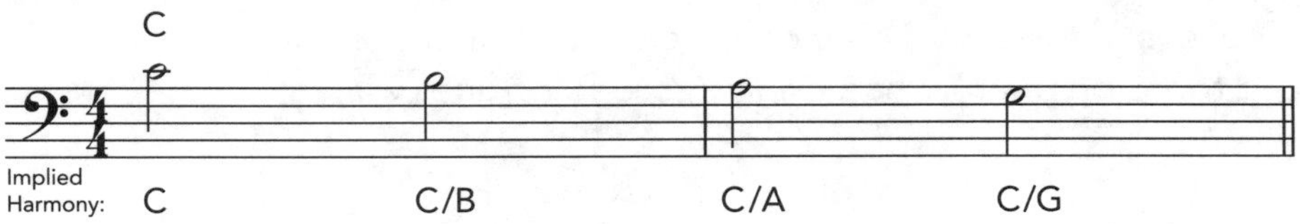

The C chord written above the measure is what the chordal player (guitar or keyboard player, for example) would actually play. The slash chords beneath the two measures are the implied harmonies supplied by a bass player's descending line.

DESCENDING BASS LINE FOR A MINOR CHORD

A minor chord that is held for multiple measures can be addressed in the same way. Simply follow a minor scale built on the root of the particular minor chord. Let's look at an example of each over an A Minor chord using the A Natural Minor scale (Aeolian mode).

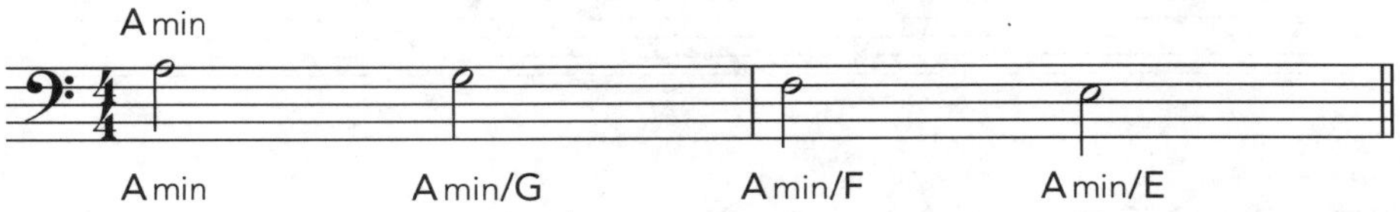

It is also common in this situation to play a line that descends chromatically.

Descending Bass Lines for Multiple Chords

One of the main responsibilities of the bass player is to create forward motion throughout chord progressions. This is not to say that every piece should have the bass line descending or moving throughout. It is sometimes the songwriter's intention to have no harmonic movement at all for multiple measures. However, when movement is desired, it is common to create descending lines that move through multiple chord changes. Once again, the bass player can imply this movement even if the chord changes stay in root position. Following are a few examples.

The following progression is I–IV–ii–V in the key of C Major. This first example bass line sticks to the chord roots and does not alter the harmony in any way.

In this example, a descending line is used to imply slash chords that descend throughout the progression.

The following example is I–vi–IV–V in the key of A Major. These bass lines are only examples, and there are certainly other options for descending lines.

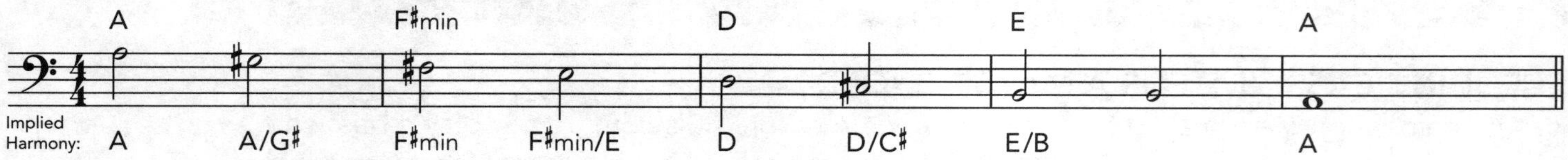

Notice that a chord tone is played on beat 1 of every measure. This creates root-position triads or inversions of those triads. Targeting chord tones on beat 1 when using descending lines will make for strong bass lines.

Common Tones

Another frequently used technique that creates interest in chord progressions is to find common tones that work over multiple chords. Using these common tones in repetitive lines will unify and stabilize harmony that is moving. Let's look at some examples.

The following progression is a I–iii–V–I progression in the key of C Major.

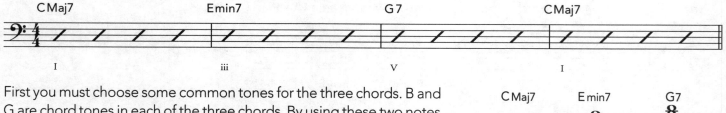

First you must choose some common tones for the three chords. B and G are chord tones in each of the three chords. By using these two notes you can create a repetitive line that works over each chord change.

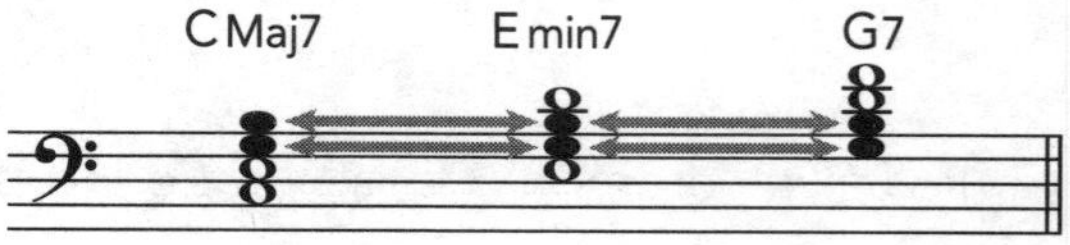

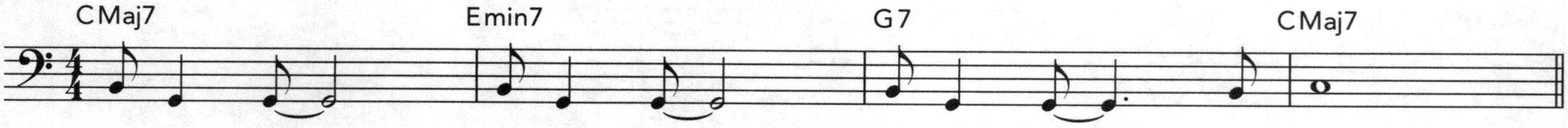

You can choose other tones to create different repetitive lines. In this example, D, E and G are used. All three notes fall in the key of C Major. Because G is the only note that is common to all three chords, it is used as the main note in the line. Making sure to revolve around and resolve to a chord tone helps this line.

This technique of altering harmony with a bass line leaves lots of room for creativity. You do not have to play the line exactly the same way every time. Altering a note or the order of notes in a mostly repetitive line to fit a chord change, for example, is certainly acceptable and sometimes necessary to avoid clashes.

Pedal Tones

While it is normal to create forward motion in bass lines, there are times when you will want to use only one tone over multiple chord changes to create tension. A single note repeated or held over moving harmonies is called a *pedal tone*.

The dominant scale degree (5) is often used as a pedal tone to create tension over a ii–V–I progression. In jazz, this pedal tone frequently occurs on beats 2 and 4. The following is an example of a pedal tone over a ii–V–I in C Major.

This pedal tone will eventually have to be released or the piece will have a constant sound of being unresolved. Your taste and mood will dictate how long you hold or repeat pedal tones.

Pedal tones can also be used to create descending lines. In this example in C Major, the pedal tone is held over two chord changes and descends in whole steps.

Notice how the E bass note acts as the root of Emin in bar 1 and the 5th of Amin7 in bar 2. The D bass note acts as the root of Dmin7 in bar 3 and the 5th of G7 in bar 4.

When using any technique covered in this book, your main objective should be to *add* to the song. If a songwriter's intention is to have a light, happy-sounding song, you probably will not want to use a pedal tone that creates tension. At the same time, don't be afraid to experiment with these techniques. Often, the bass movement can bring life to an otherwise uninteresting harmony.

Congratulations!

You have completed *Theory for the Contemporary Bassist*. You have learned a lot about the language of music. Like all languages, becoming fluent will take practice and continued study. Seek out information from any source you can find, whether it is intended for bass players or not. Check out *The Complete Electric Bass Method* by David Overthrow and any other information you can get your hands on.

Study every kind of music you can—you can learn *something* from anyone. Do a lot of listening and try to further develop your ear, which is your most important tool as a musician. Most important, enjoy!

If you love this book,
you'll love our schools!
Online...
WORKSHOPLive
The next generation of music education from the founders of the National Guitar Workshop
Take a FREE online lesson today.
workshoplive.com
...or Near You!
N · G · W
National Guitar Workshop
LOCATIONS: Connecticut, Florida, Seattle, Nashville, Los Angeles, Texas, San Francisco, Virginia ...every summer!
1-800-234-6479
guitarworkshop.com